UNDERSTANDING
dBASE III

UNDERSTANDING
dBASE III®

Alan Simpson

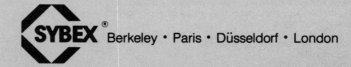
SYBEX® Berkeley • Paris • Düsseldorf • London

dBASE II and dBASE III are trademarks of Ashton-Tate
CP/M, CBASIC, and CB-80 are registered trademarks of Digital Research Incorporated
MS-DOS and MBASIC are registered trademarks of Microsoft
WordStar and MailMerge are registered trademarks of MicroPro International
PC-DOS is a registered trademark of International Business Machines
SuperCalc is a registered trademark of Sorcim
Disk Doctor is a registered trademark of Super Soft
Quickcode is a registered trademark of Fox and Gellar
Microline is a registered trademark of Okidata Corporation

SYBEX is not affiliated with any manufacturer.

Library of Congress Card Number: 84-52590
ISBN 0-89588-267-1
Printed by Haddon Craftsmen
Manufactured in the United States of America
10 9 8 7 6 5

Acknowledgments

Once again, top thanks go to Carole Alden, my editor from SYBEX, for being a great editor, teacher, and friend. And thanks to Rodnay Zaks, Rudolph Langer, and everyone else at SYBEX for helping turn this idea into yet another real live book.

Special thanks to Bill and Cynthia Gladstone, my literary agents at Waterside Productions in Del Mar, California for turning my dream of being a writer into a reality, and for being great friends too. And thanks to Susan for being a good Waterside "road trip" buddy.

Thanks to my loved ones for patiently putting up with my neglect during my work on this manuscript.

And, of course, thanks again to all of my students for teaching me what to write about.

Contents

14 A MAILING LIST SYSTEM 185

15 DEBUGGING TECHNIQUES 201

16 SETTING UP SCREEN DISPLAYS 211

17 SOME USEFUL TIPS 223

APPENDICES

A INTERFACING dBASE III WITH OTHER SOFTWARE SYSTEMS   245

B GRAPHICS WITH dBASE III   259

C dBASE III VOCABULARY   275

D CONVERTING dBASE II FILES TO dBASE III FILES   293

Introduction

dBASE III™ is a database management system for microcomputers. This is a book about putting the computer to work for you using dBASE III. We will not be too concerned here about how the computer does it. This is a book about using the computer to our benefit. When we learn to drive a car, for example, we are not too concerned about the inner workings of the clutch or voltage regulator. Instead, we just want to get from point A to point B faster and more efficiently than walking. The same is true for the majority of computer users in the world today. Knowing about bits and bytes and B-trees is great, but most of us are more concerned about getting from A to B. Point A in the computer sense is doing dull tasks inefficiently, slowly, and with human error. Point B is letting the machine do dull tasks quickly, efficiently, and accurately.

This book is written with the computer novice in mind, but certainly more experienced users can learn from our examples too. The approach for teaching you to use dBASE focuses on the practical. Rather than just tell you what dBASE does, we show you with real-life everyday examples. We'll not only tell you what the dBASE commands mean, but we'll also teach you the concepts behind using the commands correctly. We'll also give you some good techniques for using dBASE III to its fullest potential.

If you have dBASE III handy, you should follow along by trying out the examples in the book. We assume that you are using a computer with two disk drives, drive A and drive B. The examples are set up such that the dBASE III system disk is in drive A, and the databases we create are on the disk in drive B. You can use any disk configuration that you wish, however. For example, drive B is specified as the drive to put databases on by preceding the filename with the symbol B: (i.e., CREATE B:MAIL, USE B:MAIL). If you don't have a drive B, just leave off the B: (i.e., CREATE MAIL, USE MAIL).

The contents of the book include the following. Chapters 1–7 deal with dBASE III basics: creating a database; adding data to it; searching, sorting, and editing the data; and printing formatted reports and mailing labels. Chapters 8 and 9 deal with managing multiple data files, using an inventory system as the example. Chapters 10–16 discuss programming techniques which are used to go beyond the built-in capabilities of dBASE.

Appendix A discusses interfacing dBASE III with other programs such as WordStar, SuperCalc, and BASIC. Appendix B goes into graphics, and is basically just for fun. Appendix C is a summary of dBASE III commands that you can use as a reference. Appendix D discusses translating dBASE II data and programs to dBASE III.

Configuring DOS for dBASE III

To take full advantage of the capabilities of dBASE III, you should boot up the computer with a special CONFIG.SYS file on the boot-up disk. The CONFIG.SYS file you need is stored on the dBASE III system disk. If you have a hard disk system, and usually boot up from the hard disk, just copy the CONFIG.SYS file to the main directory of the hard disk. To do so, stay logged on to the C drive, put the dBASE III system disk into drive A, and type the command:

```
COPY A:CONFIG.SYS
```

If you usually boot up from a floppy disk, copy the CONFIG.SYS file to the disk that you normally boot up from. First, make sure that there is no write-protect tab on the disk you normally boot up from, then put it in drive B. Put the dBASE III system disk in drive A. From the DOS A> prompt, type in the command:

```
COPY CONFIG.SYS B:
```

If it won't fit, you may need to erase a file on the boot-up disk. You could also create a disk specifically for booting up with dBASE III. Simply put a blank, unformatted disk in drive B, and the DOS disk in drive A. Make a formatted, bootable disk with the command:

```
FORMAT B:/S
```

When the formatting is complete, remove the DOS disk from drive A, and put in the dBASE III system disk. Type in the command:

```
COPY CONFIG.SYS B:
```

To reboot the system with the CONFIG.SYS file, remove the disk from drive A and insert the new disk with the CONFIG.SYS file on it. Hold down the Ctrl and Alt keys simultaneously, and press the Del key. The system will reboot back to the A> prompt using information from the CONFIG.SYS file. When you wish to use dBASE III in the future, be sure to boot up or reboot with the disk that has the CONFIG.SYS file on it.

For more information on the CONFIG.SYS file, see the file named READ.ME on the dBASE III system disk. From the A> prompt, enter the command:

TYPE READ.ME

and press RETURN. For a printed copy, first make sure the printer is on, then hold down the CRL key and type the letter P. Then type the command:

TYPE READ.ME

or the command:

TYPE A:READ.ME

and press RETURN. After the READ.ME file is printed, hold down the CRL key and type P again.

What is a Database?

While *database management* sounds so technical, it's as ordinary as driving a car. Think, for instance, of a shoe box full of index cards with names and addresses for a mailing list in it. The shoe box and its contents are a database. Every time you juggle the index cards to get them in alphabetical order, you are *managing* the database. The average office file cabinet is a database too. It doesn't do anything, it just holds information (data). If you open a drawer and look up the Johnson account, you are searching your database, a way of managing it.

We typically keep our everyday databases in some order, either by alphabet, by date, or perhaps by zip code. We do so to *structure* our database, so that it is easier for us to work with. We human database managers do not like messy file cabinets. Ditto for computers. If we want to change the order of an alphabetical file, we might want to be able to say a magic word and have them instantly rearranged by zip code. Too bad we can't. Unfortunately, the task could take us hours of tedious labor. But with a computer, and the right magic word, the rearrangement can take place in seconds. But before we can discuss the magic words of dBASE III, we need to discuss a computer's view of a database.

In the computer world, a database is like our shoebox file, with a very rigid structure. While the shoe box is filled with index cards, a computer database is filled with *records.* And while each index card in the shoe box may contain several written lines of information, a record in a database contains *fields* of information. That is, a shoe box contains cards, each of which has several lines of information on it. A database contains records, each of which has several fields within it. Take a look at the index card in Figure 1.1.

It has four lines of information on it: (1) name, (2) address, (3) city, state, zip, and (4) phone number. This single index card represents one record on a computer database. Each of the lines roughly represents one field of information on the database.

There is a very important difference between human database managers and computer database management systems. As people, we can tell what each line on the index card represents. That is, we know who this card refers to, his first and last name, as well as his address, city, state, zip code, and phone number. We know this

John Q. Smith
123 A St.
San Diego, CA 92122

(619)455-1212

Figure 1.1: Index card record

simply by looking at the context of the information. We can tell that (619) 455-1212 is not a last name. Though this is obvious to us, it is not at all clear to a computer. A computer can't tell a phone number from a last name from a pastrami sandwich. Unfortunately, the computer doesn't understand anything about information based on its context. Thus, we have to structure our database rigidly so the computer does not mistake a name for a phone number, and we must be pretty explicit. Computers may be fast, but they are definitely not smart.

How do we structure a database with dBASE III? First we have to decide exactly what we want to store. To do so, we have to break down the information on the index card into meaningful units of information. In the above example, one card holds a name, address, city, state, zip, and phone number. We will want each record in our database to hold the same information. Recall that a given record on a database refers to one index card in a shoe box, and that each field in a record refers to one piece of information on a given card. Hence, in our database, we would want each record to contain:

NAME, ADDRESS, CITY, STATE, ZIP, PHONE

Notice that there are six fields on the record. Let me warn you here of the most common mistake that people make when structuring databases. On the index card in Figure 1.1, we see four written lines: one contains the name, one contains the address, one contains the city, state and zip, and the other contains a phone number. Looking at the card, we might be tempted to structure the database with these four fields:

NAME, ADDRESS, CSZ, PHONE

The CSZ field would contain the city, state and zip. This is misleading in reference to computer databases because if we ever wanted to sort or search our data file by zip code, we couldn't. Since the zip would be combined with city and state, the computer couldn't isolate it. Thus, you should assign each single meaningful piece of information to a unique field. Therefore, this structure:

NAME, ADDRESS, CITY, STATE, ZIP, PHONE

is preferred, because each piece of data is placed in a separate field.

Learning to define meaningful items of information is an important aspect of database management, as we shall see throughout this book. With the proper database structure we can sort individuals by zip code, or search for individuals within a given zip code range. Because the zip code field is isolated from the city and state, it becomes a meaningful, individual piece of data for the computer to sort.

So then, how does the computer know what a given piece of information means? It doesn't. In the example above, we've told the computer that on each record, there are six fields. The first field is NAME, the second is ADDRESS, the third field is CITY, etc. If we store "John Q. Smith" in the ZIP field, the computer is not going to think about this and say to us, "That looks more like a name to me!" It will just store John Q. Smith as the zip code. Therefore, it is up to us to put the correct data in the appropriate field. We're the brains of the operation, not the computer.

Introduction to Database Management

Once we've structured our database, we need to manage it by giving the computer precise instructions. Managing a database primarily involves the following tasks:

1. ADD new data to the database.
2. SORT the database into some meaningful order.
3. SEARCH the database for types of information.
4. PRINT data from our database onto formatted reports.
5. EDIT data on the database.
6. DELETE data from the database.

We need to do similar tasks with our shoe box file. Occasionally we may need to add some new index cards. We may also want to sort the index cards into some meaningful order (say, alphabetically or by zip code). We might want to search through them and find all the people who live in Los Angeles, or all the people in the 92123 zip code area, or perhaps just find out where a person named Clark

Kenney lives. If Clark Kenney moves, we may want to edit the database and change his address. Then again, if Clark Kenney stops paying his dues, we may want to delete him from the mailing list altogether. This is database management. With the shoebox, we do all the work. With the computer, we think and the computer works.

Let's move on to Chapter 2 now and start talking about dBASE III more specifically.

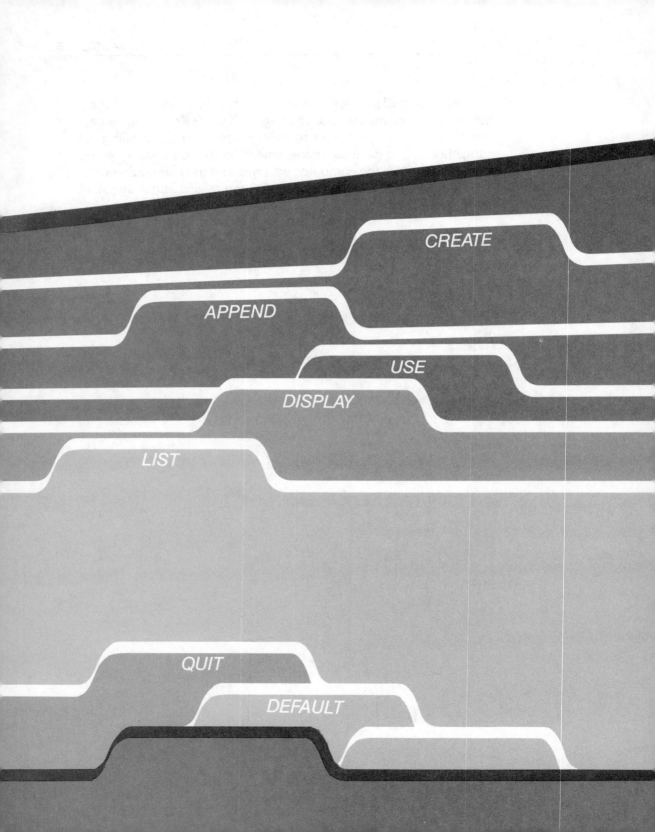

CREATE

APPEND

USE

DISPLAY

LIST

QUIT

DEFAULT

MANAGING DATA

2

In this chapter, we'll learn to create a database, add data to it, and retrieve data from it. If you have dBASE III readily available, we hope you'll load it up right now and follow every step of our examples. To load up your dBASE system, you need to place your dBASE III system disk in drive A. If you have a drive B on your computer, put a blank, formatted disk in that drive. Then boot up so that the A> prompt appears on your screen. Next, type in DBASE and press the RETURN or ENTER key on the computer.

This will cause dBASE to load up and display a copyright notice. Below the copyright notice is the dBASE dot prompt, which is a period (.) on the left-hand side of the screen. This tells you that dBASE is ready and waiting for instructions from you.

Creating a Database with CREATE

In order to create a database, we need to type in the word CREATE next to the dBASE dot prompt, and press the RETURN key. When you see the symbol <RET> on these pages, it means "press the RETURN key." Do not type <RET> on the screen.

When we ask dBASE to CREATE a database, it first asks us to

Enter the name of the new file:

Every database must have a first and last name. You assign the first name, dBASE will add the last name .DBF (which stands for database file). The name you assign can be up to eight characters long, without spaces or punctuation. For now, let's create a database called MAIL. We can also specify the disk drive in the filename. If we place a B: in front of the file name, then the database will be stored on the disk in drive B. So if you have a B drive with a disk in it, type in the filename like so:

    B:MAIL   <RET>

If you don't have a drive B, leave off the B:, and just type in the name MAIL <RET>.

Next, dBASE will want to know the structure of the database. On the screen you'll see

B:mail.dbf

field name	type	width	dec
1	Char/text		

Let's discuss what all of this means. Notice that dBASE is asking for information about the fields in each record. For each field, it needs to know the name, type, width, and number of decimal places. The name of the field can be up to ten characters long, but no spaces are allowed, and the only punctuation allowed is the underscore character (__). dBASE also needs to know the type of data being stored in the field. Data can be one of five types: 1) character (C), for non-numeric data such as name, address, etc.; 2) numeric (N), data for numbers that we want to do some math with, like dollar amounts or inventory quantity; 3) date (D) for dates in MM/DD/YY format; 4) memo (M) for long passages of text; 5) logical (L), where the field is either true or false. Then, dBASE needs to know the width of each field, the maximum number of characters that the field will contain. Finally, it needs to know how many decimal places are to be stored for numbers. For instance, in a dollar amount, we typically store two decimal places (i.e. $999.99).

To fill in information on the CREATE screen, simply type in the field name, followed by a press on the RETURN key. The cursor will move to the "type" prompt. Type in the first letter of the type of data; e.g., C for character data, N for numeric data, D for dates, M for memos, or L for logical data. In our first example, we'll just use all character types to keep things simple. The cursor will then move to the "width" field. Type in the maximum width for the field followed by a press on the RETURN key. If you make errors while typing in field data, you can use the arrow keys on the numeric keypad (on the right side of the keyboard) to position the cursor for making changes. (If they don't work at first, press the Num Lock key above the numeric keypad.)

Let's structure our MAIL database like this:

	field name	type	width	dec
1	LNAME	Char/text	15	
2	FNAME	Char/text	10	
3	ADDRESS	Char/text	25	
4	CITY	Char/text	15	
5	STATE	Char/text	5	
6	ZIP	Char/text	10	

Rather than typing in a seventh field, just press the RETURN key. dBASE will display the message

HIT RETURN to confirm—any other key to resume

Press the RETURN key.

Notice that we've broken the first and last name into separate fields. The last name field (LNAME) can take a last name 15 letters long. The first name field (FNAME) can hold up to 10 letters.

Why are there two separate fields? Because in the future, we might want to sort our data alphabetically on last name. If we just had one field for both first and last name, such as Joe Smith, when we did our sort, dBASE would sort by first name. You and I can look at Joe Smith and immediately see that Smith is the last name. Since the computer doesn't understand this, we've established the difference between first and last name by providing a separate field for each. We've also put address, city, state, and zip into separate fields. Note that C indicates that each of these is a character field.

Now you'll probably ask, "Why is zip code a character string? Isn't 92122 a number?" Yes, it is, but hyphenated zip codes like 92038-2802 could cause problems. In dBASE, the hyphen means "subtract" when dealing with numbers. So at some point, 92038-2802 might become 89236 if stored as a number (92038 minus 2802 = 89236). This could wreak havoc on our mailing system.

Another problem is that some foreign zip codes have letters in them, like A132-09. In dBASE III, letters are not allowed in numeric data. We will save ourselves a lot of trouble by making zip a character field. The only time we must make a field numeric is when we need to do math. Certainly, we'll never need to total up zip codes!

So we now have a structured database. All of our meaningful pieces of information are broken out into separate fields. Again, avoid the temptation to combine several pieces of information into one field (CITY:STATE:ZIP). dBASE III allows a maximum of 128 fields in each record, with their combined widths totalling up to a maximum of 4000 characters. There is plenty of room.

On your screen, you will now see that the computer is asking if we want to

Input data records now? (Y/N)

Type N for "no," and we will be returned to the dot prompt. There you have it. We have created a database called MAIL.DBF on the disk in drive B.

If you are anything other than a perfect typist, you are likely to make a few typographical errors along the way. Computers are not always forgiving of these. For example, if while typing in the command, DISPLAY, you accidentally type in

DISMAY

dBASE will tell you

* * * Unrecognized command verb

If you make a simple typing error such as this, dBASE will return you to the dot prompt so you can try again.

In many situations, dBASE will respond to an error with the message

Do you want some help? (Y/N)

To get some help, answer Y (yes). dBASE will present some instructions on the screen. When you are done reading these instructions, press the escape key (ESC) to return to the dot prompt.

You can also get help at any time by typing in the command HELP and pressing RETURN. On most computers, you can also get help by pressing the F1 key at the upper left corner of the keyboard.

To get help on a specific command, type in the command HELP followed by the command you need help with. For example, to get help with the DISPLAY command, type in the command:

HELP DISPLAY <RET>

and dBASE will show instructions for using the DISPLAY command. Press ESC when you are done reading the help message to return to the dot prompt.

Adding Data with APPEND

We've now got ourselves a nicely structured database waiting to be filled. Let's start putting in some data. With the dBASE dot prompt showing, we are ready to let dBASE know what database we will be referring to. The command for this is

USE B:MAIL <RET>

The USE command tells dBASE which database we will be working with. In the example above, we've told dBASE that we want to use the database MAIL.DBF on the disk in drive B. dBASE promptly responds with another dot prompt. Now let's add some names and addresses to our database.

The command for adding new data to a database is APPEND. So, type in

APPEND <RET>

This will bring us a form to fill out on the screen.

```
Record No.                    1

LNAME       :_                              :
FNAME       :                            :
ADDRESS     :                                :
CITY        :                          :
STATE       :         :
ZIP         :              :
```

dBASE is now waiting for us to fill in the blanks. Here is the first candidate for our mailing list: John Q. Smith, 123 A. St., San Diego, CA, 92123. Notice that the cursor is waiting in the LNAME field. So, we type Smith <RET>, John Q. <RET>, 123 A. St. <RET>, San Diego <RET>, CA <RET> and 92123. Before pressing the last <RET>, the screen will look like this:

```
Record No.                     1

LNAME       :Smith                          :
FNAME       :John Q.                     :
ADDRESS     :123 A. St.                       :
CITY        :San Diego                  :
STATE       :CA      :
ZIP         :92123_          :
```

We've filled in our first record. When we press <RET> after the zip code, we get a new blank form.

```
Record No.                    2

LNAME         :_                              :
FNAME         :                        :
ADDRESS       :                               :
CITY          :                      :
STATE         :          :
ZIP           :                :
```

Notice that dBASE is now waiting for the second record to be added to the list (Record 2). We can add as many names as we need to. When you want to get out of the APPEND mode, just type <RET> instead of typing in a last name. This will bring back the dot prompt.

If you need to correct mistakes while typing in data, you can use the arrow keys or *control-key* commands. Some move the cursor and some delete and insert information. The best way to learn these is to try them. The symbol ^ means "hold down the control (CTRL) key while typing." That is, ^E means hold down the CTRL key while you press E. Here are the commands:

Up-arrow or ^E	Moves cursor up one field.
Down-arrow or ^X	Moves cursor down one field.
Left-arrow or ^S	Moves cursor one space to the left.
Right-arrow or ^D	Moves cursor one space to the right.
Del or ^G	Deletes character over cursor.
Ins or ^V	Enters the Insert mode, so that newly entered data is inserted into the field without overwriting existing data.
PgUp or ^R	Moves back to previous record.
PgDn or ^C	Moves forward to next record.
^End or ^W	Saves all newly added data and returns to the dot prompt.

The arrow keys and Ins and Del keys on the numeric keypad are shown in Figure 2.1. All of the control-key commands are in the left-hand portion of the keyboard, near the CTRL key. This is so that you can hold down the CTRL key with your little finger while pressing the appropriate key. The position of the keys suggest the direction that the cursor moves, as shown in Figure 2.2.

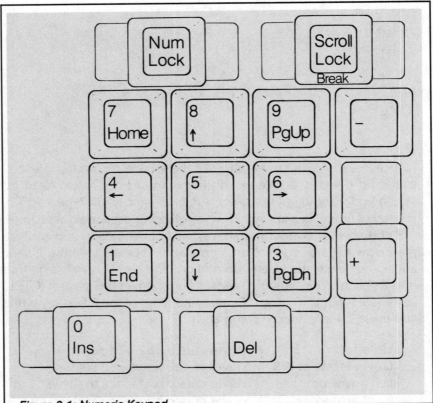

Figure 2.1: Numeric Keypad

The arrow and control-key commands hold true for all dBASE forms that appear on the screen, as we'll see throughout the following chapters.

Let's add a second record. Suppose that while adding our second record, we type in the following data:

```
Record No.                    2

LNAME          :Appleby                      :
FNAME          :Andy                       :
ADDRESS        :35 Oak St.                      :
CITY           :Los Angeless               :
STATE          :CA       :
ZIP            :_                   :
```

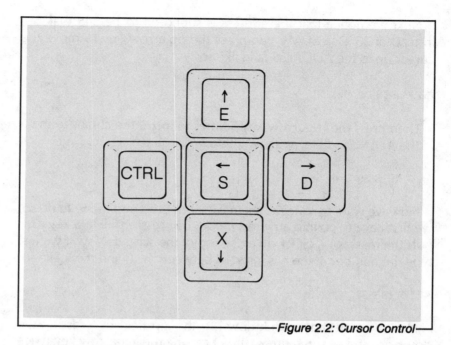

Figure 2.2: Cursor Control

Before typing in the zip code we notice a couple of errors in the field above. To fix these, first, we can move the cursor up to the CITY field by pressing the up-arrow key twice, or by holding down the CTRL key and tapping the E key twice. The cursor moves to the beginning of the CITY field like so:

CITY:Los Angeless   :

Now to move the cursor to the right, press the right-arrow key 10 times, and hold down the CTRL key. The cursor moves ten characters to the right, and should now be under the first s in Angeless.

CITY:Los Angeless   :

We can delete the character above the cursor using a ^G or by pressing the DEL key. Now the city field looks like this:

CITY:Los Angeles   :

We've eliminated the extra s.

Next we notice that the address is supposed to be 345 Oak St., instead of 35 Oak St. We can press the up-arrow key to move the cursor up to the ADDRESS field like so:

ADDRESS:35 Oak St. _

Then press the left-arrow key 9 times to move the cursor to the 5 in the ADDRESS field, as shown below:

ADDRESS:3<u>5</u> Oak St.   :

Now we want to squeeze a 4 in between the 3 and the 5. To do so, we first have to go into an _insert mode_, by pressing the INS key. This puts the message INSERT on at the top of the screen. Now if we just type the number 4, the 4 is inserted between the 3 and the 5 like so:

ADDRESS:34<u>5</u> Oak St.   :

Now we can move back down to the zip field by pressing the down-arrow key three times, then pressing the left-arrow key twice to move the cursor to the left of the entry box. Then we can type in a zip code (92123). Pressing <RET> after the zip code will then move us onto record 3 for appending.

So far so good. We've created a database and added two records to it. At this point, if you are using dBASE, we suggest that you put in more data. If the APPEND form is still showing on the screen, just start keying in the following names and addresses. If the dBASE dot prompt is showing, just USE B:MAIL <RET> then type APPEND <RET>. Here are some data (records 3–6) for you to type in which we will use for future examples:

LNAME	FNAME	ADDRESS	CITY	STATE	ZIP
Smith	Dave	619 Elm St.	San Diego	CA	92122
SMITH	Betsy	222 Lemon Dr.	New York	NY	01234
Smithsonian	Lucy	461 Adams St.	San Diego	CA	92122-1234
Doe	Ruth	1142 J. St.	Los Angeles	CA	91234

After you type in the data for the last person on the list, dBASE will still ask for more data. To stop adding names, just press the RETURN key rather than typing in a last name. Once we get them all typed in, we need to learn ways to retrieve the information.

Viewing Data with DISPLAY and LIST

There are basically two commands for viewing the contents of a database: the DISPLAY command, which displays the data of one record, and the LIST command, which displays all the records. Since DISPLAY has many other uses in dBASE, we are going to focus on the LIST command for now.

With dBASE's dot prompt showing, if we USE B:MAIL, we can view the contents of our database by typing

LIST   <RET>

This shows all of the data in our database as shown below.

Record#	LNAME	FNAME	ADDRESS	CITY	ST
ATE ZIP					
1	Smith	John Q.	123 A St.	San Diego	CA
92123					
2	Appleby	Andy	345 Oak St.	Los Angeles	CA
92123					
3	Smith	Dave	619 Elm St.	San Diego	CA
92122					
4	SMITH	Betsy	222 Lemon Dr.	New York	NY
01234					
5	Smithsonian	Lucy	461 Adams St.	San Diego	CA
92122-1234					
6	Doe	Ruth	1142 J. St.	Los Angeles	CA
91234					

The zip code for each record got stuck underneath each record number because the screen was not wide enough to handle the whole record. We can clean this up by requesting that only certain fields be listed. For example, the command

LIST LNAME,FNAME   <RET>

gives us:

Record#	lname	fname
1	Smith	John Q.
2	Appleby	Andy
3	Smith	Dave
4	SMITH	Betsy
5	Smithsonian	Lucy
6	Doe	Ruth

This is a cleaner display, with only the last and first name listed. We could reverse the order of first and last name by asking dBASE to

    LIST FNAME,LNAME   <RET>

which would give us

Record#	fname	lname
1	John Q.	Smith
2	Andy	Appleby
3	Dave	Smith
4	Betsy	SMITH
5	Lucy	Smithsonian
6	Ruth	Doe

The two fields are displayed in the order requested. We can ask for more information. Type in

    LIST FNAME,LNAME,ADDRESS,ZIP   <RET>

We will get exactly the information we request.

Record#	fname	lname	address	zip
1	John Q.	Smith	123 A. St.	92123
2	Andy	Appleby	345 Oak St.	92123
3	Dave	Smith	619 Elm St.	92122
4	Betsy	SMITH	222 Lemon Dr.	01234
5	Lucy	Smithsonian	461 Adams St.	92122-1234
6	Ruth	Doe	1142 J. St.	91234

Now, try a few other types of LISTs. Be creative. Don't worry, you won't break or ruin anything.

When you finish a session with dBASE III, you should always type the command

QUIT   <RET>

prior to removing any disks from their drives. This assures that all of your data will be safe and sound next time you wish to use dBASE III. The QUIT command returns you to the A> or C> prompt, which is the safe time to remove disks from their drives. To get back into dBASE at a later date, just put the dBASE disk in drive A, and type DBASE <RET> next to the DOS A> or C> prompt.

We've come quite a way here. We can create a database, add data to it, and display its contents. Quite the computer whizzes already. In the next chapter we'll learn how to search the database for certain types of information. For example, suppose we only want to display people who live in Los Angeles, or in the 92122 zip code area. Perhaps we just want to look up a particular address. This is called *searching*.

NOTE: dBASE III allows you to change some general parameters using the SET command. In our examples in this book, we'll assume that none of these parameters have been altered. However, where appropriate, I'll mention how a parameter may affect an example. For instance, when creating and using our MAIL database, we preceded the filename with a B: to tell dBASE that we wished to store this database on the disk in drive B. Had we not put the B: in front, dBASE would have defaulted to the drive we booted up on, drive A. To set the default to drive B, you would need to type in the command

SET DEFAULT TO B   <RET>

Once we set this parameter, dBASE will assume that the command to USE MAIL means USE B:MAIL. When you quit dBASE, all parameters are reset to their normal state. For the sake of consistency and clarity, we'll stick with the B:filename convention.

Another handy parameter in dBASE III is the SET MENU command. If you type in the command

SET MENU ON

next to the dot prompt, dBASE will display a menu of cursor-control commands at the top of the screen whenever you add or change data.

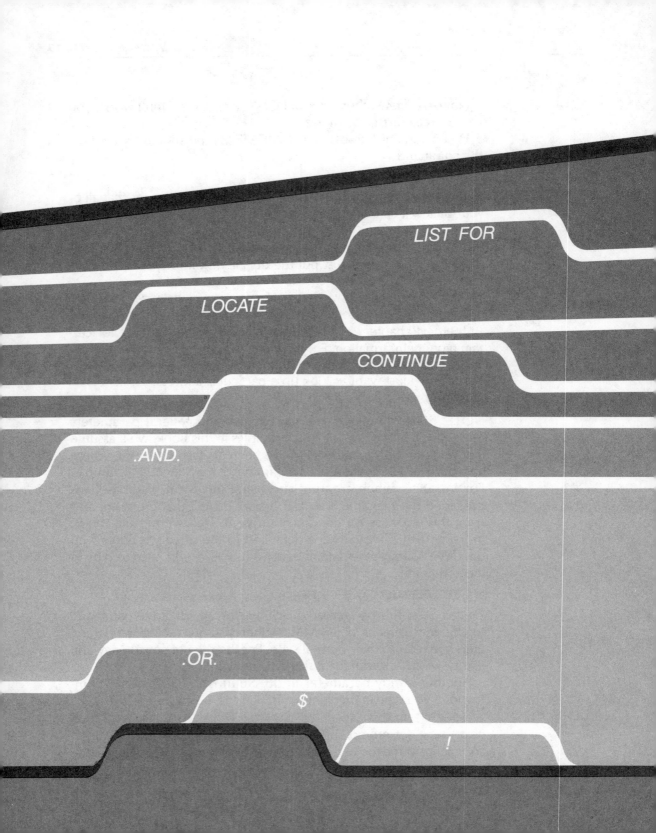

SEARCHING THE DATABASE

3

In this chapter, we will be concerned with searching our database for a particular record or records with certain characteristics in common. We'll use the LIST FOR and LOCATE commands.

Searching with LIST FOR

Let's dive in and start putting dBASE to work. Load up dBASE with the MAIL.DBF file in drive B. With the dBASE dot prompt showing, ask dBASE to

    USE B:MAIL   <RET>

Let's begin with the LIST FOR command. Suppose we want a listing of people who live in the 92123 zip code area. We could type in the command

    LIST FOR ZIP = '92123'   <RET>

Notice that we use the = to mean "equal to." The display would give us

```
Record# LNAME  FNAME   ADDRESS      CITY        STATE ZIP
     1 Smith   John Q. 123 A. St.   San Diego   CA    92123
     2 Appleby Andy    345 Oak St.  Los Angeles CA    92123
```

That is, all the people whose zip code = 92123. (From now on I'll cheat by making the LISTs fit the page, even though they might not fit the screen as shown.)

We can also display only certain fields, as usual, by specifying those fields in the LIST command. For example,

    LIST FOR ZIP = '92123' LNAME,FNAME,ADDRESS,ZIP   <RET>

gives us a list with only the fields we've requested:

```
Record#  LNAME     FNAME    ADDRESS       ZIP
     1   Smith     John Q.  123 A. St.    92123
     2   Appleby   Andy     345 Oak St.   92123
```

You can also rearrange the order in which the fields are displayed. If you wanted to see the zip code on the left, you could type in

    LIST FOR ZIP = '92123' ZIP,FNAME,LNAME,ADDRESS   <RET>

which would display:

Record#	ZIP	FNAME	LNAME	ADDRESS
1	92123	John Q.	Smith	123 A. St.
2	92123	Andy	Appleby	345 Oak St.

Now the zip code is out in front. Suppose we need to find all the people on our list who live in Los Angeles. The command

    LIST FOR CITY = 'Los Angeles'   **<RET>**

would give us all Los Angeles residents.

Record#	LNAME	FNAME	ADDRESS	CITY	STATE	ZIP
2	Appleby	Andy	345 Oak St.	Los Angeles	CA	92123
6	Doe	Ruth	1142 J. St.	Los Angeles	CA	91234

    The numbers in the left-hand column are record numbers. That is, Andy Appleby is the second record of our database, and Ruth Doe is the sixth record. The record number is useful for editing purposes, as we shall see later.

    If we need a list of everyone whose zip code is "greater than" 89999, we would use the following command:

    LIST FOR ZIP > '89999'   **<RET>**

So, our display would look like this:

Record#	LNAME	FNAME	ADDRESS	CITY	STATE	ZIP
1	Smith	John Q.	123 A. St.	San Diego	CA	92123
2	Appleby	Andy	345 Oak St.	Los Angeles	CA	92123
3	Smith	Dave	619 Elm St.	San Diego	CA	92122
5	Smithsonian	Lucy	461 Adams St.	San Diego	CA	92122-1234
6	Doe	Ruth	1142 J. St.	Los Angeles	CA	91234

If we wanted to see a list of people whose zip code is "less than" 90000, we would ask dBASE to

    LIST FOR ZIP < '90000' ZIP,LNAME,FNAME,ADDRESS   **<RET>**

which would give us:

Record#	ZIP	LNAME	FNAME	ADDRESS
4	01234	SMITH	Betsy	222 Lemon Dr.

On our database, Betsy Smith has the only zip code less than 90000. Her zip code is displayed in the column next to the record numbers because we asked for zip first in our field list.

Notice that we always use the same order even though the commands are all different. We always say LIST FOR fieldname, operator, 'condition', plus things to list <RET>. This is the proper syntax for the LIST FOR command and any deviation from this may cause an error.

Though the LIST command seems simple at first, you'll find some surprises. For example, if we want to find every Smith on our list, we would type

    LIST FOR LNAME = 'Smith' LNAME, FNAME   <RET>

Result:

Record#	LNAME	FNAME
1	Smith	John Q.
3	Smith	Dave
5	Smithsonian	Lucy

Hmmmm. There are a couple of problems here. First of all, Betsy SMITH is missing. Why? Because somebody typed in her last name as SMITH, instead of Smith. And Smith is not the same as SMITH from the computer's point of view. Second, what the heck is Smithsonian doing in there? We wanted Smiths, not everyone with Smith as the first five letters in their last name. Let's start solving these problems.

We can get rid of Smithsonian easily. Recall that dBASE pads all field data with blanks so that they fill in the field. In Chapter 2, we left 15 spaces for the last name field. So all the Smiths are actually "Smith_ _ _ _ _ _ _ _ _ _" as far as dBASE is concerned. We can omit Smithsonian in our display by specifying that only Smith, followed by a blank space, be displayed.

    LIST FOR LNAME = 'Smith ' LNAME, FNAME   <RET>

Now we see only the name Smith listed.

Record#	LNAME	FNAME
1	Smith	John Q.
3	Smith	Dave

Smithsonian didn't make it this time, because the first six letters of her last name are Smiths, not Smith_. Fooled the little devil. But we still have to deal with the absence of SMITH.

The uppercase function [UPPER()] displays all lowercase letters in a character field in uppercase. We can test this out by typing in the command

    LIST UPPER(LNAME)   <RET>

We then get

Record#	UPPER(LNAME)
1	SMITH
2	APPLEBY
3	SMITH
4	SMITH
5	SMITHSONIAN
6	DOE

Here every last name on the list is displayed in uppercase. (They're still in upper- and lowercase on the database though.) Now we can get dBASE to list all Smiths, ignoring upper- and lowercase by asking it to list all the people whose *uppercase equivalent* last name is SMITH. In dBASE, that looks like this:

    LIST FOR UPPER(LNAME) = 'SMITH '   <RET>

In English, this statement reads, "List all the people whose last name, when translated to uppercase, is 'SMITH'."

Lo and behold, we get

Record#	LNAME	FNAME	ADDRESS	CITY	STATE	ZIP
1	Smith	John Q.	123 A. St.	San Diego	CA	92123
3	Smith	Dave	619 Elm St.	San Diego	CA	92122
4	SMITH	Betsy	222 Lemon Dr.	New York	NY	01234

We finally have the correct list. You really have to spell it out for these machines. They're so literal. They hardly ever do what you *mean*, they always do exactly what you *say*. No imagination! We got rid of Smithsonian here by listing for Smith followed by a blank space, and we got SMITH in by checking to see if the uppercase equivalent (UPPER) of the last name was SMITH_.

Let's try another kind of list. Let's ask for a list of everybody except the Smiths by using the not equal to (#) sign.

    LIST FOR UPPER(LNAME) # 'SMITH' LNAME,FNAME   <RET>

We get

Record#   LNAME   FNAME
   2   Appleby   Andy
   6   Doe   Ruth

Here our list displays everyone whose last name is not Smith.

We've discussed the basics of LIST now. Let's talk about another type of searching.

Searching with the LOCATE Command

The LOCATE command is used for locating the position of a record based upon a desired characteristic. Since LOCATE does not display its data like LIST, we have to use the DISPLAY command along with it to see what dBASE has located. Like the LIST command, we use the FOR statement to indicate the characteristic we wish to find.

Let's assume we want dBASE to locate information on Dave Smith. We could ask dBASE to search for Dave Smith by last name.

    LOCATE FOR LNAME='Smith'   <RET>

This would give us the dBASE display

Record = 1

This number doesn't do us much good. We can see the contents of the record by typing

    DISPLAY   <RET>

We see this record displayed on the screen:

Record#	LNAME	FNAME	ADDRESS	CITY	STATE	ZIP
1	Smith	John Q.	123 A. St.	San Diego	CA	92123

Whoops, this isn't Dave Smith. We can continue our search for Dave with the CONTINUE command. So type in

CONTINUE   <RET>

which gives us

Record = 3

If we display this record by typing

DISPLAY   <RET>

we see that we have found Dave.

Record#	LNAME	FNAME	ADDRESS	CITY	STATE	ZIP
3	Smith	Dave	619 Elm St.	San Diego	CA	92122

Not too bad, we got it in two tries. However, if we had 10,000 names on our mailing list, this process could take a long time. A quicker approach would be to ask for the desired record more specifically. To do this we use the .AND. operator.

LOCATE FOR LNAME ='Smith ' .AND. FNAME = 'Dave'   <RET>

Now, *two* statements must be true for LOCATE to find the correct record. That is, the last name must be Smith, *and* the first name must be Dave. The result of this command is

Record = 3

on the first shot. If we DISPLAY <RET> we see the following:

Record#	LNAME	FNAME	ADDRESS	CITY	STATE	ZIP
3	Smith	Dave	619 Elm St.	San Diego	CA	92122

Got it in one try. If we type CONTINUE, we get

End of locate scope

because dBASE has checked all other records and there is not another Dave Smith to be found.

Now, last but certainly not least, we will discuss the type of search where we need to know if a field roughly matches something we are looking for. For example, suppose we want to search for people living on a street named Lemon, no matter what the address number is or whether or not they live on Lemon St., Lemon Ave., or Lemon Blvd. If we LIST or LOCATE FOR ADDRESS = 'Lemon', no match will be found, because the word Lemon is embedded in the middle of the address field (i.e. 222 Lemon Dr.). We need some way to say, "Display all records that have the word Lemon embedded in the address field." That's quite a mouthful, but not in dBASE, because the $ function will find the embedded word. So, to locate an individual living on Lemon, we would use the command

    LOCATE FOR 'Lemon' $ADDRESS   <RET>

Notice that the grammar is reversed from what we've used before. This is because the $ means "embedded in." The syntax makes sense because the above command says, "Find a record with the word Lemon embedded in the address field." When we do the above command, we see on our screen

Record = 4

If we then

    DISPLAY   <RET>

we see

Record#	LNAME	FNAME	ADDRESS	CITY	STATE	ZIP
4	SMITH	Betsy	222 Lemon Dr.	New York	NY	01234

Pretty good! It found a person living on Lemon. Keep in mind that any of the search examples we've shown with the LOCATE command work as well with the LIST command, and vice versa. That is, we could also LIST FOR 'Lemon' $ADDRESS. With this command, all individuals who live on Lemon would be displayed on the screen.

We can also combine search conditions to our heart's content. For example, if we want a listing of everyone who lives on either Elm or

Oak streets, we could:

LIST FOR 'Elm' $ADDRESS .OR. 'Oak' $ADDRESS   <RET>

which would give us

Record#	LNAME	FNAME	ADDRESS	CITY	STATE	ZIP
2	Appleby	Andy	345 Oak St.	Los Angeles	CA	92123
3	Smith	Dave	619 Elm St.	San Diego	CA	92122

   The result is a listing of the individuals who live on either Oak or
Elm streets. Be careful to distinguish *and* and *or*, though. If we had
asked for a LIST FOR 'Elm' $ADDRESS .AND. 'OAK' $ADDRESS we
would end up with nothing, because a given individual in our database can't possibly live on both Elm and Oak Streets at the same
time (unless he did happen to live at 3421 OakElm St.).
   In summary, the .OR. operator requires that only one of the conditions has to be true to get a listing. The .AND. command requires
that both search conditions be true. For instance, the command

LIST FOR 'Elm' $ADDRESS .AND. 'San Diego' $CITY   <RET>

would tell dBASE to display all of the individuals who live on Elm
St. *and* in San Diego (San Diego residents who live on Elm). The
command

LIST FOR 'Elm' $ADDRESS .OR. 'San Diego' $CITY   <RET>

would display all individuals living on Elm St., regardless of what city,
and all people living in San Diego, regardless of what street. The
.OR. command generally broadens a search, since only one condition out of two must be met for dBASE to bring the data to the
screen. On the other hand, the .AND. function narrows the search,
since both search conditions must be met to find the correct data.
   We can combine .AND. and .OR. search conditions. Try the following command:

LIST FOR STATE = 'CA' .AND. ('Oak' $ADDRESS .OR.;
   'Elm' $ADDRESS)

NOTE: Command lines that are too wide to fit on the page are broken
with a semicolon (;). You can type in the command as one long line
(without the semicolon), or press <RET> after typing in the semicolon, press the space bar, then type in the rest of the command.

This command would first require that the individual live in California. Furthermore, the individual must live on either Oak or Elm to make it to the list. In other words, this command lists all California residents who live on either Oak or Elm.

Well, perhaps we're getting carried away here. We could spend 1000 more pages discussing search possibilities, but it's better to experiment with a few searches of your own. Experience is the best teacher when it comes to computers. Don't be intimidated by errors, because they only teach you how to avoid them in the future.

In the next chapter, we will discuss dBASE commands for sorting records into some meaningful order.

NOTE: In the searching examples, I stated that a LIST or LOCATE for LNAME = 'Smith' would display Smithsonian also, since Smith represents the first five letters of Smithsonian. I suggested using 'LIST FOR LNAME = 'Smith ' (Smith followed by a blank space) to make the search more exact. There is another way to achieve the same effect. dBASE has a built-in 'EXACT' parameter which, unless specifically requested, is in the OFF mode. We can turn it on by typing in the command

    SET EXACT ON   <RET>

next to the dot prompt. This changes the results of the search to only those cases where the match is exact. Hence, if I had first SET EXACT ON, then requested a LIST FOR LNAME = 'Smith', Smithsonian would not have shown up, since this is not an EXACT match.

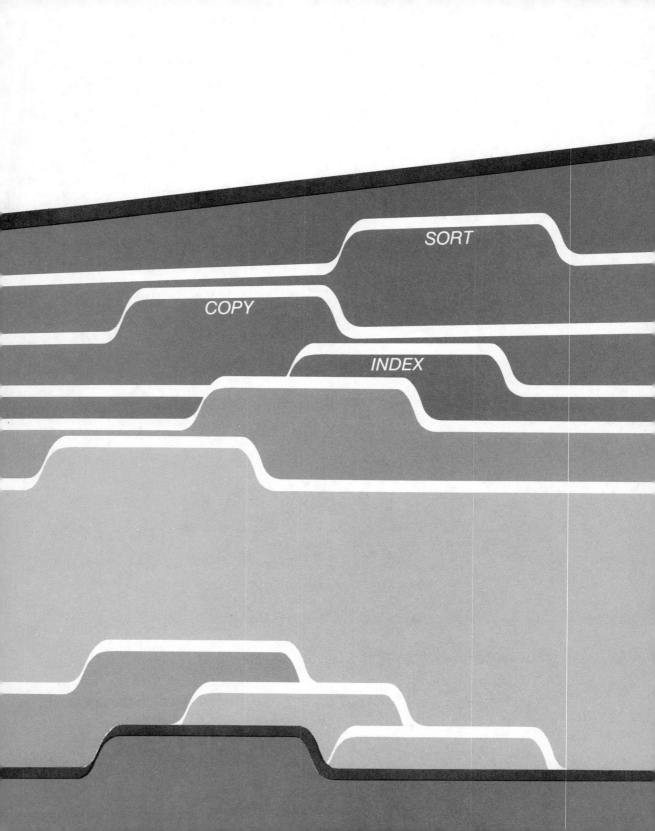

SORTING THE DATABASE

4

In most situations we add new data to our database as they become available to us. Then, at some point, we need to re-arrange the records into some meaningful order, such as by zip code for bulk mailing, or by last name for a directory. dBASE provides two commands for sorting our databases, SORT and INDEX. We'll discuss each command individually below.

Sorting with SORT

When we use the SORT command to sort our files, dBASE requires that we create a new database to store the sorted records on. Once the sorting is done, we can COPY the contents of the sorted database back into the original file. Let's try an alphabetical sort with our MAIL file on drive B. When we SORT, we'll store the newly arranged data to a file called TEMP (for temporary) on drive B (B:TEMP). After dBASE sorts the data we will copy the contents of B:TEMP back over to B:MAIL, so that the records in B:MAIL will be properly sorted.

OK, here we go. First, we want to be sure to USE B:MAIL. Take a quick look at its current state with a LIST command. You will see

1	Smith	John Q.	123 A. St.	San Diego	CA	92123
2	Appleby	Andy	345 Oak St.	Los Angeles	CA	92123
3	Smith	Dave	619 Elm St.	San Diego	CA	92122
4	SMITH	Betsy	222 Lemon Dr.	New York	NY	01234
5	Smithsonian	Lucy	461 Adams St.	San Diego	CA	92122-1234
6	Doe	Ruth	1142 J. St.	Los Angeles	CA	91234

Now, let's

SORT ON LNAME TO B:TEMP   <RET>

After the disk drives whir and buzz for a while, dBASE tells us that

100% Sorted   6 Records Sorted

Eagerly, we type LIST <RET> and again we see

1	Smith	John Q.	123 A. St.	San Diego	CA	92123
2	Appleby	Andy	345 Oak St.	Los Angeles	CA	92123
3	Smith	Dave	619 Elm St.	San Diego	CA	92122
4	SMITH	Betsy	222 Lemon Dr.	New York	NY	01234
5	Smithsonian	Lucy	461 Adams St.	San Diego	CA	92122-1234
6	Doe	Ruth	1142 J. St.	Los Angeles	CA	91234

What? These records don't look sorted to me. That's because we are listing for B:MAIL again. Remember, we sorted to B:TEMP. The sorted records are in the file B:TEMP. So, let's USE B:TEMP <RET>. Now, if we LIST, we see our sorted records.

1	Appleby	Andy	345 Oak St.	Los Angeles	CA	92123
2	Doe	Ruth	1142 J. St.	Los Angeles	CA	91234
3	SMITH	Betsy	222 Lemon Dr.	New York	NY	01234
4	Smith	John Q.	123 A. St.	San Diego	CA	92123
5	Smith	Dave	619 Elm St.	San Diego	CA	92122
6	Smithsonian	Lucy	461 Adams St.	San Diego	CA	92122-1234

Fine and dandy. So B:TEMP has the sorted records on it, but our MAIL database is still in random order. How do we put the sorted contents of B:TEMP into B:MAIL? Simple. Since B:TEMP is in use, we can just

COPY TO B:MAIL   <RET>

dBASE informs us that

mail.dbf already exists, overwrite it? (Y/N)

If you answer yes, the existing contents of the mail database will be replaced by the data in TEMP.DBF. Answer yes by typing Y.

Now if we USE B:MAIL, and do a LIST, we see

1	Appleby	Andy	345 Oak St.	Los Angeles	CA	92123
2	Doe	Ruth	1142 J. St.	Los Angeles	CA	91234
3	SMITH	Betsy	222 Lemon Dr.	New York	NY	01234
4	Smith	John Q.	123 A. St.	San Diego	CA	92123
5	Smith	Dave	619 Elm St.	San Diego	CA	92122
6	Smithsonian	Lucy	461 Adams St.	San Diego	CA	92122-1234

We have everything in alphabetical order now.

Let's illustrate what took place on the diskette in drive B with some pictures. To start with, the disk in drive B had a database called MAIL on it, with the records in random order (the order in which they were entered). Figure 4.1 shows the contents of our disk.

dBASE requires that when we SORT the database, we must sort *to* another data file. In our example, we sorted to a database called B:TEMP. After the sort was complete, we had two databases on the disk: MAIL.DBF, still in random order, and TEMP.DBF, which had the same contents as MAIL.DBF, but in sorted order, as in Figure 4.2.

In order to see the names and addresses in sorted order, we needed to USE B:TEMP, then LIST the records. However, we wanted the data on MAIL to be sorted too, so we used the COPY command to copy the sorted contents of TEMP over to MAIL. After the copy was complete, we had two identical databases, as shown in Figure 4.3.

We don't actually need the TEMP file anymore; we just needed it to temporarily hold the sorted records. We'll discuss techniques for deleting unnecessary data files in the next chapter.

Now suppose we want to do a bulk mailing, and we need these little charmers in zip code order, what do we do? I bet you can guess.

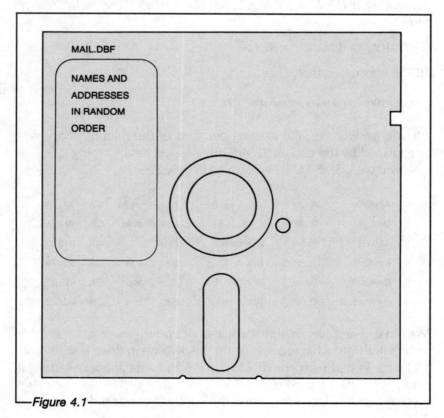

MAIL.DBF

NAMES AND
ADDRESSES
IN RANDOM
ORDER

Figure 4.1

SORT ON ZIP TO B:TEMP   <RET>

Again, dBASE will warn that we're about to overwrite the TEMP file. This is OK, so answer yes to the prompt.

Now, we'll USE B:TEMP, from there COPY TO B:MAIL, then USE B:MAIL. Doing a LIST we get

1	SMITH	Betsy	222 Lemon Dr.	New York	NY	01234
2	Doe	Ruth	1142 J. St.	Los Angeles	CA	91234
3	Smith	Dave	619 Elm St.	San Diego	CA	92122
4	Smithsonian	Lucy	461 Adams St.	San Diego	CA	92122-1234
5	Appleby	Andy	345 Oak St.	Los Angeles	CA	92123
6	Smith	John Q.	123 A. St.	San Diego	CA	92123

The records are now in zip code order, from smallest to largest. You say you want your zip codes to go from largest to smallest instead?

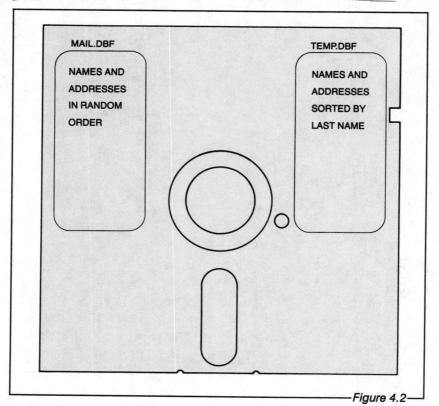

MAIL.DBF

NAMES AND
ADDRESSES
IN RANDOM
ORDER

TEMP.DBF

NAMES AND
ADDRESSES
SORTED BY
LAST NAME

Figure 4.2

Who am I to question why? Easier just to:

SORT ON ZIP/D TO B:TEMP   <RET>

When we see

100% Sorted   6 records sorted

we just

USE B:TEMP   <RET>   (wait for dot prompt to
                          reappear after each command)
COPY TO B:MAIL   <RET>
USE B:MAIL   <RET>
LIST   <RET>

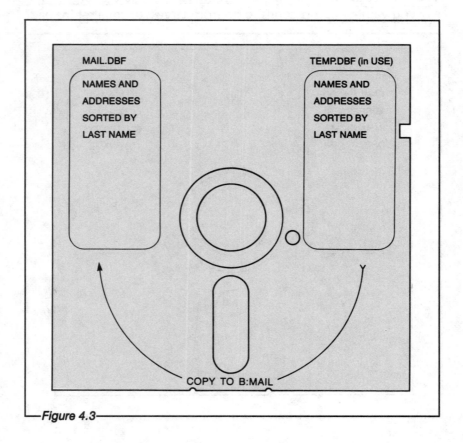

Figure 4.3

and get the following:

1	Appleby	Andy	345 Oak St.	Los Angeles	CA	92123
2	Smith	John Q.	123 A. St.	San Diego	CA	92123
3	Smithsonian	Lucy	461 Adams St.	San Diego	CA	92122-1234
4	Smith	Dave	619 Elm St.	San Diego	CA	92122
5	Doe	Ruth	1142 J. St.	Los Angeles	CA	91234
6	SMITH	Betsy	222 Lemon Dr.	New York	NY	01234

The records are now in zip code order from largest to smallest, because we specified that we wanted the SORT done in *descending (/D)* order.

Sorting in this fashion is useful, but there are disadvantages. First, sorting wastes disk space. Since dBASE does the sorting to another database file, we need at least as much empty space on the disk as the database itself fills. That means we can only use half a disk for our entire database since we need the other half to SORT TO. Second, sorting is quite slow. You may not think so with this little database, but you would if you had 5000 records. This can be especially painful when you want them sorted by name for a directory, sorted by zip code for mailings, and so forth. Also, since everyone's record number changes as the records become rearranged, we can never be sure of an individual's record number using the SORT command. This last disadvantage may seem trivial now, but with large databases, it's nice to have record numbers remain constant. What is the solution to these problems? The INDEX command is.

Sorting with INDEX

The INDEX command provides us with a much quicker and more efficient method of sorting records than does the SORT command. The command grammar is similar to the SORT command's grammar, but the approach is altogether different. Let's use the INDEX command to sort on last names. We will use a file called NAMES to do our indexing.

INDEX ON LNAME TO B:NAMES   <RET>

When we do a LIST, we see displayed on the screen

1	Appleby	Andy	345 Oak St.	Los Angeles	CA	92123
5	Doe	Ruth	1142 J. St.	Los Angeles	CA	91234
6	SMITH	Betsy	222 Lemon Dr.	New York	NY	01234
2	Smith	John Q.	123 A. St.	San Diego	CA	92123
4	Smith	Dave	619 Elm St.	San Diego	CA	92122
3	Smithsonian	Lucy	461 Adams St.	San Diego	CA	92122-1234

The records have changed to proper order, but the record numbers have remained the same. This is helpful, because that means Andy Appleby is still record 1, Ruth Doe is still record 5, etc. Also, we didn't have to go through the COPY TO rigamarole to see the records listed in proper order.

In our command, we asked dBASE to INDEX to B:NAMES. Isn't B:NAMES a data file? Yes, but it is not a database. It is a special file, an *index file* named NAMES.NDX. Its contents look very much like an index in a book. A book's index has a list of keywords in alphabetical order, and page numbers where the keywords appear in text. Our database index has a list of last names in alphabetical order, and the record numbers where they appear on the database, like so:

Appleby	1
Doe	5
SMITH	6
Smith	2
Smith	4
Smithsonian	3

After the index is complete, when we LIST, dBASE automatically uses information from the index file to determine the proper order to display the records in MAIL.DBF. The records in the MAIL.DBF database are still in their original order; the index file, however, tells dBASE the proper order in which to display the records.

After we do an index, the MAIL.DBF and NAMES.NDX files exist on the disk, as in Figure 4.4.

Let's try another example. This time we'll index on the ZIP field. First, we'll

USE B:MAIL   <RET>

then

INDEX ON ZIP TO B:ZIP   <RET>

Doing a LIST, we see

6	SMITH	Betsy	222 Lemon Dr.	New York	NY	01234
5	Doe	Ruth	1142 J. St.	Los Angeles	CA	91234
4	Smith	Dave	619 Elm St.	San Diego	CA	92122
3	Smithsonian	Lucy	461 Adams St.	San Diego	CA	92122-1234
1	Appleby	Andy	345 Oak St.	Los Angeles	CA	92123
2	Smith	John Q.	123 A. St.	San Diego	CA	92123

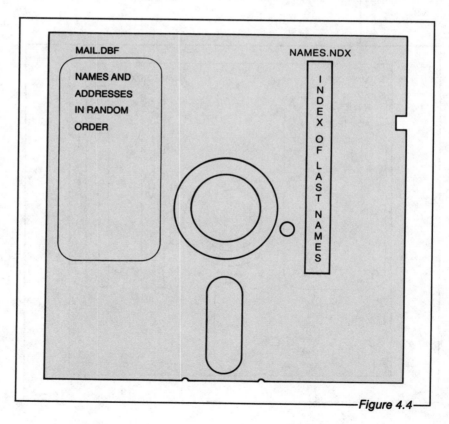

MAIL.DBF

NAMES AND
ADDRESSES
IN RANDOM
ORDER

NAMES.NDX

INDEX OF LAST NAMES

Figure 4.4

The records are now displayed in zip code order. Furthermore, we have a file on drive B called ZIP.NDX which tells dBASE the order in which to display records, as in Figure 4.5.

If we want a quick view of our mailing list sorted alphabetically by name, we don't have to sort it again. We just tell dBASE to

USE B:MAIL INDEX B:NAMES   <RET>

then LIST <RET>, which gives us

1	Appleby	Andy	345 Oak St.	Los Angeles	CA	92123
5	Doe	Ruth	1142 J. St.	Los Angeles	CA	91234
6	SMITH	Betsy	222 Lemon Dr.	New York	NY	01234
2	Smith	John Q.	123 A. St.	San Diego	CA	92123
4	Smith	Dave	619 Elm St.	San Diego	CA	92122
3	Smithsonian	Lucy	461 Adams St.	San Diego	CA	92122-1234

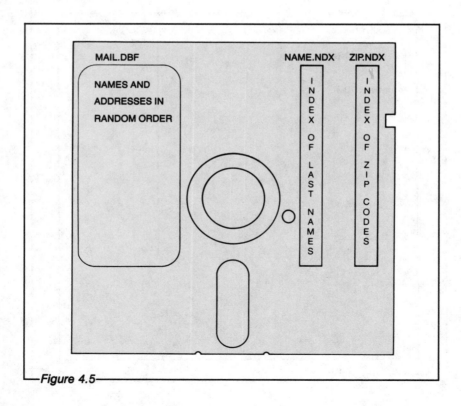

Figure 4.5

When we want a quick look at our mailing list in zip code order we don't have to re-sort anything since we've already indexed on zip, and ZIP.NDX still exists. We just tell dBASE to

USE B:MAIL INDEX B:ZIP   <RET>

then LIST <RET> immediately gives us

6	SMITH	Betsy	222 Lemon Dr.	New York	NY	01234
5	Doe	Ruth	1142 J. St.	Los Angeles	CA	91234
4	Smith	Dave	619 Elm St.	San Diego	CA	92122
3	Smithsonian	Lucy	461 Adams St.	San Diego	CA	92122-1234
1	Appleby	Andy	345 Oak St.	Los Angeles	CA	92123
2	Smith	John Q.	123 A. St.	San Diego	CA	92123

Furthermore, an index (.NDX) file takes up much less disk space than a SORT TO file, so we don't have to worry about reserving half of a disk's capacity for the SORT TO file. The INDEX command does everything that the SORT command does, but faster and better.

The beauty of the INDEX command is that it allows you to add new records and change information on the database, then view the records in sorted order immediately without re-sorting or going through the INDEX ON procedure again. It is important to keep in mind, however, that this only works with *active* index files. For example, suppose you want to display data from the MAIL database in last name and zip code order regularly. You could type in the command:

USE B:MAIL INDEX B:NAMES,B:ZIP   <RET>

next to the dot prompt. You could then add as many new records as you wish with the APPEND command. After adding new records to the database, just type in the LIST command to view the records listed alphabetically by last name. There is no need to go through the INDEX ON procedure first.

To view the records in zip code order, just make the ZIP index file the first-listed active index file, as below:

USE B:MAIL INDEX B:ZIP,B:NAMES   <RET>

Typing in the LIST command will now display the records in zip code order, once again without going through the INDEX ON procedure first.

You must remember to make the index files active, as below:

```
USE B:MAIL INDEX B:ZIP,B:NAMES   <RET>
```

before you add or change data on the database. If you don't, the index files will become *corrupted*. That is, they'll need to be recreated. If you only make one index file active before adding, changing, or deleting data, as below:

```
USE B:MAIL INDEX B:NAMES   <RET>
```

then the active index file will still be OK, but the unlisted index files (the ZIP index in ths example) will be corrupted.

You know when an index file has been corrupted because either

1. dBASE does not display newly added records when you enter the LIST command.
2. dBASE will not display the error message RECORD OUT OF RANGE when you attempt to list the records.

In either case, the index file(s) will have to be recreated from scratch. There are two methods to do so. First, just use the the database without the index files, then recreate the index files with the INDEX ON command again, as in the series of commands below:

```
USE B:MAIL   <RET>
INDEX ON LNAME TO B:NAMES   <RET>
INDEX ON ZIP TO B:ZIP   <RET>
```

Optionally, you can use the database with the existing index files, then use the REINDEX command to recreate the index files, as in the commands below:

```
USE B:MAIL INDEX B:NAMES,B:ZIP   <RET>
REINDEX   <RET>
```

dBASE III allows you to have up to seven index files active at a time. You may want to wait until you have more experience before you try managing that many index files, but you should practice working with index files and experiment a bit. Don't worry about damaging the database; it's impossible to do so. Remember, if you have problems using a database with an index file, you can make the index file(s) active again by specifying them in the USE command, then typing in the REINDEX command again. That should get everything back in shape.

Sorts within Sorts

Let's take a look at our B:MAIL file indexed by LNAME. That is, let's USE B:MAIL INDEX B:NAMES, then LIST the file. We see

1	Appleby	Andy	345 Oak St.	Los Angeles	CA	92123
5	Doe	Ruth	1142 J. St.	Los Angeles	CA	91234
6	SMITH	Betsy	222 Lemon Dr.	New York	NY	01234
4	Smith	John Q.	123 A. St.	San Diego	CA	92123
2	Smith	Dave	619 Elm St.	San Diego	CA	92122
3	Smithsonian	Lucy	461 Adams St.	San Diego	CA	92122-1234

It is sorted on last names, but if we look closely at all the Smiths, we can see that the first names are not alphabetized. That is, John Smith comes before Dave Smith. To really shape up this database, we want to SORT (or INDEX) by last name, and then within each last name, sort by first name, so that Dave Smith comes before John Smith. "Ahaa!" you say, "Do two sorts!" Sorry, it doesn't work that way. We need to do one sort on two separate fields. That is, we need to

INDEX ON LNAME + FNAME TO B:BOTH   <RET>

If we now LIST <RET> the records are displayed in the requested order.

1	Appleby	Andy	345 Oak St.	Los Angeles	CA	92123
5	Doe	Ruth	1142 J. St.	Los Angeles	CA	91234
6	SMITH	Betsy	222 Lemon Dr.	New York	NY	01234
4	Smith	Dave	619 Elm St.	San Diego	CA	92122
2	Smith	John Q.	123 A. St.	San Diego	CA	92123
3	Smithsonian	Lucy	461 Adams St.	San Diego	CA	92122-1234

John Smith is now properly placed after Dave Smith. In our INDEX command line, we've told dBASE to index on last name, and to index on first name within the last names. That was easy.

Now suppose we want the records sorted by zip code, and within each zip code batch, we want the names in alphabetical order. Easy enough. We would just ask dBASE to index on zip code as the primary sort order, and last name as the secondary sort order. How do we say that in dBASE?

    INDEX ON ZIP + LNAME TO B:ZNAMES   <RET>

If you don't like ZNAMES, use any filename you like. Either way, the records will be sorted by zip code, and within each zip code batch, names will appear in alphabetical order by last name. After typing it in, we then

    LIST   <RET>

Our file is sorted as we asked.

6	SMITH	Betsy	222 Lemon Dr.	New York	NY	01234
5	Doe	Ruth	1142 J. St.	Los Angeles	CA	91234
4	Smith	Dave	619 Elm St.	San Diego	CA	92122
3	Smithsonian	Lucy	461 Adams St.	San Diego	CA	92122-1234
1	Appleby	Andy	345 Oak St.	Los Angeles	CA	92123
2	Smith	John Q.	123 A. St.	San Diego	CA	92123

We can see the ordering more clearly if we just list the zip code and last name fields, like so:

    LIST ZIP,LNAME   <RET>

The response is

6	01234	SMITH
5	91234	Doe
4	92122	Smith
3	92122-1234	Smithsonian
1	92123	Appleby
2	92123	Smith

Within the common 92123 zip codes near the bottom of the list, the last names are alphabetized. Piece o' cake. But, we still only have the last names sorted within each zip code batch. If we had a very large database, it might behoove us to sort by zip code, alphabetically by last name within each zip code batch, and alphabetically by first name within common last names. This sounds complicated, but we just have to ask dBASE to index on the three fields:

INDEX ON ZIP + LNAME + FNAME TO B:ALL   <RET>

and our wish comes true. When you USE B:MAIL INDEX B:ALL, your mailing list would appear in zip code order, with last names alphabetized within each zip code batch, and first names alphabetized within each last name. Our present B:MAIL database is too small to demonstrate this. But trust me, it works.

Now I want to fill you in on a little trick I learned while managing my own mailing list system. I was concerned about the size of it, so I thought I'd check to see if there were any duplicate street addresses on the database. I didn't feel like writing an elaborate program to do this, so I decided to

USE B:MAIL   <RET>
INDEX ON B:ADDRESS TO B:STREETS   <RET>

When I got the dot prompt, I just asked for a list of addresses, last names, first names, and cities. That is, I asked dBASE to

LIST ADDRESS,LNAME,FNAME,CITY   <RET>

and I got this:

9	123 A. St.	Jones	John	San Diego
97	123 A. St.	Jones	John	San Diego
321	1291 Adams Ave.	Smith	Robert	Los Angeles
932	1300 Curie Way	Bragg	Andy	San Diego
1943	1410 Pacific Dr.	Quinn	Mary	Los Angeles
32	1410 Pacific Dr.	Gorton	John	Los Angeles
761	1492 Ingraham St.	Hammer	Fanny	San Diego
7	1510 Metropolis Rd.	Kenney	Clark	Metropolis

Running my finger down the address column, I could see that 123 A. St. appeared twice on my mailing list, in both record 9 and record 97. Furthermore, I could see that two people at 1410 Pacific Dr. were getting mail from me. I decided to delete the second occurrence of John Jones from the database. I also decided that I'd call one of the folks at 1410 Pacific Drive and ask if they really needed two mailings.

Hmmm. We didn't think to put phone numbers on our database. Even though we wouldn't need them for mailings, they could come in handy at other times. We'll discuss techniques for adding new fields to an existing database in the next chapter, as well as techniques for editing and deleting data.

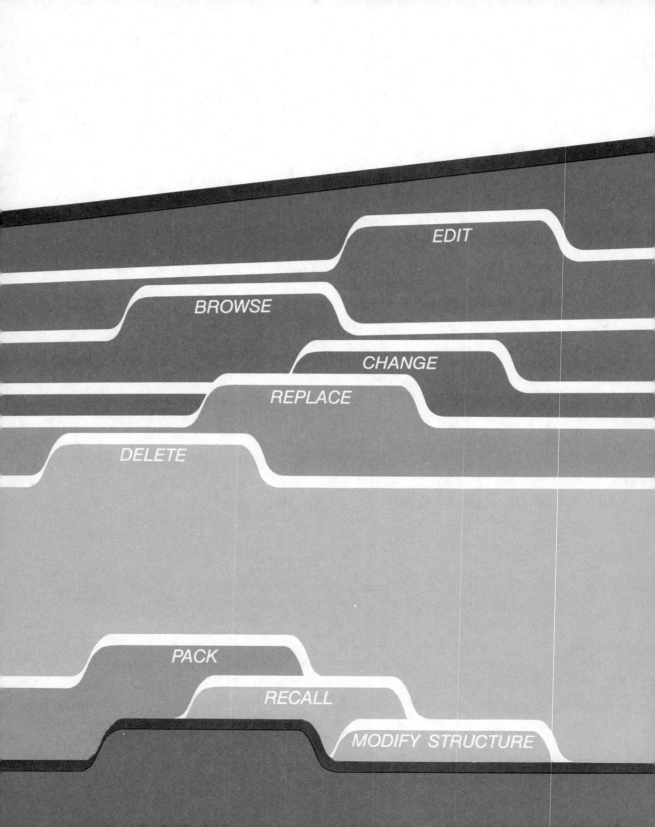

EDIT

BROWSE

CHANGE

REPLACE

DELETE

PACK

RECALL

MODIFY STRUCTURE

EDITING AND MODIFYING DATABASES

5

When working with computers, the term *edit* means to change existing data on the database. For instance, if a certain individual who is already on our database moves to a new house, we would want to change his street address. That would be a database edit. Suppose we decide that we want to include phone numbers for each individual on our database, even though we did not originally designate a field for storing phone numbers. We would have to modify the structure of the database. The commands we can use to perform such feats are discussed in this chapter.

Editing with EDIT

Computer databases need editing for a variety of reasons. People move and change their addresses, we make mistakes while entering data and have to fix them, and so forth. Editing with dBASE is a rather simple task if we know the number of the particular record we are looking for. We can't possibly remember all those numbers, but we can use the knowledge we've gained thus far to look up a record number quickly.

NOTE: If you want dBASE to display a menu of cursor-control commands while editing records, just enter the command SET MENU ON next to the dot prompt.

Let's suppose that Dave Smith from our MAIL database moves and we need to change his address. We have no idea what Dave's record number is, so we set out to find it. This is not difficult. We just load up dBASE, and

    USE B:MAIL   <RET>

Then we

    LIST FOR LNAME = 'Smith ' .AND. FNAME = 'Dave'   <RET>

This would give us the following display on the screen:

    4   Smith   Dave   619 Elm St.   San Diego   CA   92122

dBASE informs us that we have only one Dave Smith, and his record number is 4. Of course, if we had many Dave Smiths on our database, we might have to pick out the appropriate one from the display based on context. But for this example, suffice it to say that we've located our Dave Smith. He is record 4, as the left-most column informs us.

    EDIT 4   <RET>

next to the dBASE dot prompt. This gives us a new form to fill out which looks like this on our screen:

Record No.   4

LNAME   :Smith   :
FNAME   :Dave   :

```
ADDRESS        :619 Elm St.                              :
CITY           :San Diego                       :
STATE          :CA        :
ZIP            :92122             :
```

Notice that the cursor is under the S in Smith. Now we can use the arrow keys and cursor-control keys to position the cursor around to make changes. (Remember, the ^ symbol means "hold down the Ctrl key while pressing the next key.") Cursor commands for the EDIT mode are:

up-arrow	or	^E	Moves cursor up one line.
down-arrow	or	^X	Moves cursor down one line.
left-arrow	or	^S	Moves cursor left one space.
right-arrow	or	^D	Moves cursor right one space.
backspace			Moves cursor left and erases.
Del	or	^G	Deletes character over cursor.
^T			Erases one word to the right.
^Y			Erases all field contents to the right of the cursor
^U			Deletes entire record (*DEL* appears at the top of the screen).
Ins	or	^V	Turns Insert mode on/off.
PgUp	or	^R	Moves back one record.
PgDn	or	^C	Moves forward one record.
^End	or	^W	Saves changes and returns to dot prompt.
Esc	or	^Q	Abandons changes and returns to dot prompt.

To change Dave's address here, press the down-arrow key twice to move down two lines. This positions the cursor to the beginning of the ADDRESS field. Type ^Y to empty out the current address field, and type in the new address, 123 B St. Press the down-arrow key, then the left-arrow key a few times to move the cursor to the beginning of the CITY field. Type ^Y to erase the current city and type in Los Angeles as the new city. Press the down-arrow key twice, then the left-arrow key a few times to move to the beginning of the

ZIP field. Press ^Y to delete the current zip code and type in the new zip code, 90123. Now Dave Smith's data looks like this:

```
Record No.                     4
LNAME           :Smith                         :
FNAME           :Dave                  :
ADDRESS         :213 B St.                          :
CITY            :Los Angeles               :
STATE           :CA     :
ZIP             :90123_                    :
```

At this point, it is important that we check to see if the data looks ok. If it does, we next save the new data by pressing a ^W or ^End. This will bring us back to the dot prompt.

If you practice using the EDIT mode, you will find it easy to use. It is a straightforward procedure; there is nothing particularly tricky about it. At this point, you can try editing a few records of your own.

Editing with BROWSE

The BROWSE command allows us to scroll through the database, both horizontally and vertically to edit or add records. As we pan, dBASE shows as much data as will fit on the screen. We can move the cursor to change whatever information we please. This is a very useful technique for locating obvious errors, like misspellings, that can be easily corrected. To enter the BROWSE mode, we simply type in the command

BROWSE   <RET>

The screen then displays as much information as will fit. The BROWSE display looks something like this:

```
Record No.                     1          mail


LNAME————————FNAME————————ADDRESS————————CITY————————STATE

Smith          John Q.        123 A. St.      San Diego    CA

Appleby        Andy           345 Oak St.     Los Angeles  CA
```

Smith	Dave	123 B. St.	Los Angeles	CA
SMITH	Betsy	222 Lemon Dr.	New York	NY
Smithsonian	Lucy	461 Adams St.	San Diego	CA
Doe	Ruth	1142 J. St.	Los Angeles	CA

Now we can move the cursor to alter whatever information we like. The control-key commands used with the BROWSE command are:

Up-arrow	or	^E	Moves cursor up one line.
Down-arrow	or	^X	Moves cursor down one line.
Left-arrow	or	^S	Moves cursor one space to the left.
Right-arrow	or	^D	Moves cursor one space to the right.
Home	or	^A	Moves cursor one field to the left.
End	or	^F	Moves cursor one field to the right.
^Right-arrow	or	^B	Pans one field to the right.
^Left-arrow	or	^Z	Pans one field to the left.
Del	or	^G	Deletes character over cursor.
^Y			Deletes information to the right of cursor in the field.
Ins	or	^V	Enters INSERT mode, so that newly entered data is inserted into the field without overwriting existing data.
^Home			Displays/erases help menu on the top of the BROWSE screen.
^End	or	^W	Saves all newly edited data and returns to dot prompt.
Esc	or	^Q	Returns to dot prompt without saving changes made in the BROWSE mode.

To change the information of a field or record, just position the cursor where you want to make the change, and type the new data on top of the old data.

In the above example, the zip field is not displayed because it can't fit on the screen with all the other information. To look at that field, we need to pan to the right. Typing in a ^Right-arrow will pan to the right one field, so the zip code would be displayed and the last name would be invisible. Typing ^Left-arrow pans the screen back to the left again.

When we are done browsing, we can use a ^W or ^End to save all data and return to the dot prompt.

Global Editing with CHANGE and REPLACE

In some cases we may wish to make the same change to numerous records in the database. This is called *global editing*. For example, here in San Diego we recently had our area code changed from 714 to 619. Our MAIL database doesn't have a field for phone numbers yet, so we can't try out this example. But if we had a database with a field for phone numbers in it, we might want to scan through all the individuals who live in San Diego, and change their area codes. This could be accomplished by asking dBASE to

   CHANGE FIELD PHONE FOR CITY = 'San Diego'   <RET>

The effect would be to display the phone number for each San Diego resident one at a time, so that we could change the area code. We tacked on the FOR CITY = 'San Diego' condition so that only the phone numbers for San Diego residents would be displayed. The resulting conversation might look something like this:

Record No. 1
PHONE   :(714)555-1212:

Record No. 3
PHONE   :(714)555-9090:

Record No. 9
PHONE   :(714)555-1234:

etc.

dBASE will step through the database, show us each San Diego resident's phone number, and allow us to change each one until we get to the end of the database. This is a slow though safe means of performing a global edit. We can do things more quickly with the REPLACE command.

The REPLACE command is similar to the CHANGE command in that it changes the contents of a given field on a record. The REPLACE command, however, makes the change without asking questions. Here's a hypothetical example. Suppose that secretary A types in 500 names and addresses. She uses L.A. to stand for Los Angeles in the CITY field. Secretary B comes in and adds 500 more names to the list, but she spells out Los Angeles rather than using the abbreviation. The dilemma? Anytime we want to do a mailing to Los Angeles, we have to do two: one for L.A. and one for Los Angeles. Lots of problems arise because our mindless computer has no idea that L.A. means Los Angeles. What's the solution? We could just change all the L.A.s to Los Angeles, or vice versa, but it would take a long time. This is where the REPLACE ALL command comes in handy. Observe how this command works:

REPLACE ALL CITY WITH 'Los Angeles' FOR CITY = 'L.A.'
   <RET>

This one sentence says, "Anywhere you see L.A. as the city replace it with Los Angeles."

We must be very careful with this type of global editing, though, as the slightest mistake could ruin our database. For example, *don't* type in the command to

REPLACE ALL CITY WITH 'Los Angeles'   <RET>

or you will move everyone in the database to Los Angeles. The hasty command above says, "Change *every* CITY field in *every* record to Los Angeles." Everyone in the database would have Los Angeles as their city, whether their city was originally L.A., Cucamonga, or Seattle. The FOR CITY = 'L.A.' is necessary to make sure that only the L.A.s get changed.

We can try out the the REPLACE ALL command on our small MAIL database just for fun. With MAIL in use, if we LIST the database, we see

1	Appleby	Andy	345 Oak St.	Los Angeles	CA	92123
2	Smith	John Q.	123 A. St.	San Diego	CA	92123
3	Smithsonian	Lucy	461 Adams St.	San Diego	CA	92122-1234
4	Smith	Dave	123 B. St.	Los Angeles	CA	90123
5	Doe	Ruth	1142 J. St.	Los Angeles	CA	91234
6	SMITH	Betsy	222 Lemon Dr.	New York	NY	01234

Now let's type in the command to

    REPLACE ALL STATE WITH 'HI' FOR STATE = 'CA'   <RET>

dBASE informs us that

    5 records replaced

Now if we do a LIST, we see that we just moved everyone in California to Hawaii.

1	Appleby	Andy	345 Oak St.	Los Angeles	HI	92123
2	Smith	John Q.	123 A. St.	San Diego	HI	92123
3	Smithsonian	Lucy	461 Adams St.	San Diego	HI	92122-1234
4	Smith	Dave	123 B. St.	Los Angeles	HI	90123
5	Doe	Ruth	1142 J. St.	Los Angeles	HI	91234
6	SMITH	Betsy	222 Lemon Dr.	New York	NY	01234

This could create a great deal of undeliverable mail for us, so we better reverse it. Simply type in the command to

    REPLACE ALL STATE WITH 'CA' FOR STATE = 'HI'   <RET>

and the MAIL database will be back to its original form.

   Like the LIST and DISPLAY commands, CHANGE and REPLACE can be used with any searching conditions to achieve a desired result. For example, the command

    REPLACE ALL LNAME WITH 'Smith' FOR LNAME = 'SMITH'

would change all the uppercase SMITHs to Smith. Likewise the command

    CHANGE FIELD ZIP FOR ZIP<'10000'

would step us through all the records with zip codes less than 10000 and allow us to change them. The possibilities are endless, and practice is the best teacher. With the REPLACE ALL command, however, it is best to practice on a backup database rather than one that is important. The REPLACE ALL command has a high whoops factor. By the time you get done saying "whoops," dBASE has already made the erroneous change to all records in the database. Be careful.

Deleting from the Database
with DELETE, PACK, and RECALL

Sometimes we need to get rid of records in our database. The DELETE command is used to mark records for deletion, and the PACK command is used to permanently delete records. Let's use Dave Smith as an example again. This time he does not renew his membership to our mailing list, so we want to eliminate him from our database. First we need to find him on the database. To do so, we

LIST FOR LNAME = 'Smith' .AND. FNAME = 'Dave'   <RET>

which gives us

| 4 | Smith | Dave | 123 B St. | Los Angeles | CA | 90123 |

We could ask dBASE to EDIT 4 (edit record 4), and then use a ^U to delete. A more direct approach would be to simply ask dBASE to

DELETE RECORD 4   <RET>

and dBASE displays the message

1 record deleted

Now, taking another look at our database with a LIST, we see

1	Appleby	Andy	345 Oak St.	Los Angeles	CA	92123
2	Smith	John Q.	123 A. St.	San Diego	CA	92123
3	Smithsonian	Lucy	461 Adams St.	San Diego	CA	92122-1234
4 *	Smith	Dave	123 B. St.	Los Angeles	CA	90123
5	Doe	Ruth	1142 J. St.	Los Angeles	CA	91234
6	SMITH	Betsy	222 Lemon Dr.	New York	NY	01234

Dave is still there, but he is marked for deletion with an asterisk. Now we can say goodbye to Dave once and for all using this command:

PACK   <RET>

dBASE replies

5 records copied

If we LIST our file now, we don't see Dave Smith.

1	Appleby	Andy	345 Oak St.	Los Angeles	CA	92123
2	Smith	John Q.	123 A. St.	San Diego	CA	92123
3	Smithsonian	Lucy	461 Adams St.	San Diego	CA	92122-1234
4	Doe	Ruth	1142 J. St.	Los Angeles	CA	91234
5	SMITH	Betsy	222 Lemon Dr.	New York	NY	01234

Notice that everyone underneath Dave's original place in the database has moved up a notch, and their record numbers have changed. We've packed in the empty spaces left open by deletions with active records. Remember, once you do a PACK, the record is gone forever. Prior to performing a PACK, however, we can reclaim records that are marked for deletion. For instance, let's

DELETE RECORD 2   <RET>

If we now LIST the database, we see

1	Appleby	Andy	345 Oak St.	Los Angeles	CA	92123
2 *	Smith	John Q.	123 A. St.	San Diego	CA	92123
3	Smithsonian	Lucy	461 Adams St.	San Diego	CA	92122-1234
4	Doe	Ruth	1142 J. St.	Los Angeles	CA	91234
5	SMITH	Betsy	222 Lemon Dr.	New York	NY	01234

Now John Q. Smith is marked for deletion. If we wish to call him back to the database, we simply ask dBASE to

RECALL RECORD 2

Doing another LIST, we see

1	Appleby	Andy	345 Oak St.	Los Angeles	CA	92123
2	Smith	John Q.	123 A. St.	San Diego	CA	92123
3	Smithsonian	Lucy	461 Adams St.	San Diego	CA	92122-1234
4	Doe	Ruth	1142 J. St.	Los Angeles	CA	91234
5	SMITH	Betsy	222 Lemon Dr.	New York	NY	01234

John Q. Smith is no longer marked for deletion, so a PACK procedure would not eliminate him from our database.

We can also perform global deletions, using the command to DELETE ALL FOR (some condition). If we wanted to do a quick job of deleting all the people in California from our database, we could simply type in the command to

DELETE ALL FOR STATE = 'CA'   <RET>

dBASE would respond with

4 records deleted

The effect of this command would be to mark all records with CA in the state field for deletion. If we were to list the contents of the database now, we'd see

1 *	Appleby	Andy	345 Oak St.	Los Angeles	CA	92123
2 *	Smith	John Q.	123 A. St.	San Diego	CA	92123
3 *	Smithsonian	Lucy	461 Adams St.	San Diego	CA	92122-1234
4 *	Doe	Ruth	1142 J. St.	Los Angeles	CA	91234
5	SMITH	Betsy	222 Lemon Dr.	New York	NY	01234

All individuals who live in California are marked for deletion. Don't PACK them now, or we'll end up with only one record in our database, Betsy SMITH, since she lives in New York. Rather than packing, let's

RECALL ALL   <RET>

so that we don't lose all our California residents permanently. (The big earthquake hasn't hit yet, but the practice might be useful.) If we LIST after recalling all the records we'll see

1	Appleby	Andy	345 Oak St.	Los Angeles	CA	92123
2	Smith	John Q.	123 A. St.	San Diego	CA	92123
3	Smithsonian	Lucy	461 Adams St.	San Diego	CA	92122-1234
4	Doe	Ruth	1142 J. St.	Los Angeles	CA	91234
5	SMITH	Betsy	222 Lemon Dr.	New York	NY	01234

Everyone is back in shape.

Global deletes are useful for getting the job done quickly, but there is an element of danger: we might accidentally delete records we wanted to keep. It's a good idea always to LIST the records that are marked for deletion prior to packing the database. For example, suppose we decided to take a shortcut method for deleting John Smith from the database using the command

DELETE ALL FOR LNAME = 'Smith'   <RET>

We would end up with the response

2 records deleted

Whoops. We had actually only planned to delete one Smith, but ended up with two deletions. So to see who else we've accidentally deleted, we would ask dBASE to

LIST FOR DELETED()   <RET>

That is, list all the records that are marked for deletion. The result would be

2 * Smith	John Q.	123 A. St.	San Diego	CA	92123
3 * Smithsonian	Lucy	462 Adams St.	San Diego	CA	92122-1234

Apparently we've gotten a little carried away with our global delete here. We only meant to delete John Q. Smith, but, unfortunately our global delete marked Lucy Smithsonian for deletion also. We can bring back Lucy with the command to

RECALL RECORD 3   <RET>

dBASE would release record 3 from deletion. Global deletes are useful in cases where we want to delete records of a certain type, but be sure to LIST FOR DELETED() prior to PACKing to make sure you won't be deleting any innocents. Now type in the command

RECALL ALL   <RET>

so that we don't lose John Q. Smith permanently.

The ERASE command can be used to delete an entire database. Remember when we were using the SORT command, we would SORT TO B:TEMP. That means old B:TEMP.DBF is still taking up space on the disk. We can get rid of TEMP right now by typing in the command

ERASE B:TEMP.DBF   \<RET\>

dBASE will respond with the comment

File has been deleted

Once you delete an entire file, you can't get it back without extra help. So do be careful. If you should ever accidentally delete a whole database that was important to you, there are several software packages on the market that might bring them back to life. The Norton Utilities by Peter Norton is one such commercially available product. If you ever realize that you've accidentally deleted an important file, do not put anything else on that disk prior to attempting to reclaim it with the appropriate software, or it will be too late.

MODIFY STRUCTURE of a Database

The issue of adding telephone numbers to our database has popped up a couple of times. Let's take care of that now by modifying the structure of our database to include a field for phone numbers. The command for this is MODIFY STRUCTURE. Let's get started. Type in the command to

USE B:MAIL   \<RET\>

Then type in the command

MODIFY STRUCTURE   \<RET\>

The screen displays the current structure of the database as below

B:mail.dbf

	field name	type	width	dec
1	LNAME	Char/text	15	
2	FNAME	Char/text	10	

3	ADDRESS	Char/text	25
4	CITY	Char/text	15
5	STATE	Char/text	5
6	ZIP	Char/text	10

We can see the cursor ready under LNAME. Now, pop quiz. What type of data will the phone number be, character or numeric? If you guessed numeric, then you indeed just guessed. Perhaps the word "number" in "phone number" threw you off. What might a typical phone number look like? Perhaps 453-0121, or (619) 555-1212, or maybe there are two: W:555-1212 and H:555-1313. There are lots of nonnumeric characters floating around these numbers, especially the infamous hyphen sign, which means "subtract" in computer talk. A phone number is a character type. Its width? Well, let's take a liberal case: W:(619) 453-7120 H:(619) 455-1212. That one is 35 characters wide, so we'll make our PHONE field 35 characters wide.

Field 7 seems as good as any for putting in the phone number, so we can just move the cursor down to that field in the usual fashion (Down arrow or ^X). When we get there, type in

    PHONE   C   035   <RET>

so that the screen display looks like this:

B:mail.dbf

	field name	type	width	dec
1	LNAME	Char/text	15	
2	FNAME	Char/text	10	
3	ADDRESS	Char/text	25	
4	CITY	Char/text	15	
5	STATE	Char/text	5	
6	ZIP	Char/text	10	
7	PHONE	Char/text	35	
8		Char/text		

After adding the new field to the database, save the new structure by typing in a ^W or ^End. dBASE displays the message:

Database records will be APPENDED from backup fields of the same name only!!
Hit RETURN to confirm—any other key to resume

This somewhat cryptic message is a little easier to understand if you know how the MODIFY STRUCTURE command works. When you ask dBASE to MODIFY STRUCTURE, it first copies all of the records from the database to a separate database. Then, it deletes all records in the current database and allows the user to make changes. When you are done changing the structure, it reads all the records from the backup database back into the current database. However, if you changed the name of any field, it does not read in data for the new field name. For example, if you had changed the LNAME field to LAST_NAME, you would have lost all of the last names in the database. This is a useful reminder, because if you have changed a field name, you can press any key, then change the field name back to its original name.

In this example, we didn't change any field names; we just added a new field; so it's safe to proceed. Press the RETURN key now to complete the modification of the database. You'll be returned to the dot prompt.

Now, I'm afraid there is no command to fill in the phone numbers automatically on the MAIL database. To add new phone numbers, you'll need to do so one record at a time. For example, to fill in the phone number for record number 2, type in the command:

EDIT 2   <RET>

The data for record 2 appears on the screen as below:

```
Record No.                      2
LNAME         :Smith                      :
FNAME         :John Q.                  :
ADDRESS       :123 A. St.                      :
CITY          :San Diego             :
STATE         :CA     :
ZIP           :92123               :
PHONE         :                                :
```

Notice that there is now a new field at the bottom of the EDIT display in which to put phone numbers. We can move the cursor down by pressing the down-arrow key six times, so that the cursor would be in the PHONE field, like so:

PHONE:_

Then we can type in the phone number:

PHONE:(555) 453-1212_

and save the new data with a ^End or ^W. The APPEND command would permit phone numbers too. So in this last example, we've modified the structure of the database, and created a new field so that we can add phone numbers to each record.

NOTE: You've probably noticed by now that whenever you fill up any field in an EDIT screen format (as well as any APPEND screen format), the computer beeps and the cursor jumps down to the next field in the display. If you find this bell irritating, you can get rid of it by changing a basic dBASE parameter. The command

    SET BELL OFF   <RET>

typed in next to the dBASE dot prompt will keep the bell from beeping or ringing when you fill up one of the fields on the EDIT or APPEND screens.

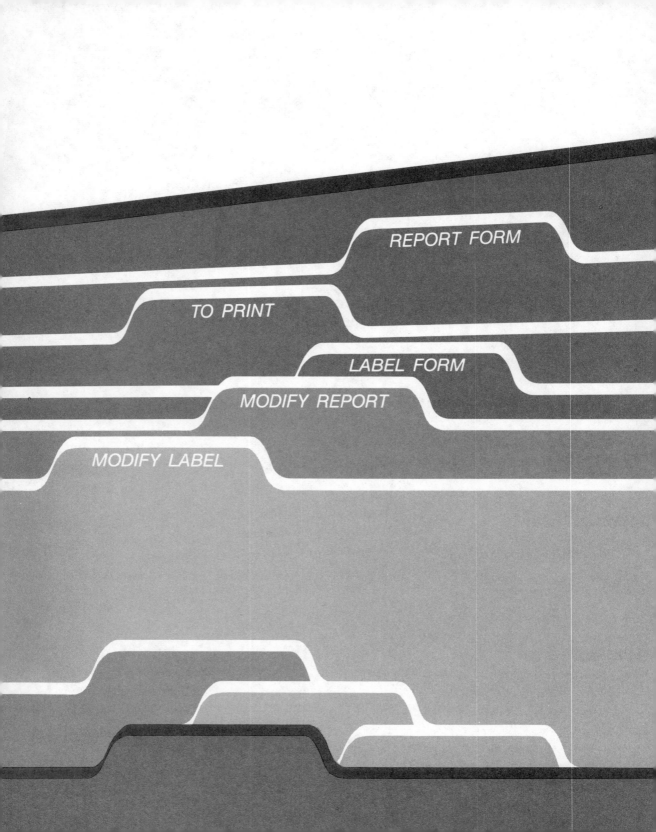

REPORT FORM

TO PRINT

LABEL FORM

MODIFY REPORT

MODIFY LABEL

CREATING AND PRINTING FORMATTED REPORTS

6

So far we've been displaying our data on the screen without any particular format. I've even cheated a little in displaying LISTs in this book so that they would fit the page. If we don't provide dBASE with an exact format for displaying our data, dBASE will list records and fields in its own fashion. To print formatted reports with dBASE III, we use its built-in report generator.

REPORT FORM

The procedure for creating report formats is simple. Whenever we create a report format, we need to give it a file name so that dBASE can easily find it later. The names used for report forms can be up to eight characters in length. Remember that spaces and punctuation marks should not be used. dBASE stores the report format on a data file and adds the last name .FRM. So if we create a report format called BYNAME, dBASE will store this format in a file called BYNAME.FRM. Let's create a report format now for our MAIL file that displays the records on our database in a directory fashion. First we need to get dBASE up and running. Then we need to

USE B:MAIL

Now, let's create a formatted report, called BYNAMES.FRM, to display the mailing list data. From the dot prompt, type in the command:

MODIFY REPORT B:BYNAME   <RET>

This brings up the first screen of the REPORT questionnaire, as displayed in Figure 6.1.

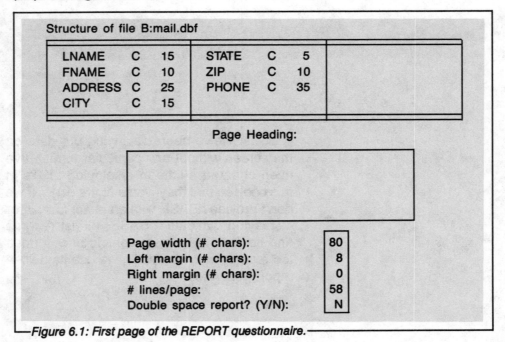

Structure of file B:mail.dbf

LNAME	C	15	STATE	C	5
FNAME	C	10	ZIP	C	10
ADDRESS	C	25	PHONE	C	35
CITY	C	15			

Page Heading:

Page width (# chars):	80
Left margin (# chars):	8
Right margin (# chars):	0
# lines/page:	58
Double space report? (Y/N):	N

Figure 6.1: First page of the REPORT questionnaire.

For our sample report, we'll type in the heading "Mailing List by Name" and set the left margin to zero spaces. Type in the title, then press the down-arrow key to move the cursor to the *left margin* prompt. Enter 0 into the left margin prompt, so that the first page of the REPORT questionnaire looks like Figure 6.2.

After filling in the first page, press the PgDn key to move to the next page. (You can use the PgUp key to move back a page if necessary.) The second page asks for information about grouping or totals, as shown in Figure 6.3.

There is no need to use groups or totals in this report, so just press the PgDn key to move to the next page of the REPORT questionnaire.

Starting with the third page of the questionnaire, dBASE asks for the specific contents of each field. Figure 6.4 shows this page.

We'll put the last name in the first column of the report, and put the heading *Last Name* at the top of this column. Type in LNAME as the field contents, and *Last Name* as the field heading, as in Figure 6.5.

Structure of file B:mail.dbf

LNAME	C	15	STATE	C	5		
FNAME	C	10	ZIP	C	10		
ADDRESS	C	25	PHONE	C	35		
CITY	C	15					

Page Heading:

Mailing List by Name

Page width (# chars):	80
Left margin (# chars):	0
Right margin (# chars):	0
# lines/page:	58
Double space report? (Y/N):	N

Figure 6.2: First page of the filled in REPORT questionnaire.

Structure of file B:mail.dbf

LNAME	C	15	STATE	C	5	
FNAME	C	10	ZIP	C	10	
ADDRESS	C	25	PHONE	C	35	
CITY	C	15				

Group/subtotal on:

Summary report only? (Y/N) ☐   Eject after each group/subtotal? ☐

Group/subtotal heading:

Subgroup/sub-total on:

Subgroup/subtotal heading:

Figure 6.3: Second page of the REPORT questionnaire.

After filling in information for the first column, press the RETURN key until dBASE asks for information about the second column. We'll put the first name in this column, with the appropriate heading, so that the screen looks like Figure 6.6.

Notice that near the top of the screen, dBASE displays a skeleton structure of how the report is shaping up. The heading *Last Name* appears with 15 X's below it, indicating the heading and width of the first column.

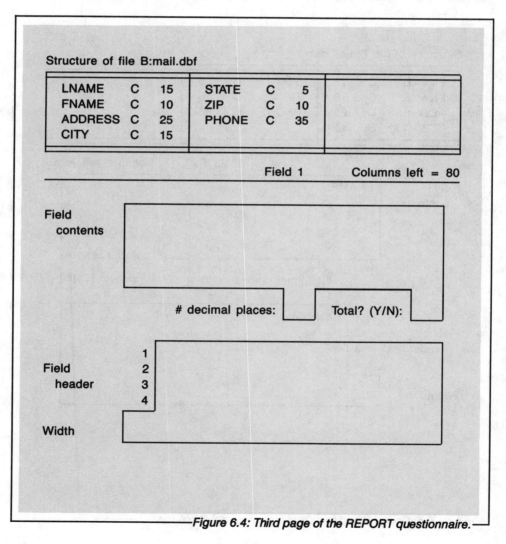

Structure of file B:mail.dbf

LNAME	C	15	STATE	C	5			
FNAME	C	10	ZIP	C	10			
ADDRESS	C	25	PHONE	C	35			
CITY	C	15						

Field 1   Columns left = 80

Field contents

decimal places: Total? (Y/N):

Field header   1 2 3 4

Width

Figure 6.4: Third page of the REPORT questionnaire.

After filling in information for the second column, press the RETURN key to bring up a page for entering the contents of the third column. We'll put the ADDRESS field in this column, along with the heading *Address.* We'll make the column 15 characters wide, just to ensure that we don't end up going beyond the 80-column maximum width of (most) printers. Figure 6.7 shows the REPORT page for the ADDRESS column of the report.

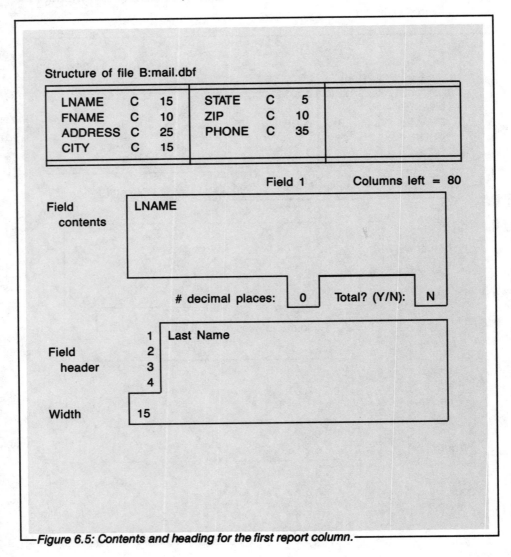

Structure of file B:mail.dbf

LNAME	C	15	STATE	C	5			
FNAME	C	10	ZIP	C	10			
ADDRESS	C	25	PHONE	C	35			
CITY	C	15						

Field 1   Columns left = 80

Field contents   LNAME

decimal places: 0   Total? (Y/N):   N

Field header
1   Last Name
2
3
4

Width   15

Figure 6.5: Contents and heading for the first report column.

After filling in the ADDRESS column data, put the CITY field in the fourth column by filling in the screen as in Figure 6.8.

Then add the state, with the heading *State* in the fifth column, as in Figure 6.9.

We'll put the zip code in the sixth column, as in Figure 6.10.

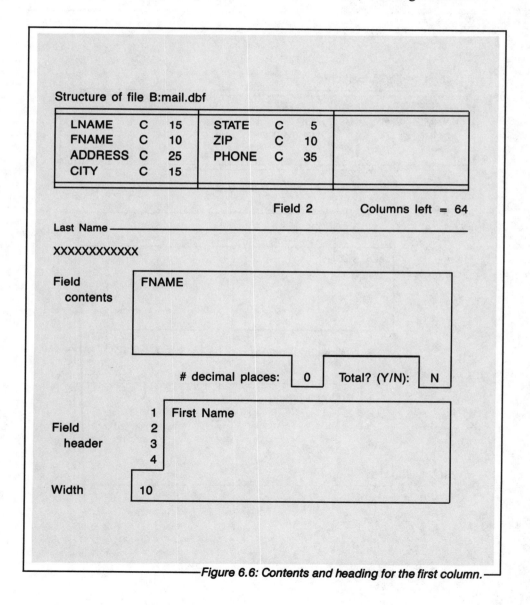

Structure of file B:mail.dbf

LNAME	C	15	STATE	C	5	
FNAME	C	10	ZIP	C	10	
ADDRESS	C	25	PHONE	C	35	
CITY	C	15				

Field 2   Columns left = 64

Last Name

XXXXXXXXXXXX

Field contents   FNAME

decimal places: 0   Total? (Y/N): N

Field header
1 First Name
2
3
4

Width 10

Figure 6.6: Contents and heading for the first column.

After filling in the column information for the sixth column, dBASE will ask for the contents of the seventh column. To complete the report format, just press RETURN instead of keying in data. The dot prompt reappears on the screen.

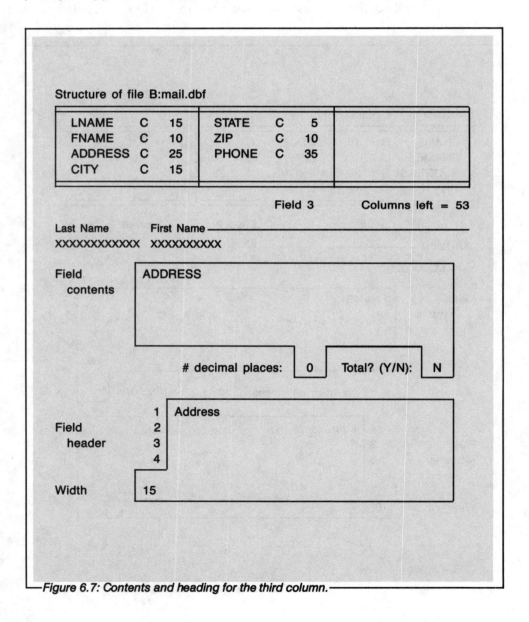

Structure of file B:mail.dbf

LNAME	C	15	STATE	C	5
FNAME	C	10	ZIP	C	10
ADDRESS	C	25	PHONE	C	35
CITY	C	15

Field 3   Columns left = 53

Last Name   First Name
XXXXXXXXXXXX XXXXXXXXXX

Field contents   ADDRESS

decimal places: 0   Total? (Y/N):   N

Field header
1 Address
2
3
4

Width   15

Figure 6.7: Contents and heading for the third column.

To view the data on the formatted report, type in the command REPORT FORM along with the name of the format file. In this example, type in the command:

REPORT FORM B:BYNAME   <RET>

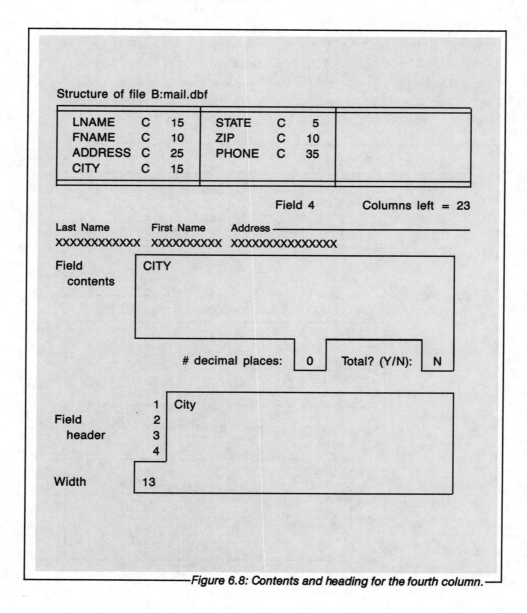

Structure of file B:mail.dbf

LNAME	C	15	STATE	C	5	
FNAME	C	10	ZIP	C	10	
ADDRESS	C	25	PHONE	C	35	
CITY	C	15				

Field 4   Columns left = 23

Last Name   First Name   Address —————————————
XXXXXXXXXXXX XXXXXXXXXX XXXXXXXXXXXXXX

Field contents
CITY

decimal places: 0   Total? (Y/N): N

Field header
1 City
2
3
4

Width 13

Figure 6.8: Contents and heading for the fourth column.

Page No. 1
05/30/83

Mailing List by Name

Last Name	First Name	Address	City	State	Zip Code
Appleby	Andy	345 Oak St.	Los Angeles	CA	92123
Smith	John Q.	123 A St.	San Diego	CA	92123
Smithsonian	Lucy	461 Adams St.	San Diego	CA	92122-1234
Doe	Ruth	1142 J. St.	Los Angeles	CA	91234
SMITH	Betsy	222 Lemon Dr.	New York	NY	01234

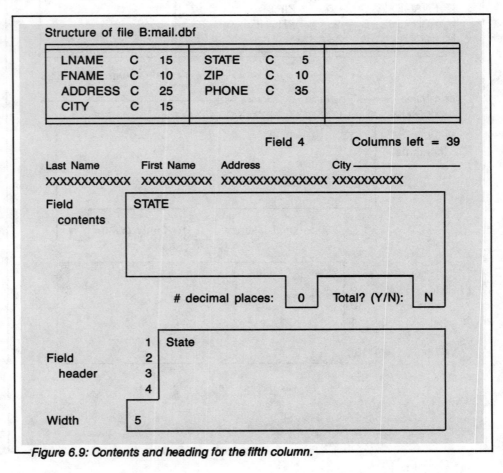

Structure of file B:mail.dbf

LNAME	C	15	STATE	C	5
FNAME	C	10	ZIP	C	10
ADDRESS	C	25	PHONE	C	35
CITY	C	15			

Field 4   Columns left = 39

Last Name   First Name   Address   City ————
XXXXXXXXXXXXX   XXXXXXXXXX   XXXXXXXXXXXXXXXXX XXXXXXXXXX

Field
contents

STATE

decimal places: 0   Total? (Y/N): N

Field
header

1 State
2
3
4

Width   5

Figure 6.9: Contents and heading for the fifth column.

To see the data in alphabetical order, first index the database, as in the command below:

INDEX ON LNAME TO B:NAMES   <RET>

Then once again type in the command:

REPORT FORM B:BYNAME   <RET>

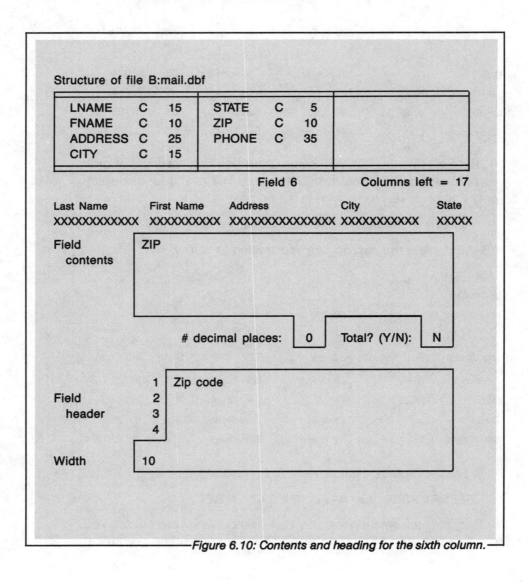

Figure 6.10: Contents and heading for the sixth column.

The same report is printed, but this time the names are in alphabetical order as below:

Page No. 1

05/30/83

Mailing List by Name

Last Name	First Name	Address	City	State	Zip Code
Appleby	Andy	345 Oak St.	Los Angeles	CA	92123
Doe	Ruth	1142 J. St.	Los Angeles	CA	91234
SMITH	Betsy	222 Lemon Dr.	New York	NY	01234
Smith	John Q.	123 A St.	San Diego	CA	92123
Smithsonian	Lucy	461 Adams St.	San Diego	CA	92122-1234

Like the LIST and LOCATE commands, you can specify that only certain records be printed on the report. For example, to display only California residents, type in the command

REPORT FORM B:BYNAME FOR STATE = "CA"   <RET>

dBASE displays the appropriate information as below

Page No. 1

05/30/83

Mailing List by Name

Last Name	First Name	Address	City	State	Zip Code
Appleby	Andy	345 Oak St.	Los Angeles	CA	92123
Doe	Ruth	1142 J. St.	Los Angeles	CA	91234
Smith	John Q.	123 A St.	San Diego	CA	92123
Smithsonian	Lucy	461 Adams St.	San Diego	CA	92122-1234

To see the report on paper, use this command:

REPORT FORM B:BYNAME TO PRINT   <RET>

To display information for only certain records on the printer, you can use both the FOR and the TO PRINT options. The command below displays records for all individuals in the 92XXX zip code area on the printer:

```
REPORT FORM B:BYNAME FOR ZIP = "92" TO;
    PRINT   <RET>
```

The printed report contains all 92XXX zip code residents, as shown below:

```
Page No. 1
05/30/83
                        Mailing List by Name
```

Last Name	First Name	Address	City	State	Zip Code
Appleby	Andy	345 Oak St.	Los Angeles	CA	92123
Smith	John Q.	123 A St.	San Diego	CA	92123
Smithsonian	Lucy	461 Adams St.	San Diego	CA	92122-1234

The TO option can also be used to send the report to a separate disk file. This is very useful if you wish to use a copy of a report in a word processing document. The command below sends a copy of the report to a disk file named DSKFILE.TXT (dBASE automatically adds the extension .TXT to the file name):

```
REPORT FORM B:BYNAME TO B:DSKFILE   <RET>
```

You can use the dBASE TYPE command to view the report, as shown below:

```
TYPE B:DSKFILE.TXT   <RET>
```

You can use the DOS TYPE command in the same manner to view the report. Appendix A discusses techniques for pulling reports into a word processing document.

To change the date on the report, type in the command

```
RUN DATE   <RET>
```

and type in the new date using MM/DD/YY format. Then use the REPORT FORM command once again to print the report.

Modifying Reports

If you change your mind about the format of a report, you can use the MODIFY REPORT command again to change its appearance. First, make sure the database is in use as shown below:

```
USE B:MAIL   <RET>
MODIFY REPORT B:BYNAME   <RET>
```

The first page of the report questionnaire will appear on the screen. You can use the PgUp and PgDn keys to move from page to page in the format file. Optionally, you can press ^Home (hold down Ctrl and press Home) to jump to a particular page. Pressing ^Home brings up a small menu of options as below:

Title   Grouping   First   Middle   Last   Append   Save   Quit

You can use the arrow keys to jump to the appropriate page, or type in the first letter of the desired option. For example, to jump to the middle of the questionnaire, highlight the word *Middle* and press RETURN, or just type in the letter M. Select the report column to edit from the menu that appears on the screen as below:

```
1   LNAME
2   FNAME
3   ADDRESS
4   CITY
5   STATE
6   ZIP
```

Use the up- and down-arrow keys to move the highlighting on the numbers. When the column you wish to edit is highlighted, press RETURN. dBASE will skip to the appropriate page of the REPORT questionnaire, and then you can use the arrow keys once again to change any information.

After making changes to the appropriate report column, type ^End or ^W to return to the dot prompt. Use the REPORT FORM command again to see the results of the changes.

Mailing Labels

To create a mailing label format for the membership system, bring the dBASE dot prompt to the screen, and use the MAIL database. Then think of a name for the label format. In this example, we'll create a two-column label format, so we'll use the name TWOCOL. Type in the commands below to create a label format called TWO-COL.LBL for the MAIL database:

```
USE B:MAIL    <RET>
MODIFY LABEL B:TWOCOL    <RET>
```

A screen displaying the contents of the current database and label format parameters appears as in Figure 6.11.

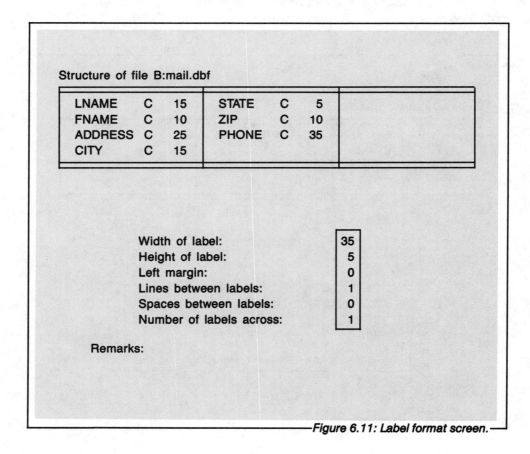

Structure of file B:mail.dbf

LNAME	C	15	STATE	C	5	
FNAME	C	10	ZIP	C	10	
ADDRESS	C	25	PHONE	C	35	
CITY	C	15				

Width of label:	35
Height of label:	5
Left margin:	0
Lines between labels:	1
Spaces between labels:	0
Number of labels across:	1

Remarks:

Figure 6.11: Label format screen.

You can change any of the parameters on the screen to modify the appearance of the labels. Most printers print 10 characters to the inch (CPI) across and 6 lines to the inch. So, for 2-across mailing labels, 3.5 inches wide, you only need to change the *Number of labels across* option to 2. Use the arrow keys to move the cursor around the label screen and make changes. Remember, you are free to set up the label format in any way you please. The prompt titled *Remarks* is just for adding comments for future reference. The information in the Remarks field is never printed.

After changing the appropriate format settings, the Label Contents screen appears. Figure 6.12 shows label contents information filled in for the MAIL database.

The TRIM function is used in the example above to trim off blank spaces that dBASE adds to the contents of each field. The '+", "+ ' puts a comma and a blank space between the city and the state, so

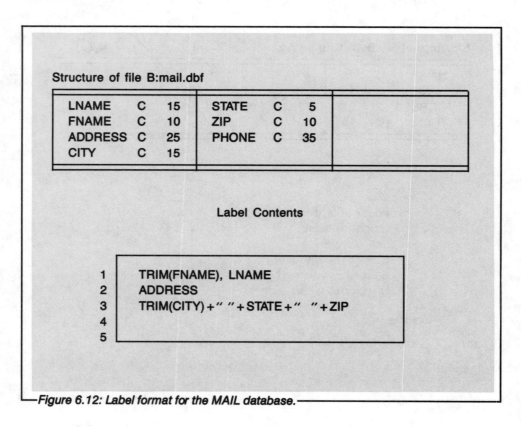

Figure 6.12: Label format for the MAIL database.

that they appear as *San Diego, CA*. When you're done filling in the field contents portion of the screen, keep pressing the RETURN key until the dot prompt appears. To print labels, type in the command:

LABEL FORM B:TWOCOL   <RET>

The labels will appear on the screen as below:

Andy Appleby	John Q. Smith
345 Oak St.	123 A St.
Los Angeles, CA 92123	San Diego, CA 92123
Lucy Smithsonian	Ruth Doe
461 Adams St.	1142 J. St.
San Diego, CA 92122-1234	Los Angeles, CA 91234

To display labels on the printer rather than on the screen, use the command:

LABEL FORM B:TWOCOL TO PRINT   <RET>

An indexed file will print labels in sorted order. For example, to print labels in zip code order for bulk mailing, create an index of zip codes as shown below:

USE B:MAIL   <RET>
INDEX ON ZIP TO B:ZIP   <RET>

Then again use the LABEL FORM command to print the labels, as below

LABEL FORM B:TWOCOL   <RET>

To print labels for only certain individuals, use the standard FOR option. For example, to print labels for only Los Angeles residents, use the command

LABEL FORM B:TWOCOL FOR CITY = "Los Angeles" TO;
**   PRINT   <RET>**

When printing mailing labels, sometimes you'll have to experiment to get the labels lined up properly in the printer. You can do a few test runs to help you get the labels lined up. Use the dBASE

NEXT option to print only a few labels at a time. For example, to do a test run with the two-column format, start at the top of the database and print the next four labels using the commands below:

```
GO TOP   <RET>
LABEL FORM B:TWOCOL NEXT 4 TO PRINT   <RET>
```

You can repeat this process until the labels are properly aligned in the printer. Then, use the LABEL FORM B:TWOCOL TO PRINT command as usual to print the labels.

To modify the TWOCOL label format, use the command

```
MODIFY LABEL B:TWOCOL   <RET>
```

Use the arrow keys to move the cursor around and make changes, and use the PgUp and PgDn keys to flip between pages in the label format. When you are done making changes, enter ^W or ^End to save the modifications.

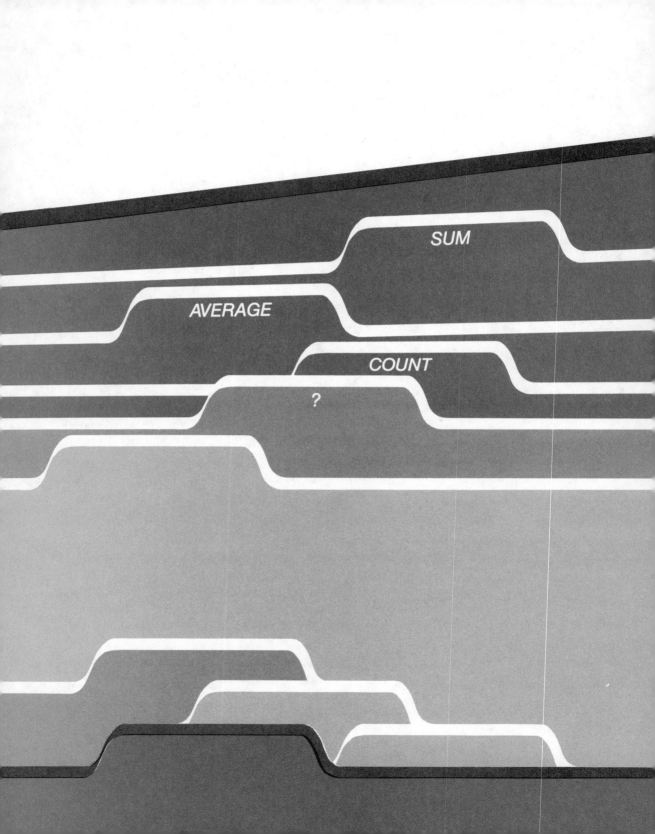

MANAGING NUMBERS AND DATES

7

dBASE III has several capabilites for doing basic arithmetic in databases. Our MAIL database did not require such manipulations, so in this chapter we'll create a new database and try out some new commands. We'll discuss the totaling and subtotaling capabilities of the REPORT command, and also experiment with SUM, AVERAGE, COUNT, and ? techniques for handling dates.

Managing Numeric Data

To learn techniques for managing numbers we'll create a new database called SALES. It will have fields for product code, product description, quantity sold, amount of sale, and date of sale. To create this database we need to have the dBASE dot prompt ready on our screen, then we

CREATE B:SALES   <RET>

We've selected drive B once again for storing the data. As usual, dBASE gives us a form to fill in describing the structure of the database. Here's how the form should look on the screen after we've filled in all the information:

	field name	type	width	dec
1	CODE	Char/text	5	
2	TITLE	Char/text	15	
3	QTY	Numeric	5	0
4	AMOUNT	Numeric	12	2
5	DATE	Date	8	
6				

Notice that CODE and TITLE are character (Char/text) types. QTY (quantity) is a numeric type with a maximum width of five and no decimal places. AMOUNT is also numeric, with a maximum of twelve digits, including two digits for decimal places. Two decimal places are necessary because this is a dollar amount. You make a field numeric by typing N when the cursor is in the *type* identification field on the screen. DATE is the Date data type, specified by assigning D as the type. dBASE automatically assigns a width of eight spaces, because dates are always entered in MM/DD/YY format. When we get to the sixth field, press RETURN and dBASE asks

Hit RETURN to confirm—any other key to resume.

Press the RETURN key. dBASE asks if you are ready to add new data. If you are ready to type in the data below, answer Y. Otherwise, you can answer N and APPEND the data later. Here are the data we will be using for our examples. Let's type these in.

CODE	TITLE	QTY	AMOUNT	DATE
AAA	Rakes	3	15.00	03/01/83
BBB	Hoes	2	12.50	03/01/83
CCC	Shovels	3	21.00	03/01/83
AAA	Rakes	2	10.00	03/01/83
CCC	Shovels	4	26.50	03/01/83
AAA	Rakes	2	11.00	03/02/83
CCC	Shovels	1	7.50	03/02/83
BBB	Hoes	2	12.50	03/02/83
AAA	Rakes	5	23.50	03/02/83

When dBASE asks for the tenth record, just press RETURN so that the dot prompt appears.

SUM and COUNT

Now we can experiment with some new commands. Suppose we wanted to know how much our gross sales were. We would need to sum the amounts using the command

SUM AMOUNT   <RET>

dBASE replies with

9 records summed
AMOUNT
139.50

We might want to know both the quantity of items sold and the total sales. The command to find out is

SUM QTY,AMOUNT   <RET>

to which dBASE replies

9 records summed
QTY AMOUNT
24   139.50

We may want to sum data for specific records only. For example, suppose we want to know how product AAA, rakes, is selling. We could ask dBASE to

SUM QTY,AMOUNT FOR CODE = 'AAA'   <RET>

dBASE sums the quantities and amounts for product code AAA, and displays the answer as

4 records summed
QTY AMOUNT
12   59.50

The AVERAGE command will average a field for records in the database. For example, to average all the AMOUNT fileds, type in the command:

AVERAGE AMOUNT   <RET>

dBASE replies with the answer:

9 records averaged
AMOUNT
15.50

You can use the FOR option to specify that only certain records be included in the average. For example, to average the AMOUNT field for records that have part number AAA, use the command

AVERAGE AMOUNT FOR CODE = "AAA"   <RET>

dBASE replies with

4 records averaged
AMOUNT
14.88

If you want the average selling price of part AAA, you need to take into account the quantity sold for each transaction. That is, the average selling price is the average of the amounts divided by the quantities. So, we will tell dBASE to average the amount divided by the quantity for part number AAA with the following command:

AVERAGE (AMOUNT/QTY) FOR CODE = "AAA"   <RET>

(The / symbol stands for divided by, as in the fraction 3/4.) dBASE
displays

4 records averaged

(AMOUNT/QTY)

5.05

The average selling price for part number AAA is $5.05.

In some cases we might prefer to know how many records contain certain information, rather than knowing about sums of fields.
For example, we might wish to know how many transactions
involved part AAA. We use the COUNT command for this. To find
out how many records on the database have AAA as the part number, we would ask dBASE to

COUNT FOR CODE = "AAA"   <RET>

dBASE will tell us

4 records

There are four records with part AAA.

In short, the SUM command adds up numeric fields, AVERAGE
will average numeric fields, and the COUNT command counts how
many records in the database have some particular characteristic.
The SUM FOR, AVERAGE FOR, and COUNT FOR commands can use
all the searching conditions that the LIST FOR command can use, so
we can be pretty specific about our sums and countings.

Managing Dates

In our SALES database, we've included a field named DATE, and
assigned it the type Date. dBASE III contains many *functions* for managing dates. The DATE() function displays today's date, as it was typed in
when you first booted up your system. For example, if you ask dBASE

what the date is (using the **?** command), as shown below:

    ? DATE()   <RET>

you'll see today's date on the screen. To change that date, type in the command

    RUN DATE   <RET>

The screen will display the current date, and allow you to change it, as shown below:

    Current date is Tue 11-06-1984
    Enter new date:_

To try out some new exercises, fill in the new date as 03/01/84, then press RETURN, as shown below:

    Current date is Tue 11-06-1984
    Enter new date: 03/01/84   <RET>

Now, let's try out some new exercises. First, with the SALES database still in use, ask dBASE to display all records that match today's date, using the command

    LIST FOR DATE = DATE()   <RET>

dBASE displays

Record#	CODE	TITLE	QTY	AMOUNT	DATE
1	AAA	Rakes	3	15.00	03/01/83
2	BBB	Hoes	2	12.50	03/01/83
3	CCC	Shovels	3	21.00	03/01/83
4	AAA	Rakes	2	10.00	03/01/83
5	CCC	Shovels	4	26.50	03/01/83

Next, ask dBASE to display all records that have dates that are later than today's date, as shown below:

    LIST FOR DATE > DATE()   <RET>

Record#	CODE	TITLE	QTY	AMOUNT	DATE
6	AAA	Rakes	2	11.00	03/02/83
7	CCC	Shovels	1	7.50	03/02/83
8	BBB	Hoes	2	12.50	03/02/83
9	AAA	Rakes	5	23.50	03/02/83

dBASE contains many *functions* for managing dates, as listed below:

Function name	Purpose
CDOW	Day of week as a Character type (e.g. Monday).
CMONTH	Month as a Character type (e.g. January).
CTOD	Character-to-date conversion.
DAY	Day of month (e.g. 31).
DOW	Day of week as number (e.g. Sunday = 1, Monday = 2, etc.).
DTOC	Date-to-character conversion.
MONTH	Month as number (e.g. 1–12).
TIME	Time expressed as HH:MM:SS.
YEAR	Year of date (e.g. 1985).

We can test these out with the SALES database. The command below asks dBASE to list the date, day of week (DOW), month (CMONTH), day (DAY) and year (YEAR) of each date in the SALES database:

LIST
DATE,CDOW(DATE),CMONTH(DATE),DAY(DATE),YEAR(DATE)   <RET>

dBASE displays

Record#	DATE	CDOW(DATE)	CMONTH(DATE)	DAY(DATE)	YEAR(DATE)
1	03/01/83	Tuesday	March	1	1983
2	03/01/83	Tuesday	March	1	1983
3	03/01/83	Tuesday	March	1	1983
4	03/01/83	Tuesday	March	1	1983

5	03/01/83	Tuesday	March	1	1983
6	03/02/83	Wednesday	March	2	1983
7	03/02/83	Wednesday	March	2	1983
8	03/02/83	Wednesday	March	2	1983
9	03/02/83	Wednesday	March	2	1983

If you need to see which records in a database have dates that fall on a Wednesday (for scheduling purposes), use the CDOW function as shown below:

    LIST FOR CDOW(DATE) = "Wednesday"   <RET>

dBASE displays

Record#	CODE	TITLE	QTY	AMOUNT	DATE
6	AAA	Rakes	2	11.00	03/02/83
7	CCC	Shovels	1	7.50	03/02/83
8	BBB	Hoes	2	12.50	03/02/83
9	AAA	Rakes	5	23.50	03/02/83

To see which records have dates in March, use the CMONTH function as shown below:

    LIST FOR CMONTH(DATE) = "March"   <RET>

dBASE displays

Record#	CODE	TITLE	QTY	AMOUNT	DATE
1	AAA	Rakes	3	15.00	03/01/83
2	BBB	Hoes	2	12.50	03/01/83
3	CCC	Shovels	3	21.00	03/01/83
4	AAA	Rakes	2	10.00	03/01/83
5	CCC	Shovels	4	26.50	03/01/83
6	AAA	Rakes	2	11.00	03/02/83
7	CCC	Shovels	1	7.50	03/02/83
8	BBB	Hoes	2	12.50	03/02/83
9	AAA	Rakes	5	23.50	03/02/83

To display a specific date, you need to convert the date in the database to a Character type with the DTOC function. The command below lists all records with the date March 2:

        LIST FOR DTOC(DATE) = "03/02"   <RET>

dBASE displays

Record#	CODE	TITLE	QTY	AMOUNT	DATE
6	AAA	Rakes	2	11.00	03/02/83
7	CCC	Shovels	1	7.50	03/02/83
8	BBB	Hoes	2	12.50	03/02/83
9	AAA	Rakes	5	23.50	03/02/83

Incidentally, in case you should need to know the time at any given moment, you can use the TIME function

        ? TIME()   <RET>

dBASE will display the time in HH:MM:SS format

        14:26:18

(That's 2:26 pm, plus 18 seconds.) The time that dBASE displays is based upon the time you keyed in when you first booted up the system. To change the time, enter the command

        RUN TIME   <RET>

Date Arithmetic

You can perform *date arithmetic*, too. For example, if you want to know at what date the amounts in the SALES file became 90 days overdue, just add 90 to each of the dates

        LIST DATE + 90

dBASE displays

Record#	date + 90
1	05/30/83
2	05/30/83

3	05/30/83
4	05/30/83
5	05/30/83
6	05/31/83
7	05/31/83
8	05/31/83
9	05/31/83

Let's reverse the order of the operation a bit. Suppose today is May 30, and you want to know which records on the SALES database are 90 or more days past due. You would want to list for those dates in which the difference between the current date minus the database DATE was greater than or equal to ($>=$) 90, as in the command below:

LIST FOR CTOD("05/30/83") – DATE $>$ = 90   <RET>

dBASE displays the appropriate records:

Record#	CODE	TITLE	QTY	AMOUNT	DATE
1	AAA	Rakes	3	15.00	03/01/83
2	BBB	Hoes	2	12.50	03/01/83
3	CCC	Shovels	3	21.00	03/01/83
4	AAA	Rakes	2	10.00	03/01/83
5	CCC	Shovels	4	26.50	03/01/83

When you want to do determine how many days have passed between two dates, just subtract the smaller, earlier date from the larger, later date. Make sure the dates are Date data types. If not, use the CTOD function to convert them. For example, suppose you were born on March 31, 1956, and today is November 6, 1984. To find out how many days you've been alive, subtract your birth date from today's date. If you forget to convert the data first and type in the equation below

? "11/06/84" – "03/31/56"

You get a strange result:

11/06/8403/31/56

However, if you remember to use the CTOD conversion function, as below:

? CTOD("11/06/84")-CTOD("03/31/56")   <RET>

dBASE will tell you exactly how many days have passed between the two dates

10447

Similarly, if you forget to do the date conversion when working with a database

list DATE – "01/01/83"

dBASE will produce the error message *Data type mismatch,* because you are trying to subtract the character string "01/01/83" from a date (the DATE field). On the screen, you'll see

Data type mismatch
                                 ?
list DATE – "01/01/83"
Do you want some help? (Y/N)

Just remember to use the CTOD function to convert the character string surrounded by quotation marks: "01/01/83" to a date:

LIST DATE – CTOD("01/01/83")

and everything will be fine.

Sorting by Date

If you want your records to be displayed in chronological order, you can index on the DATE field

INDEX ON DATE TO DATES   <RET>

When you list the database, or print a report, the records will be in order by date

Record#	CODE	TITLE	QTY	AMOUNT	DATE
1	AAA	Rakes	3	15.00	03/01/83
2	BBB	Hoes	2	12.50	03/01/83
3	CCC	Shovels	3	21.00	03/01/83

4	AAA	Rakes	2	10.00	03/01/83
5	CCC	Shovels	4	26.50	03/01/83
6	AAA	Rakes	2	11.00	03/02/83
7	CCC	Shovels	1	7.50	03/02/83
8	BBB	Hoes	2	12.50	03/02/83
9	AAA	Rakes	5	23.50	03/02/83

In some cases, you might want to combine the date with another field for sorting. For example, you might want the SALES database to be sorted by date, and within common dates be further sorted by product code (CODE). In this case, you need to convert the date to a Character type, using the DTOC function, like so:

INDEX ON DTOC(DATE)+CODE TO DATECODE   <RET>

When you list the database

LIST DATE,CODE,TITLE,QTY,AMOUNT   <RET>

the records will be sorted properly

Record#	DATE	CODE	TITLE	QTY	AMOUNT
1	03/01/83	AAA	Rakes	3	15.00
4	03/01/83	AAA	Rakes	2	10.00
2	03/01/83	BBB	Hoes	2	12.50
3	03/01/83	CCC	Shovels	3	21.00
5	03/01/83	CCC	Shovels	4	26.50
6	03/02/83	AAA	Rakes	2	11.00
9	03/02/83	AAA	Rakes	5	23.50
8	03/02/83	BBB	Hoes	2	12.50
7	03/02/83	CCC	Shovels	1	7.50

If you want the records in descending order by date, that is, from the most-recent to least-recent date, then you'll either have to use the SORT command with the /D option, or index on the *inverse* of the date. To index, specify the DATE field subtracted from a large date, such as 12/31/99:

INDEX ON CTOD("12/31/99")−DATE TO INVDATE   <RET>

When you list the database, the records will be in descending chronological order

Record#	CODE	TITLE	QTY	AMOUNT	DATE
6	AAA	Rakes	2	11.00	03/02/83
7	CCC	Shovels	1	7.50	03/02/83
8	BBB	Hoes	2	12.50	03/02/83
9	AAA	Rakes	5	23.50	03/02/83
1	AAA	Rakes	3	15.00	03/01/83
2	BBB	Hoes	2	12.50	03/01/83
3	CCC	Shovels	3	21.00	03/01/83
4	AAA	Rakes	2	10.00	03/01/83
5	CCC	Shovels	4	26.50	03/01/83

Note to advanced users: the FIND or SEEK command will not work with this index file, unless you first subtract the date you are trying to find from CTOD("12/31/99").

Totals and Subtotals in Reports

When you have a database with numbers and dates in it, you might want to print reports that include totals and subtotals. When you want a report with subtotals, the database must be indexed by the field that you are subtotaling on. For example, if we want to print a report of sales, subtotaled according to product code, we'd first need to create an index file of product codes:

```
USE B:SALES   <RET>
INDEX ON CODE TO B:CODES   <RET>
```

Then create a name (SUBTOTS in this example), and start creating the report format with the command

```
MODIFY REPORT SUBTOTS   <RET>
```

For this report, fill out the first page of the REPORT questionnaire with the information below:

```
Page Heading: Sales By Product Code
Page width (# chars):            80
Left margin (# chars):            0
Right margin (# chars):           0
# lines/page:                    58
Double space report? (Y/N)        N
```

The second page of the report, which controls subtotaling and grouping, should be filled out with the following information:

```
Group/subtotal on:              CODE
Summary report only?:           No
Eject after each group?         No
Group/subtotal heading:         Product Code
```

The remaining pages of the REPORT questionnaire ask for information about individual column contents. The information used for the SUBTOTS report is displayed below:

Field name	Decimal places	Total?	Title	Width
CODE	0	No	Code	5
TITLE	0	No	Title	15
QTY	0	Yes	Qty	5
AMOUNT	2	Yes	Amount	12
DATE	0	No	Date	8

After filling in the various pages of the REPORT questionnaire, you'll be returned to the dot prompt. To view the SALES data on the report, type in the command

REPORT FORM SUBTOTS   <RET>

dBASE will display the SALES data, subtotaled by product code

Page No. 1
03/01/83

Sales By Product Code

Code	Title	Qty	Amount	Date
* * Product Code AAA				
AAA	Rakes	3	15.00	03/01/83
AAA	Rakes	2	10.00	03/01/83
AAA	Rakes	2	11.00	03/02/83
AAA	Rakes	5	23.50	03/02/83
* * Subtotal * *				
		12	59.50	
* * Product Code BBB				
BBB	Hoes	2	12.50	03/01/83
BBB	Hoes	2	12.50	03/02/83
* * Subtotal * *				
		4	25.00	
* * Product Code CCC				
CCC	Shovels	3	21.00	03/01/83
CCC	Shovels	4	26.50	03/01/83
CCC	Shovels	1	7.50	03/02/83
* * Subtotal * *				
		8	55.00	
* * * Total * * *				
		24	139.50	

You can also create a report format that includes subtotals and sub-subtotals. For example, suppose we want to see the data on the SALES database subtotaled by date. Furthermore, we would like to see the data sub-subtotaled by product code within each date. First, we'd need to create an index file of the subtotal (DATE) and sub-subtotal (CODE) fields. Since DATE is a Date type, we'll need to use the DTOC function in the index command:

```
USE SALES   <RET>
INDEX ON DTOC(DATE)+CODE TO DATECODE   <RET>
```

To create the report format, type in the command

```
MODIFY REPORT DATECODE   <RET>
```

Then fill in the first page of the REPORT questionnaire as follows:

Page Heading: Sales By Date and Product Code	
Page width (# chars):	80
Left margin (# chars):	0
Right margin (# chars):	0
# lines/page:	58
Double space report? (Y/N)	N

The second page of the report will need information for both the sub-total and sub-subtotal fields

Group/subtotal on:	DATE
Summary report only?:	No
Eject after each group?	No
Group/subtotal heading:	Date
Subgroup/sub-subtotal on:	CODE
Subgroup/subsubtotal heading:	Product Code

Fill in the remaining pages of the REPORT questionnaire with individual column data as summarized here:

Field name	Decimal places	Total?	Title	Width
DATE	0	No	Date	8
CODE	0	No	Code	5
TITLE	0	No	Title	15
QTY	0	Yes	Qty	5
AMOUNT	2	Yes	Amount	12

After you fill in all the blanks on the REPORT questionnaire, you'll see the dot prompt. To print the report, type in the command

REPORT FORM DATECODE   <RET>

dBASE will display this report:

Page No.   1
03/01/83

                                          Sales by Date and Product Code

Date	Code	Title	Qty	Amount
* * Date 03/01/83				
* Product Code AAA				
03/01/83	AAA	Rakes	3	15.00
03/01/83	AAA	Rakes	2	10.00
* Subsubtotal *				
			5	25.00
* Product Code BBB				
03/01/83	BBB	Hoes	2	12.50
* Subsubtotal *				
			2	12.50
* Product Code CCC				
03/01/83	CCC	Shovels	3	21.00
03/01/83	CCC	Shovels	4	26.50
* Subsubtotal *				
			7	47.50
* * Subtotal * *				
			14	85.00
* * Date 03/02/83				
* Product Code AAA				
03/02/83	AAA	Rakes	2	11.00

03/02/83	AAA	Rakes	5	23.50
* Subsubtotal *				
			7	34.50
* Product Code BBB				
03/02/83	BBB	Hoes	2	12.50
* Subsubtotal *				
			2	12.50
* Product Code CCC				
03/02/83	CCC	Shovels	1	7.50
* Subsubtotal *				
			1	7.50
* * Subtotal * *				
			10	54.50
* * * Total * * *				
			24	139.50

The report shows sub-subtotals of each product code within each date. It also presents an overall total for each date, and a grand total, under *** Total *** for all the data in the report.

We've covered a lot of ground in this chapter. You've seen how dBASE III can help you manage and organize your data, but we've hardly scratched the surface of dBASE III's potential uses. In the next chapter, we'll discuss techniques for managing multiple data files.

NOTE: Once you get a feel for the basic commands used in managing a database, you might want to try the dBASE ASSIST mode. From the dot prompt, type ASSIST <RET>. A menu describing keystrokes appears. Press <RET> to go to the first page of ASSIST. Use the left- and right-arrow keys to highlight menu options at the top of the screen, and <RET> to select a highlighted option. To return to the dot prompt, press Esc a few times.

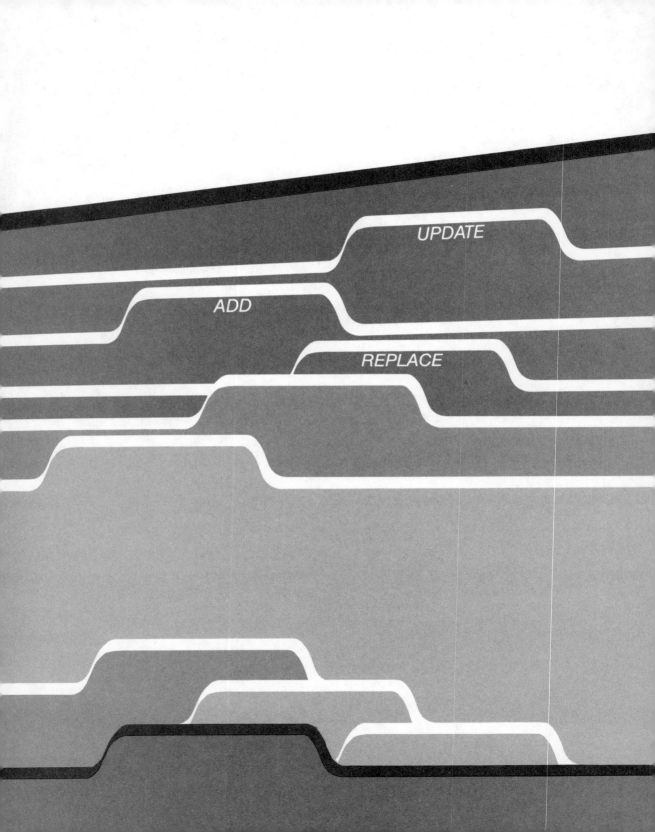

In the last chapter, we created a database called SALES to keep track of business sales figures. Most businesses also need to keep a record of goods received and overall inventory too. To allow dBASE to manage this much data, we need to develop three separate databases: one for sales, one for new stock, and a master inventory database. We can envision the relationship among the three databases in Figure 8.1.

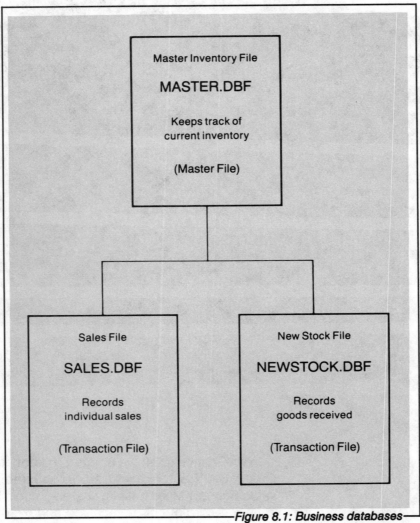

Figure 8.1: Business databases

We refer to the sales and new stock files as transaction files, because they contain information about individual transactions involved in buying and selling goods. The inventory file is the master file, because it represents the status of the inventory, based upon information from the two transaction files. We must occasionally update the master file from the transaction files, and that is what this chapter explains.

An Inventory System

First, let's create the master inventory file, and give it the filename MASTER.

CREATE B:MASTER   <RET>

Let's give it the following structure:

Structure for database : B:master.dbf

fld	field name	type	width	dec
1	CODE	Char/text	5	
2	TITLE	Char/text	15	
3	QTY	Numeric	5	
4	PRICE	Numeric	5	2
5	REORDER	Numeric	5	

When dBASE asks if we want to Input data records now, we'll answer Y and type in the following data:

CODE	TITLE	QTY	PRICE	REORDER
AAA	Rakes	30	3.50	25
BBB	Hoes	30	4.50	25
CCC	Shovels	30	5.00	25

When we're done typing in the data, we can

USE B:MASTER   <RET>
LIST   <RET>

We should see three records on the database.

Record#	CODE	TITLE	QTY	PRICE	REORDER
1	AAA	Rakes	30	3.50	25
2	BBB	Hoes	30	4.50	25
3	CCC	Shovels	30	5.00	25

The first record tells us that product code AAA is rakes, we have 30 in stock, our purchase price is $3.50, and we reorder when the stock on hand gets below 25. We have 30 hoes in stock (product code BBB), each costing $4.50, and we reorder when stock gets below 25. Product code CCC is shovels, we have 30 in stock, each costs us $5.00, and we reorder when stock is below 25.

Now let's create a database to keep track of new stock received. We'll call it NEWSTOCK, so use the command

CREATE B:NEWSTOCK   <RET>

to create it. Structure it like so:

Structure for database : B:newstock.dbf

	field name	type	width	dec
1	CODE	Char/text	5	
2	QTY	Numeric	5	
3	PRICE	Numeric	12	2
4	DATE	Date	8	

When dBASE asks INPUT DATA NOW? (Y/N), say Y. Let's assume we've just received two orders from our wholesalers, one order of ten rakes, each costing $4.00, and another order for six shovels, each costing $4.50. Furthermore, let's assume that we received them on March 1, 1983. To add these new items to NEWSTOCK, we'd need to type in the following data:

Code	Qty	Price	Date
AAA	10	4.00	03/01/83
BBB	6	4.50	03/01/83

When dBASE asks for data from record 3 press <RET>, and the dot prompt will appear. So if we now

USE B:NEWSTOCK   <RET>
LIST   <RET>

we see our new stock listed in our database format.

Record#	CODE	QTY	PRICE	DATE
1	AAA	10	4.00	03/01/83
2	BBB	6	4.50	03/01/83

Now we need to come up with a method to update the master inventory so that it reflects the new goods received.

Updating Databases with UPDATE

The dBASE UPDATE command allows us to update the contents of one database based upon information from another. We can specify that the update either add, subtract or replace entire fields. This is best explained with an example. Suppose we wish to add the new stock items to our MASTER file. Furthermore, if there is a change in the price we are paying for an item, we want the MASTER file to record the new price. In that case, we need to replace the existing price in the MASTER file with the price in the NEWSTOCK file.

Let's review what we have on both files first. If we

```
USE B:MASTER   <RET>
LIST   <RET>
```

we see our original inventory.

Record#	CODE	TITLE	QTY	PRICE	REORDER
1	AAA	Rakes	30	3.50	25
2	BBB	Hoes	30	4.50	25
3	CCC	Shovels	30	5.00	25

That is, we have 30 rakes in stock, at a wholesale price of $3.50. We have 30 hoes, wholesale priced at $4.50. We have 30 shovels, wholesale priced at $5.00. Now let's

```
USE B:NEWSTOCK   <RET>
LIST   <RET>
```

We see our new items in stock.

Record#	CODE	QTY	PRICE	DATE
1	AAA	10	4.00	03/01/83
2	BBB	6	4.50	03/01/83

We've received ten product AAA (rakes) at $4.00 each. We've also received six product BBB (hoes) at $4.50 each. So we need to add these items to our inventory, and note that the wholesale price of rakes has increased from $3.50 to $4.00. Here is the procedure to do so.

First we must identify a *key field*, one that relates the contents of the MASTER file with the NEWSTOCK file. Both files must have this field in common. In this example, CODE is the key field, because we want dBASE to add ten items of product code AAA to the master file, and six of product code BBB.

Second, we must open both the MASTER and NEWSTOCK files simultaneously. We use the SELECT command to do so. For this example, we'll open the MASTER file in a work area labeled A, and the NEWSTOCK file in a work area labeled B. Here are the correct commands:

```
SELECT A   <RET>
USE MASTER   <RET>

SELECT B   <RET>
USE NEWSTOCK   <RET>
```

Now, we need to specify the MASTER file by selecting work area A, then use the UPDATE command to perform the update. Here are the commands:

```
SELECT A   <RET>
UPDATE ON CODE FROM NEWSTOCK REPLACE QTY WITH;
   QTY + B->QTY, PRICE WITH B->PRICE   <RET>
```

These commands mean "Update the MASTER file from the data in NEWSTOCK using as the comparison (key) field; replace the QTY field with its current value plus the value of the QTY field in NEWSTOCK (QTY + B->QTY), and replace the PRICE with the price from the NEW-STOCK file (B->PRICE). The B-> symbol is used to specify data from the NEWSTOCK file opened in work area B. (The arrow symbol is formed by typing a hyphen followed by a greater-than sign).

As soon as the update procedure is complete, list the contents of the MASTER file.

LIST   <RET>

We see

1	AAA	Rakes	40	4.00	25
2	BBB	Hoes	36	4.50	25
3	CCC	Shovels	30	5.00	25

which is exactly as it should be. That is, there are now 40 rakes (AAA) in stock, because we've received 10. The price of rakes is now $4.00, as opposed to $3.50, because we REPLACED PRICE. There are now 36 hoes (BBB) in stock, because we received six. The price of hoes is still the $4.50. Shovels (CCC) were not affected, because the NEWSTOCK file did not have any information about shovels.

Now, let's discuss updating the MASTER file from the SALES database. As stated in the dBASE manual, the FROM (transaction) file in an UPDATE command must be sorted or indexed by the key field. We can see that these are certainly not sorted by the key field, CODE. If we

USE B:SALES   <RET>
LIST   <RET>

we see

1	AAA	Rakes	3	15.00	03/01/83
2	BBB	Hoes	2	12.50	03/01/83
3	CCC	Shovels	3	21.00	03/01/83
4	AAA	Rakes	2	10.00	03/01/83
5	CCC	Shovels	4	26.50	03/01/83
6	AAA	Rakes	2	11.00	03/02/83
7	CCC	Shovels	1	7.50	03/02/83
8	BBB	Hoes	2	12.50	03/01/83
9	AAA	Rakes	5	23.50	03/02/83

We can use INDEX in this case, so let's try it.

```
INDEX ON CODE TO B:SALES   <RET>
LIST   <RET>
```

Now we see the inventory sorted by product code.

1	AAA	Rakes	3	15.00	03/01/83
2	AAA	Rakes	2	10.00	03/01/83
3	AAA	Rakes	2	11.00	03/02/83
4	AAA	Rakes	5	23.50	03/02/83
5	BBB	Hoes	2	12.50	03/01/83
6	BBB	Hoes	2	12.50	03/02/83
7	CCC	Shovels	3	21.00	03/01/83
8	CCC	Shovels	4	26.50	03/01/83
9	CCC	Shovels	1	7.50	03/02/83

Now we need to open the MASTER and SALES files, along with the SALES index file to perform the update. First, let's cancel all previous SELECT assignments by typing in the command

```
CLEAR ALL   <RET>
```

Now we'll select the MASTER file as A, and the SALES file and index as B:

```
SELECT A   <RET>
USE MASTER   <RET>

SELECT B   <RET>
USE SALES INDEX SALES   <RET>
```

To perform the update, reselect the MASTER file, and perform the update, subtracting the quantities in the SALES file from the quantities in the MASTER file. (Note: the -> symbol is formed by typing a hyphen followed by a "greater-than" symbol.)

```
SELECT A   <RET>
UPDATE ON CODE FROM SALES REPLACE QTY WITH;
  QTY-B->QTY   <RET>
```

To see the effect, LIST the MASTER file:

```
LIST   <RET>
```

dBASE displays:

Record#	CODE	TITLE	QTY	PRICE	REORDER
1	AAA	Rakes	28	4.00	25
2	BBB	Hoes	32	4.50	25
3	CCC	Shovels	22	5.00	25

There are now 28 rakes in stock because we've sold 12. There are 32 hoes because we've sold 4, and 22 shovels, because we've sold 8. dBASE subtracted the appropriate quantities from the MASTER file based upon the quantities and product codes in the SALES file.

Now, to see which items need to be reordered, type in the command:

LIST FOR QTY < REORDER   <RET>

The result is

Record#	CODE	TITLE	QTY	PRICE	REORDER
3	CCC	Shovels	22	5.00	25

The amount of shovels in stock (22) has fallen below the reorder point (25).

Now, to keep future exercises in order let's "unassign" the SELECT commands by typing in the command

CLEAR ALL   <RET>

We have a managerial problem on our hands now. Our master file is accurate, but SALES and NEWSTOCK still have data in them. If we were to add new records to these transaction databases and do another update, our master file would then be incorrect. It would add or subtract these items a second time from our MASTER file. Therefore, we must come up with a managerial scheme for getting rid of data we've already updated. If we wished to update our MASTER file daily, a good approach might be to do the following:

1. Use the NEWSTOCK and SALES files during the course of the day to record goods received and sold.

2. At the end of the day, print a REPORT of all sales and goods received from the SALES and NEWSTOCK files for a permanent record.

3. UPDATE the MASTER file from the SALES and NEWSTOCK files.

4. DELETE and PACK (or ZAP) all records from the SALES and NEWSTOCK file, so future updates are not confused with previous updates.

The disadvantage to this approach is that we lose all the data from the SALES and NEWSTOCK files. Here's a better approach, which leaves the SALES and NEWSTOCK files intact. Let's use NEWSTOCK as the example. Suppose on March 2 we receive 10 rakes at $4.00 each. Let's

```
USE B:NEWSTOCK    <RET>
APPEND    <RET>
```

and add the following information:

```
Record no. 3
CODE   :AAA :
QTY    :10:
PRICE  :4.00:
DATE   :03/02/83:
```

When we LIST, we'll see the new record added at the bottom.

Record#	CODE	QTY	PRICE	DATE
1	AAA	10	4.00	03/01/83
2	BBB	6	4.50	03/01/83
3	AAA	10	4.00	03/02/83

When we do another UPDATE, we won't want records 1 and 2 to be used again. So we could move only our newest entry to a file named B:TEMP.

```
COPY TO B:TEMP FOR DTOC(DATE) = "03/02/83"    <RET>
```

If we now

```
USE B:TEMP    <RET>
LIST    <RET>
```

we'll see

Record#	CODE	QTY	PRICE	DATE
00003	AAA	10	4.00	03/02/83

Now we can update the MASTER file from TEMP, without worrying about updating records 1 and 2 again. That is, we can

```
SELECT A
USE B:MASTER
SELECT B
USE B:TEMP

SELECT A
UPDATE ON CODE FROM B:TEMP REPLACE QTY WITH;
    QTY + B->QTY, PRICE WITH B->PRICE    <RET>
```

Note: Remember to sort or index the TEMP file first. Since there was only one record in our TEMP file, we had no need to sort or index it first.

When we LIST the MASTER file now, we'll see

1	AAA	Rakes	38	4.00	25
2	BBB	Hoes	32	4.50	25
3	CCC	Shovels	22	5.00	25

Ten rakes have been added to the inventory. Our NEWSTOCK file still contains records of all goods received.

In this chapter, we've seen how we can design a series of databases to manage a small business inventory. We stored individual sales and new stock items on transaction files, and used the UPDATE command to keep the master file up to date. In the next chapter, we'll explore other methods for managing multiple databases.

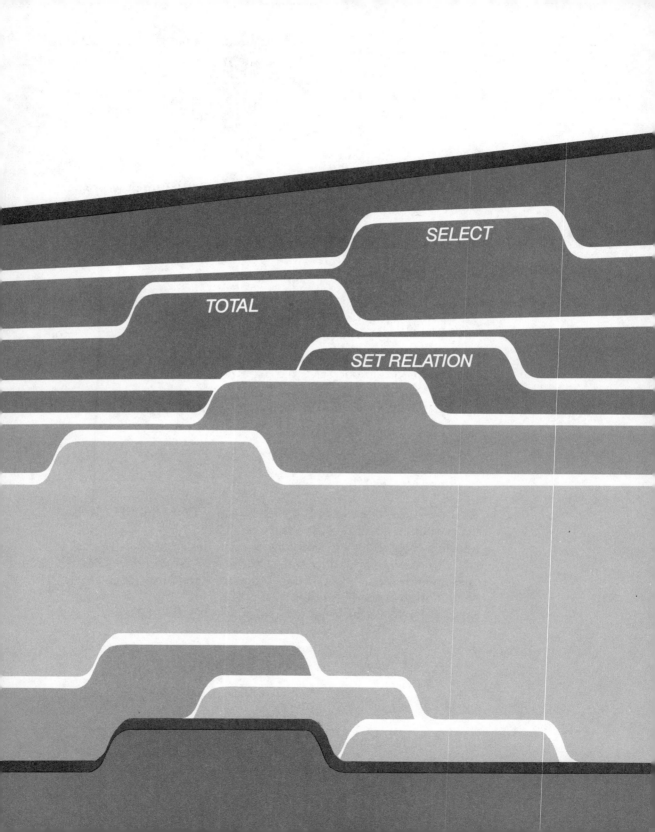

SELECT

TOTAL

SET RELATION

COMBINING AND SUMMARIZING DATABASES

9

dBASE III allows us to set up relationships among multiple databases. The SET RELATION command can be used in conjunction with the SELECT command to create relational databases.

Multiple Databases

When using the SELECT command to open multiple databases, files can be assigned numbers (1–10) or letters (A–J). With the dBASE dot prompt showing on the screen, let's designate the MASTER file as the database in work area number 1:

```
SELECT 1   <RET>
USE B:MASTER   <RET>
```

Now, let's define NEWSTOCK as the database in work area 2:

```
SELECT 2   <RET>
USE B:NEWSTOCK   <RET>
```

We can now refer to the databases as simply 1 or 2. For example, type in

```
SELECT 1   <RET>
```

and ask dBASE to display the structure of the primary-use database

```
DISPLAY STRUCTURE   <RET>
```

We now see

```
Structure for database    :   B:master.dbf
Number of data records    :   3
Date of last update       :   03/01/83
```

Field	Field name	Type	Width	Dec
1	CODE	Character	5	
2	TITLE	Character	15	
3	QTY	Numeric	5	
4	PRICE	Numeric	5	2
5	REORDER	Numeric	5	
** Total **			36	

We can also look at its contents. If we

```
LIST   <RET>
```

we see it contains:

Record#	CODE	TITLE	QTY	PRICE	REORDER
1	AAA	Rakes	38	4.00	25
2	BBB	Hoes	32	4.50	25
3	CCC	Shovels	22	5.00	25

Now let's take a look at our second database, NEWSTOCK. Type

> SELECT 2 <RET>

and ask dBASE to show us the structure of the database:

> DISPLAY STRUCTURE <RET>

We see

Structure for database : B:newstock.dbf
Number of data records : 2
Date of last update : 03/01/83

Field	Field name	Type	Width	Dec
1	CODE	Character	5	
2	QTY	Numeric	5	
3	PRICE	Numeric	12	2
4	DATE	Date	8	

To see its contents, we

> LIST <RET>

and get

Record#	CODE	QTY	PRICE	DATE
1	AAA	10	4.00	03/01/83
2	BBB	6	4.50	03/01/83
3	AAA	10	4.00	03/02/83

Our databases have some common field names (CODE, QTY, PRICE). Let's try a little experiment here with the two files. First of all, let's ask dBASE to display record 3:

```
GOTO 3    <RET>
DISPLAY   <RET>
```

We see

Record#	CODE	QTY	PRICE	DATE
3	AAA	10	4.00	03/02/83

the third record in NEWSTOCK. If we now

```
SELECT 1    <RET>
GOTO 3      <RET>
DISPLAY     <RET>
```

we see the third record in MASTER:

Record#	CODE	TITLE	QTY	PRICE	REORDER
3	CCC	Shovels	22	5.00	25

At this point we can ask dBASE for the code, quantity, and price from the third record of the MASTER file:

```
? CODE,QTY,PRICE    <RET>
```

We see

```
CCC   22   5.00
```

the code, quantity, and price from the MASTER file (1). To see data from the NEWSTOCK file, we use the B-> symbol, as in the previous chapter. (Even though you might select data files with numbers such as 1, 2, 3, you use letters in the arrow symbols, such as A->, B->, C->.) So, to view the code, quantity, and price from the NEWSTOCK file, type in the command:

```
? B->CODE,B->QTY,B->PRICE    <RET>
```

which gives the result, the CODE, QTY, and PRICE from the NEWSTOCK file:

```
AAA   10   4.00
```

If you have a lot of databases open, and you don't remember which is A, B, or C, you can use the file name with the arrow symbol instead:

? newstock->CODE, newstock->QTY, newstock->DATE   <RET>

which displays the CODE, QTY, and DATE from the NEWSTOCK file:

AAA   10 03/02/83

We'll see a very practical example of this shortly. For now, keep in mind that you use the SELECT command to open several databases at the same time. You can use either numbers or letters with the SELECT command. To refer to fields from a specific file, use the letter designator with an arrow (e.g. B->DATE), or the name of the file (e.g. newstock->DATE). With these relationships in mind, we can learn how to set up *relational* databases.

Relational Databases

Relational databases are files that are related to one another through a common field. Let's create a relational database with our NEWSTOCK and MASTER databases. First, let's take a look at the current structure and contents of the NEWSTOCK database with the commands:

```
USE NEWSTOCK   <RET>
DISPLAY STRUCTURE   <RET>
```

dBASE shows the structure of the database:

Structure for database   :   B:newstock.dbf
Number of data records   :   3
Date of last update   :   03/01/83

Field	Field name	Type	Width	Dec
1	CODE	Character	5	
2	QTY	Numeric	5	
3	PRICE	Numeric	12	2
4	DATE	Date	8	
** Total **			31	

Notice that there is no field for the name (TITLE) of each part. If we list the database, we'll see that there are no part names, only codes:

LIST   <RET>

Record#	CODE	QTY	PRICE	DATE
1	AAA	10	4.00	03/01/83
2	BBB	6	4.50	03/01/83
3	AAA	10	4.00	03/02/83

Now suppose you want to display the information from the NEW-STOCK file, with part names included. You could get this information directly from the MASTER file. Let's use the MASTER file, and take a look at its structure and contents:

USE MASTER   <RET>
DISPLAY STRUCTURE   <RET>

Structure for database   :   B:master.dbf
Number of data records   :   3
Date of last update   :   03/01/83

Field	Field name	Type	Width	Dec
1	CODE	Character	5	
2	TITLE	Character	15	
3	QTY	Numeric	5	
4	PRICE	Numeric	5	2
5	REORDER	Numeric	5	
** Total **			36	

LIST   <RET>

Record#	CODE	TITLE	QTY	PRICE	REORDER
1	AAA	Rakes	28	4.00	25
2	BBB	Hoes	32	4.50	25
3	CCC	Shovels	22	5.00	25

There is the information we need to display the NEWSTOCK data with part names (the TITLE field from the MASTER file).

To be able to combine the MASTER file TITLE field with information from the NEWSTOCK file, we need to set up a relationship between the two databases. That is, when we display records in the NEWSTOCK file, we want dBASE to look up the title for each product code in the NEWSTOCK file, and display that title along with the product code. The SET RELATION TO command can set up just such a relationship.

First of all, you need to index the field that you will be looking up in a database. In this example, we will index the product code in the MASTER file so that we can look it up to determine the part title. Let's create an index file of the CODE field in the MASTER file first:

```
USE MASTER    <RET>
INDEX ON CODE TO MASTER    <RET>
```

Now, let's set up the relationship between the NEWSTOCK and MASTER file. First, make sure that there are no databases already in use:

```
CLEAR ALL    <RET>
```

Then select NEWSTOCK as the first file:

```
SELECT 1    <RET>
USE NEWSTOCK    <RET>
```

Next, set up MASTER with the MASTER index as the second database:

```
SELECT 2    <RET>
USE MASTER INDEX MASTER    <RET>
```

Now, select NEWSTOCK as the file to use for our LIST:

```
SELECT 1    <RET>
```

Then, set up a relationship based upon the CODE field, between NEWSTOCK and MASTER. That is, set the relation to the CODE field to look up from NEWSTOCK *into* MASTER. Here is the command to do so:

```
SET RELATION TO CODE INTO MASTER    <RET>
```

Now, if you just LIST the NEWSTOCK file, it will appear as it normally would, without the TITLE field:

LIST   <RET>

Record#	CODE	QTY	PRICE	DATE
1	AAA	10	4.00	03/01/83
2	BBB	6	4.50	03/01/83
3	AAA	10	4.00	03/02/83

But, if you specify the TITLE field from the MASTER file (B->TITLE) with the LIST command as below:

LIST CODE,B->TITLE,QTY,PRICE,DATE   <RET>

the data from NEWSTOCK will be displayed with the appropriate titles:

Record#	CODE	B->TITLE	QTY	PRICE	DATE
1	AAA	Rakes	10	4.00	03/01/83
2	BBB	Hoes	6	4.50	03/01/83
3	AAA	Rakes	10	4.00	03/02/83

Although this is not the most powerful relational database possible, it gives you a good idea of how such a database works. Let's look at another hypothetical example to show the power of relational databases.

Let's suppose you have an accounts payable system with a few dozen vendors from whom you regularly purchase goods. For each vendor, you purchase several hundred items a year. Along with the amount and date of each bill, you want to record the vendor's name and address. You could manage this information by putting the vendor name and address, along with the date and amount of the bill, on a single database, using this structure:

Structure for database   :   B:ar.dbf

Field	Field name	Type	Width	Dec
1	BILL_DATE	Date	8	
2	AMOUNT	Numeric	9	2

3	VENDOR	Character	20
4	ADDRESS	Character	20
5	CITY	Character	20
6	STATE	Character	20
7	ZIP	Character	20

This would do the job, but not very efficiently, because the vendor name and address would be repeated unnecessarily throughout the database. You might even have to type this information in over and over again through the APPEND command. A sample listing from this hypothetical database shows how much information would be repeated:

BILL_DATE	AMOUNT	VENDOR	ADDRESS	CITY
06/01/85	734.75	American Iceberg Co.	345 No. Pole St.	Gnome
06/01/85	8456.32	Thompson Twins, Inc.	466 Chesapeake Way	San Francisco
06/01/85	2956.70	Logitek Microcode	256 Eprom Blvd.	Van Nuys
06/01/85	624.88	DBMS Software	256 K. St.	Solana Beach
06/05/85	1115.60	Antioch Petroleum	8776 Fossil St.	Denver
06/15/85	534.94	Hockleed Aeronautics	1777 Cannard Blvd.	Augusta
07/01/85	4236.54	Hockleed Aeronautics	1777 Cannard Blvd.	Augusta
07/01/85	2352.54	DBMS Software	256 K. St.	Solana Beach
07/06/85	3426.43	Thompson Twins, Inc.	466 Chesapeake Way	San Francisco
07/15/85	8351.76	American Iceberg Co.	345 No. Pole St.	Gnome
07/15/85	6342.75	Logitek Microcode	256 Eprom Blvd.	Van Nuys
07/20/85	946.38	Antioch Petroleum	8776 Fossil St.	Denver
08/01/85	684.34	Logitek Microcode	256 Eprom Blvd.	Van Nuys
08/12/85	12354.34	DBMS Software	256 K. St.	Solana Beach
08/15/85	1234.56	American Iceberg	345 No. Pole St.	Gnome
08/15/85	232.12	Thompson Twins, Inc.	466 Chesapeake Way	San Francisco
08/15/85	877.43	Antioch Petroleum	8776 Fossil St.	Denver
08/21/85	3214.45	Hockleed Aeronautics	1777 Cannard Blvd.	Augusta

This repetition wastes disk space and causes unnecessary repetitive typing. A better approach would be to use two databases: one containing the amount and date of each bill, as well as a simple code to identify who the bill is to be paid to, and a second one that stores the name, address, city, state, and zip code for the individual vendors.

The first database, which we'll name BILLINGS, could have the structure below:

```
Structure for database  :  B:billings.dbf
Field        Field name        Type            Width          Dec
  1          BILL_DATE         Date              8
  2          AMOUNT            Numeric           9              2
  3          VEND_CODE         Character         5
```

A listing of the data in this database might appear as below:

```
Record#  BILL_DATE   AMOUNT  VEND_CODE
      1   06/01/85    734.75  AIC
      2   06/01/85   8456.32  TTI
      3   06/01/85   2956.70  LM
      4   06/01/85    624.88  DBMS
      5   06/05/85   1115.60  AP
      6   06/15/85    534.94  HA
      7   07/01/85   4236.54  HA
      8   07/01/85   2352.54  DBMS
      9   07/06/85   3426.43  TTI
     10   07/15/85   8351.76  AIC
     11   07/15/85   6342.75  LM
     12   07/20/85    946.38  AP
     13   08/01/85    684.34  LM
     14   08/12/85  12354.34  DBMS
     15   08/15/85   1234.56  AIC
     16   08/15/85    232.12  TTI
     17   08/15/85    877.43  AP
     18   08/21/85   3214.45  HA
```

Notice that the only repetitive data is the small VEND_CODE field, so the excess space wasted by repeating vendor names and addresses is eliminated.

Now a second database, which we'll call VENDORS, can be created to store vendor names and addresses, along with vendor codes, as in the example below:

```
Structure for database   :   B:vendors.dbf
        1       VEND_CODE       Character       5
        2       VENDOR          Character       20
        3       ADDRESS         Character       20
        4       CITY            Character       20
        5       STATE           Character       20
        6       ZIP             Character       20
```

Notice that both databases have a VEND_CODE (vendor code) field for relating the information in the two databases. A listing of this database might appear as below:

	VEND_CODE	VENDOR	ADDRESS	CITY	STATE	ZIP
1	AIC	American Iceberg Co.	345 No. Pole St.	Gnome	AL	00001
2	AP	Antioch Petroleum	8776 Fossil St.	Denver	CO	55555
3	DBMS	DBMS Software	256 K. St.	Solana Beach	CA	93221
4	HA	Hockleed Aeronautics	1777 Cannard Blvd.	Augusta	GA	32212
5	LM	Logitek Microcode	256 Eprom Blvd.	Van Nuys	CA	93323
6	TTI	Thompson Twins, Inc.	466 Chesapeake Way	San Francisco	CA	91121

To set up the relationship between the two databases, you first need to index the lookup database by the *key field,* the field that relates the two databases. VEND_CODE is the relating field in this example, so you need to index the VENDORS database by VEND_CODE:

```
USE VENDORS
INDEX ON VEND_CODE TO CODES
```

To set up the relationship between the two files, open both databases simultaneously with the SELECT command, then set up the relationship with the SET RELATION TO command, as shown below:

```
SELECT 1
USE BILLINGS
```

```
SELECT 2
USE VENDORS INDEX CODES
SELECT 1
SET RELATION TO VEND_CODE INTO VENDORS
```

Now both databases are open and related via the VEND_CODE field. To display the data from the BILLINGS database along with vendor name, address, city, state, and zip code, you could LIST the BILLINGS database, using the B-> symbol to specify related information from the VENDORS database:

```
LIST BILL_DATE,AMOUNT,B->VENDOR,B->ADDRESS
```

The listing on the screen or printer would display the billing information along with the vendor names and addresses:

#	BILL_DATE	AMOUNT	B->VENDOR	B->ADDRESS
1	06/01/85	734.75	American Iceberg Co.	345 No. Pole St.
2	06/01/85	8456.32	Thompson Twins, Inc.	466 Chesapeake Way
3	06/01/85	2956.70	Logitek Microcode	256 Eprom Blvd.
4	06/01/85	624.88	DBMS Software	256 K. St.
5	06/05/85	1115.60	Antioch Petroleum	8776 Fossil St.
6	06/15/85	534.94	Hockleed Aeronautics	1777 Cannard Blvd.
7	07/01/85	4236.54	Hockleed Aeronautics	1777 Cannard Blvd.
8	07/01/85	2352.54	DBMS Software	256 K. St.
9	07/06/85	3426.43	Thompson Twins, Inc.	466 Chesapeake Way
10	07/15/85	8351.76	American Iceberg Co.	345 No. Pole St.
11	07/15/85	6342.75	Logitek Microcode	256 Eprom Blvd.
12	07/20/85	946.38	Antioch Petroleum	8776 Fossil St.
13	08/01/85	684.34	Logitek Microcode	256 Eprom Blvd.
14	08/12/85	12354.34	DBMS Software	256 K. St.
15	08/15/85	1234.56	American Iceberg Co.	345 No. Pole St.
16	08/15/85	232.12	Thompson Twins, Inc.	466 Chesapeake Way
17	08/15/85	877.43	Antioch Petroleum	8776 Fossil St.
18	08/21/85	3214.45	Hockleed Aeronautics	1777 Cannard Blvd.

The information is readily available from both databases, but no space is wasted by repeating all the vendor information in each record of the BILLINGS file.

If you would like to display data from two related databases in a formatted report, you can use the MODIFY REPORT command as usual to define the report format. Use the B-> symbol with field names in the report to refer to fields in a related database. Just remember to go through the SET RELATION procedure before setting up the report.

The examples above should give you a feel for the power of a relational database system and dBASE III's SET RELATION command. As you gain experience with database management, you'll find many applications for the SET RELATION command. But for now, let's return to our inventory system of databases (MASTER, SALES, and NEWSTOCK), and look at a technique for summarizing the contents of a database.

Summarizing Databases with TOTAL

We can summarize data in a database using the TOTAL command. For example, suppose the end of March rolls around, and we want to get a summary view of how much we sold. To find out, we could USE the sales database and total up all the sales by code. First, we'll terminate the SELECT commands by typing in the command CLEAR ALL. Then we'll USE and LIST the database:

```
CLEAR ALL   <RET>
USE B:SALES   <RET>
LIST   <RET>
```

we see

Record#	CODE	TITLE	QTY	AMOUNT	DATE
1	AAA	Rakes	3	15.00	03/01/83
2	BBB	Hoes	2	12.50	03/01/83
3	CCC	Shovels	3	21.00	03/01/83
4	AAA	Rakes	2	10.00	03/01/83
5	CCC	Shovels	4	26.50	03/01/83
6	AAA	Rakes	2	11.00	03/02/83
7	CCC	Shovels	1	7.50	03/02/83
8	BBB	Hoes	2	12.50	03/02/83
9	AAA	Rakes	5	23.50	03/02/83

The TOTAL command requires that the file be either sorted or indexed by the key field. In this example, we want to summarize sales based upon product code, so we'll index by the CODE field as shown below:

    INDEX ON CODE TO SALES <RET>

Now when we LIST the database, we see the records sorted into CODE order:

1	AAA	Rakes	3	15.00	03/01/83
2	AAA	Rakes	2	10.00	03/01/83
3	AAA	Rakes	2	11.00	03/02/83
4	AAA	Rakes	5	23.50	03/02/83
5	BBB	Shovels	2	12.50	03/02/83
6	BBB	Shovels	2	12.50	03/02/83
7	CCC	Hoes	3	21.00	03/01/83
8	CCC	Hoes	4	26.50	03/01/83
9	CCC	Hoes	1	7.50	03/02/83

Now we can use the TOTAL command to create the summary database by product code. Enter the command:

    TOTAL ON CODE TO SALESUMM <RET>

dBASE will respond with:

    9 Record(s) totalled
    3 Records generated

Now let's take a look at the contents of the summary database we've just created and named SALESUMM:

    USE SALESUMM <RET>
    LIST <RET>

We see it contains one record for each unique code in the SALES database, along with the total quantity (QTY) and amount

(AMOUNT) for each code:

Record#	CODE	TITLE	QTY	AMOUNT	DATE
1	AAA	Rakes	12	59.50	03/01/83
2	BBB	Hoes	4	25.00	03/01/83
3	CCC	Shovels	8	55.00	03/01/83

The summary database tells us at a glance that we've sold 12 rakes for a total of $59.50, 4 hoes for $25.00 total, and 8 shovels for a total of $55.00.

As we can see, there is much we can do with multiple data files in dBASE. The commands we've discussed here do a great deal of work, and therefore require more study and thinking than do simpler commands like CREATE and LIST. Acquiring the skills to manage several databases and more complex commands takes some practice, but we now have some techniques to do so. The dBASE III user's manual provides more examples of the various commands but, as with all aspects of learning to use computers, you will learn best by trying them.

Starting with the next chapter, we will begin to explore another facet of dBASE III, command files. But first we must get a feel for the computer's main memory (RAM) and memory variables.

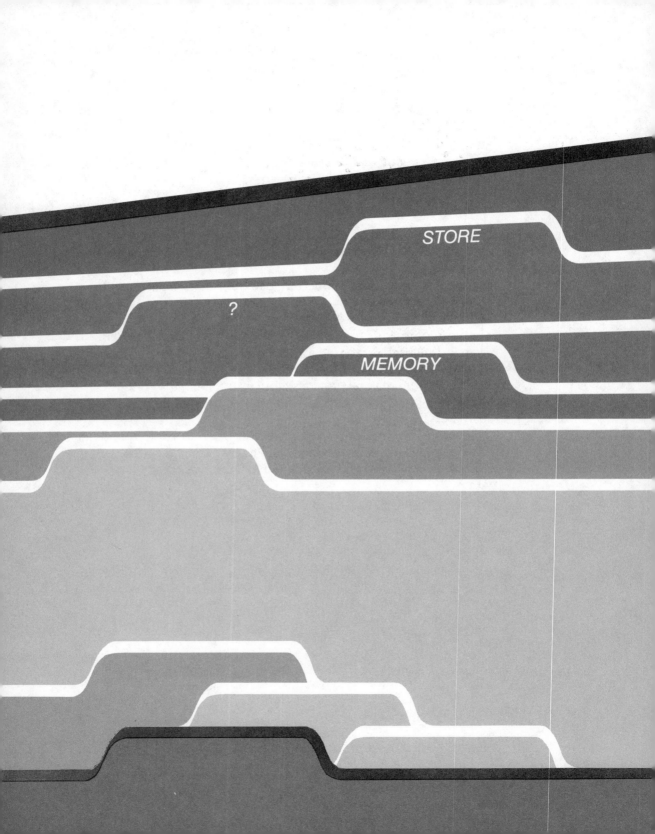

A computer's main memory is called *random access memory*, or *RAM*. All of this memory is available when the computer is turned on; whatever was stored in RAM is lost when you shut off the power. With dBASE III, we can store data in the temporary RAM similar to the way we store data in fields of databases on disk. Data in fields have field names. Data in RAM also have names, which are stored in *memory variables* instead of databases. Memory variables are temporary storage places for pieces of information you are using while working out a problem. In dBASE III, you can store 64 of these variables. The name you use for a memory variable can be up to ten characters. Let's start by getting a good feel for memory variables by examining the arithmetic capabilities of RAM.

Managing Data in RAM

Using RAM memory in your computer is much like using any pocket calculator. We ask dBASE to calculate some numbers, and it displays the answer. Let's load up dBASE and get the dot prompt to show on the screen. Then let's put the computer's main memory (RAM) to work. Next to the dot prompt, type in this command:

    ? 1 + 1   <RET>

dBASE responds with

2

the sum of 1 plus 1. Let's give it a tougher problem. Let's ask dBASE to

    ? 25/5   <RET>

It responds with

5.00

the quotient of 25 divided by 5. Not bad. dBASE is performing as well as our $5.00 calculator.

Now we can give it an even tougher problem. Suppose we need to know what the cost of an item selling for $181.93 is if we must pay 6% sales tax. That is, we need to know how much 181.93 + 6% of 181.93 is. Type in

    ? 181.93 + (.06 * 181.93)   <RET>

dBASE tells us that the total cost is

192.8458

The four decimal places give us more accuracy than necessary, but it beats paper and pencil.

We can also work with non-numeric data (called *character strings* or just *strings*) in RAM too. For instance, if we type in

? 'Hi' + 'there'   <RET>

we get the result

Hithere

Notice when we "added" two strings, they were linked together rather than summed. At first you might think that dBASE was naturally clever enough to figure this out on its own, but it was not dBASE's idea. Rather, it was the fact that we enclosed "hi" and "there" in apostrophes that told dBASE to link rather than sum. So does this mean that if we enclose the ones in 1+1 in apostrophes, it will also link rather than sum? Try it. Type in

? '1' + '1'   <RET>

and, yes, dBASE responds with

11

two ones linked together, not summed. Interesting. The apostrophes told dBASE to treat the ones as character strings, not as numbers. This leaves us another possibility: to print hi + there without the apostrophes. Type in

? hi + there   <RET>

dBASE informs us that it can't perform this operation. It says

Variable not found
  ?
? HI + there
Do you want some help? (Y/N) _

Hmmmm. It looks like these apostrophes carry quite a bit of meaning in RAM. There is a very good reason for this, as we shall see in a moment. For now, keep in mind that if we wish to do math with numbers, we do not use apostrophes (i.e. 1 + 1). If we wish to link strings together, we must use apostrophes (i.e. ? 'hi ' + 'there').

Now let's explore the reason for the error that occurred when we attempted to ? hi + there without the apostrophes.

Storing Data to Memory Variables with STORE

How do we store data in memory variables? First, we pick a name for the memory variable, and ask dBASE to store some information in it. A variable in the computer sense is exactly the same as a variable in the mathematical sense. That is, if we know that variable $X = 10$, and variable $Y = 5$, then we know that $X + Y = 15$. The same is true with computers. In order to store a value (such as 10) to a variable (such as X), we use the STORE command. Let's name our first variable X, and store 10 under that name.

    STORE 10 TO X   <RET>

dBASE displays the brief message

10

Now let's create another variable name, Y, and store 5 under that name:

    STORE 5 TO Y   <RET>

dBASE displays

5

When we ask dBASE for the sum of $X + Y$, like so:

    ? X+Y   <RET>

it should respond with 15, which it does.

15

While the variables are invisible to us right now, we can take a look at them by typing in the command to

    DISPLAY MEMORY   <RET>

and dBASE displays our variable names and what we've stored in them.

X	pub N	10	(	10.00000000)
Y	pub N	5	(	5.00000000)

2 variable defined, 18 bytes used
254 variables available, 5982 bytes available

It informs us that two memory variables exist: X and Y. Furthermore, we know that each is numeric (N), and that the value of X is 10 and the value of Y is 5. Since they are numeric, we can do basic math with them. For example, we can subtract them:

    ? X–Y   <RET>

and get the result

5

which is the difference of 10–5. To multiply them, we type

    ? X*Y   <RET>

We get the product

50

ten times five. If we wish to divide the numbers stored in the memory variables, we type

    ? X/Y   <RET>

We get the quotient

2.00

the answer to ten divided by five.

We are not limited to simple equations. For example, if we wish to get the answer to X plus Y times X, we type

    ? X+Y*X   <RET>

The result is:

60

dBASE automatically follows the standard order of precedence in math computation. That is, when an equation involves both multiplication and addition, the multiplication is performed first. We can alter the order of computations by using parentheses.

> ? (X + Y) * X   <RET>

We get the result

150

In this case, the addition was performed first. At this point, we have stored data to two memory variables, X and Y. So if we ask dBASE to

> ? A + B   <RET>

we get an error

Variable not found
  ?
? A + B
Do you want some help? (Y/N)

because we've asked dBASE to sum A and B, variables we have not yet used for storing data.

If we again examine our memory variables by typing

> DISPLAY MEMORY   <RET>

we see that we have numbers stored in X and Y.

X	pub N	10	(	10.00000000)
Y	pub N	5	(	5.00000000)

A while back we got a syntax error when we asked dBASE to ? hi + there. That is because memory variables "hi" and "there" do not exist. Of course, we could create a couple of memory variables called HI and THERE. That is, we can

STORE 'Hello' TO HI   <RET>

and then

STORE ' yourself' TO THERE   <RET>

Now we can type in the command

? HI+THERE   <RET>

and dBASE will respond with

Hello yourself

That is, the contents of memory variables HI and THERE linked together. Why are they linked? Let's see what we have stored in our memory variables.

DISPLAY MEMORY   <RET>

Now we have four memory variables:

X	pub N	10	(	10.00000000)
Y	pub N	5	(	5.00000000)
HI	pub C	"Hello"		
THERE	pub C	" yourself"		

Memory variables HI and THERE are of the character (C) type. We told dBASE they were character types by putting apostrophes around them when we stored them (STORE 'Hello' TO HI). Notice an important difference between fields and memory variables here. When we define types of data in fields, we specifically state C or N when we CREATE the database. In memory variables, dBASE automatically assumes that data stored without apostrophes (STORE 10 TO X) are numbers, and data stored with apostrophes (STORE 'Hello' TO HI) are characters.

If we wish to link the words "hi" and "there," rather than asking for the contents of the memory variables HI and THERE, we use apostrophes.

```
? 'Hi' + ' there'   <RET>
```

This gives us the result

Hi there

on the screen. The apostrophes told dBASE that we want to link the words 'Hi' and ' there' literally. To use the same principle with X and Y, if we were to ask dBASE to

```
? X+Y   <RET>
```

we'd get

15

as the answer, the sum of numeric variable X (10) plus numeric variable Y (5). On the other hand, if we use apostrophes,

```
? 'X' + 'Y'   <RET>
```

we get

XY

This is literally an X and a Y linked together.

The important aspect of memory variables you should remember is that they are not permanent like field data are. RAM memory is temporary. Disk storage is permanent. When we QUIT dBASE and turn off our computer, our databases are still safe and sound on disk. However, memory variables are erased completely. Memory variables are available as a sort of computer scratch pad, as we will see in the coming chapters.

Math Functions

Besides simple addition, subtraction, multiplication, and division, dBASE III can work with exponents and logarithms. The symbols ^ or ** can be used as an exponent symbol. For example, to see the result of three squared, ask dBASE to display 3 ^ 2

```
? 3^2   <RET>
```

dBASE responds with:

9.00

To see the value of three cubed, using the ** option, type in:

? 3**3   <RET>

dBASE responds with

27.00

To see the cube root of 27, raise 27 to the 1/3 power:

? 27^(1/3)   <RET>

dBASE responds with

3.00

The SQRT function will display the square root of any positive number. For example, to see the square root of 81, type in the command

? SQRT(81)   <RET>

dBASE responds with

9.00

You can use memory variables in place of numbers, of course. For example, you can store 81 to a memory variable called Z as shown below:

STORE 81 TO Z   <RET>

Then ask for the square root of Z

? SQRT(Z)   <RET>

dBASE displays the square root of 81

9.00

The ROUND and INT (integer) functions are used to control the number of decimals displayed. For example, we'll store the number 1.234567 to a memory variable called TEST

STORE 1.234567 TO TEST   <RET>

To see the number rounded to two decimal places, use the ROUND function:

> **? ROUND(TEST,2)   <RET>**

dBASE displays

> 1.230000

The ,2 in the ROUND function specifies two decimal places. To see the same number rounded to four decimal places, use the command

> **? ROUND(TEST,4)   <RET>**

dBASE displays

> 1.234600

To see the integer (whole number) portion only, you can round to zero decimal places

> **? ROUND(TEST,0)   <RET>**

which displays

> 1.000000

Similarly, the INT (integer) function will display the number without decimal places

> **? INT(TEST)   <RET>**

which displays

> 1

There is a difference between rounding and using the INT function, however. For example, if we store 1.9999 to a variable called TEST

> **STORE 1.9999 TO TEST   <RET>**

then print TEST rounded to zero decimal places

> **? ROUND(TEST,0)   <RET>**

we get the number rounded up to 2

2.0000

However, the INT function *truncates* the decimal portion without rounding. So if we print the integer portion of TEST

    ? INT(TEST)   <RET>

we get

1

For those of you who use logarithms on your work, dBASE III provides the EXP and LOG functions. For example, to view the natural exponent (e) of 1, type in the command

    ? EXP(1)   <RET>

dBASE responds with

2.72

To see the natural logarithm of 2.72, type in the command

    ? LOG(2.72)   <RET>

and dBASE displays

1.00

If you need more decimals, just use them in the number you're working with. For example, the command

    ? EXP(1.00000000)   <RET>

displays

2.7182818

In later chapters, we'll have a chance to work with additional dBASE III functions. Starting with the next chapter, we'll explore one of dBASE III's most powerful features: command files.

MODIFY COMMAND

DO

DO WHILE . . . ENDDO

EOF()

SKIP

GO TOP

GO BOTTOM

RETURN

CREATING COMMAND FILES

11

A *command file* is a disk file that has a series of commands in it. We record commands in files because it is more convenient to have dBASE do a whole batch of commands than for us to type in each command one at a time. The potential of command files goes far beyond saving time, however, as we shall see. A command file is actually a computer program, and from now on we'll use the words command file and program interchangeably.

A *computer program* is similar to the program we receive when we go to the theater. The theater's program displays the series of events that are to be carried out, and the order in which they will occur. Likewise, the computer program presents a series of commands to the computer in the order in which they are to be carried out. Of course, the computer program is more difficult to read than the theater program because it is not in plain English. It is written in a computer language. In this book, our programs will be written in dBASE III, the computer language that we're already familiar with.

The basic procedure for working with command files goes something like this. First, we write the command file, and save it using a filename. Then, we run the command file by asking dBASE to DO the command file. Sometimes we make mistakes when we create a command file, so then we have to edit it. Correcting these errors is called *debugging*. Let's deal with creating command files first.

Creating Command Files with MODIFY

For our first command file, we'll create a program to print mailing labels. This might seem a bit redundant since dBASE III has a LABEL FORM command to print labels. But a mailing label program is an ideal example for explaining the basics of programming, such as loops and decision making. Later, we'll use the same skills to create more practical programs such as menus and custom screens.

Let's write a mailing label command file now. Use the disk that we put our MAIL.DBF database on as the disk in drive B. We'll call our command file LABELS, and we'll store it on the disk in drive B too. The command to create a new command file, or edit an existing one, is MODIFY COMMAND plus the name of the command file. So let's ask dBASE to

    MODIFY COMMAND B:LABELS   <RET>

dBASE displays the prompt

dBASE Word Processor

then gives us a blank screen on which to write our command file. Let's go ahead and type it in. Make sure you type it exactly as it appears on the page here, or it may not work properly when you run it.

```
?   TRIM(FNAME),LNAME
?   ADDRESS
?   TRIM(CITY) + ', ' + STATE + ZIP
```

Press the RETURN key after typing in each line to get down to the next blank line. If you make errors while you're typing in the program, you can move the cursor around to make changes. The cursor control keys are the same as we use in the EDIT and APPEND modes. Once you have it typed in exactly as above, save it by typing in a ^W.

We have just written our first command file, and stored it on the disk in drive B as LABELS.PRG. (As you've probably guessed, dBASE added the .PRG, which stands for program.) Now let's run our program.

Running Command Files with DO

First of all, let's tell dBASE to use the MAIL as the database.

USE B:MAIL   \<RET\>

Now to run our command file, we need to tell dBASE to

DO B:LABELS   \<RET\>

and we see on the screen

Andy Appleby
345 Oak St.
Los Angeles, CA 92123

dBASE did all three lines in the command file in the order they were placed. That is, dBASE printed the first name with the blanks trimmed off followed by the last name (? TRIM(FNAME),LNAME). Then it printed the address (? ADDRESS), then the city, followed by a comma, the state and the zip (? TRIM(CITY)+','+STATE+ZIP). This is the first mailing label.

Let's review the steps. We created the command file, using the MODIFY COMMAND command, and called it LABELS.PRG. We saved the command file, using a ^W. When the dot prompt reappeared, we asked dBASE to DO B:LABELS. dBASE then did each of the commands in the command file in the order in which they appeared. That is, dBASE read the command file left to right, top to bottom, just as we read English. The results came out in that order.

This is not bad for a first command file, but we can see one major weakness right off the bat: it only prints one label. In order to get dBASE to print all the labels in the database, we need to set up a *loop* in the command file.

Setting Up Loops in Programs with DO WHILE and ENDDO

dBASE has a pair of commands called DO WHILE and ENDDO which can be used in a program to repeat a series of commands indefinitely. All we have to do is enclose the commands to be repeated between a DO WHILE and an ENDDO command. Every DO WHILE begins a loop, and must have an ENDDO command to end it. We also need to tell dBASE what the condition is for performing the commands inside the loop. Let's give it a try in our LABELS program. First we'll ask dBASE to

    MODIFY COMMAND B:LABELS   <RET>

at which point dBASE will redisplay LABELS.PRG on the screen and let us make some changes. We see this on the screen:

```
? TRIM(FNAME),LNAME
? ADDRESS
? TRIM(CITY) + ', ' + STATE + ZIP
```

To make dBASE print labels for every person in the mailing list, we need to put these commands inside a loop. So, type a ^N to make room for a new line, and add the DO WHILE command at the top, as shown below.

You will also need to add a SKIP command to have dBASE skip down to the next name in the database as it performs the commands in the loop. Then we need an ENDDO to end the loop. Finally, a RETURN command will tell dBASE to return to the dot prompt after the program is done. The command file should be like the one below:

```
DO WHILE .NOT. EOF()
?  TRIM(FNAME),LNAME
?  ADDRESS
?  TRIM(CITY)+', '+STATE+ZIP
SKIP
ENDDO
RETURN
```

Now save the edited version of the command file with a ^W. When the dot prompt reappears, let's

```
USE B:MAIL    <RET>
DO B:LABELS   <RET>
```

and we get

Andy Appleby

345 Oak St.

Los Angeles, CA 92123

Record no. 2

John Q. Smith

123 A. St.

San Diego, CA 92123

Record no. 3

Lucy Smithsonian

461 Adams St.

San Diego, CA 92122-1234

Record no. 4

Ruth Doe

1142 J. St.

Los Angeles, CA 91234

Record no. 5

Betsy SMITH

222 Lemon Dr.

New York, NY 01234

Record no. 6

If something goes wrong when you try this, check to see if you typed it in exactly as it appears in the book. If your program seems to be running on and on endlessly, press the escape (ESC) key on your keyboard to cancel the run and get back to the dot prompt. Then, you'll need to MODIFY COMMAND B:LABELS again, and make the appropriate corrections so that it *exactly* matches the LABELS.PRG program in the book.

Now all the names on the database are on the screen in a mailing label format. Let's summarize what we did here. In the command file, we told dBASE to DO WHILE .NOT. EOF(). In English, this translates to, "Do everything between here and the ENDDO command as long as you haven't reached the EOF(), end of the database file." The next three lines in the command file then print one label. Then the SKIP command causes dBASE to SKIP down to the next record in the database. The ENDDO command marks the end of the loop, but the loop is repeated because the end of the file [EOF()] has not been reached yet. Hence, another label is printed, dBASE skips down to the next name and address, and another label is printed, until all the labels have been printed. At that point dBASE has reached the end of the database. This causes the loop to end and the first command under the ENDDO command to be processed, then to return. The RETURN command simply tells dBASE to RETURN to the dot prompt in this case.

One problem with our mailing labels is that they have record numbers on them. We can get rid of the record numbers by asking dBASE to SET TALK OFF. Let's run the program again. This time, let's first

   USE B:MAIL   <RET>

then, tell dBASE to get rid of the record numbers with

   SET TALK OFF   <RET>

If you have a printer hooked up, you can also

   SET PRINT ON   <RET>

Now let's run our LABELS program. Tell dBASE to

DO B:LABELS   <RET>

and we see on the printer (or screen, if you don't have a printer) that the record numbers have been removed.

Andy Appleby

345 Oak St.

Los Angeles, CA 92123

John Q. Smith

123 A. St.

San Diego, CA 92123

Lucy Smithsonian

461 Adams St.

San Diego, CA 92122-1234

Ruth Doe

1142 J. St.

Los Angeles, CA 91234

Betsy SMITH

222 Lemon Dr.

New York, NY 01234

If you did SET PRINT ON, I suggest that you now type in the command to

SET PRINT OFF   <RET>

otherwise everything else that you type on the screen will go to your printer too.

We've got a little problem here. Most mailing labels are one inch tall, and the names are spaced evenly on each one. It just so happens that most printers print six lines to the inch, so if we modify our command file to print six lines for each label, each name and address should fit perfectly on one label. So let's

MODIFY COMMAND B:LABELS   <RET>

Now press the down-arrow key four times to get the cursor on the SKIP command. Then type three ^Ns to make room for three new lines, so the command file looks like this:

```
DO WHILE .NOT. EOF()
?  TRIM(FNAME),LNAME
?  ADDRESS
?  TRIM(CITY)+', '+STATE+ZIP
—

SKIP
ENDDO
RETURN
```

Now we'll put in commands to print three blank lines on each mailing label. That is, we will begin each blank line with a ? command.

```
DO WHILE .NOT. EOF()
?  TRIM(FNAME),LNAME
?  ADDRESS
?  TRIM(CITY)+', '+STATE+ZIP
?
?
?
SKIP
ENDDO
RETURN
```

Save it with a ^W. Now let's

```
USE B:MAIL   <RET>
DO B:LABELS   <RET>
```

and we should see the names and addresses properly formatted for 1-inch-tall mailing labels.

Andy Appleby
345 Oak St.
Los Angeles, CA 92123

John Q. Smith
123 A. St.
San Diego, CA 92123

Lucy Smithsonian
461 Adams St.
San Diego, CA 92122-1234

Ruth Doe
1142 J. St.
Los Angeles, CA 91234

Betsy SMITH
222 Lemon Dr.
New York, NY 01234

Much better. The labels have the extra three blank lines between them. You may wonder why we repeatedly type in USE B:MAIL. We do so to get back to the top of the database. If we *don't* USE our file at this point, we'll get nothing on the screen when we type DO B:LABELS. Try it.

    DO B:LABELS   <RET>

All we get is the dot prompt. Yet we know that there are several records in the database. The reason that no labels were printed is because dBASE is already at the end of the file. We can prove this by typing in the command

    ? EOF()   <RET>

dBASE responds with

.T.

which is dBASE's way of saying, "True, I'm at the end of the database." Recall that in our command file, we said to print labels while we were *not* at the end of the database (DO WHILE .NOT. EOF). So that's why when we ran our program this time, we got nothing. We can return to the top of the database by typing

    GO TOP   <RET>

If we then type

```
DO B:LABELS    <RET>
```

we'll see our labels. It might be to our benefit to put the GO TOP command right into the command file, so we don't have to remember to type it in ourselves every time we do LABELS. We can now add GO TOP at the top of our program by editing the command file again with MODIFY COMMAND B:LABELS:

```
GO TOP
DO WHILE .NOT. EOF()
?  TRIM(FNAME),LNAME
?  ADDRESS
?  TRIM(CITY) + ', ' + STATE + ZIP
?
?
?
SKIP
ENDDO
RETURN
```

Then the program will always start with dBASE at the top (first record) of the database. Notice that the GO TOP command is outside and above the loop. This is so that dBASE will start at the first record, then start the loop. Had we put the GO TOP command inside the loop, the command file would print a label for the first record, skip to the next record, go back to the first record, print that label again, skip to the next record, back to the first record . . . on and on. The command file would print countless mailing labels for the first record on the database.

Now we have a good mailing label program to use with our MAIL file. We could spruce it up a bit so that it's nicer to look at. Take a look at this version of LABELS.PRG.

```
* * * * * * * * * Mailing Labels Program.
GO TOP

DO WHILE .NOT. EOF()
        ?  TRIM(FNAME),LNAME
        ?  ADDRESS
        ?  TRIM(CITY) + ', ' + STATE + ZIP
        ?
```

```
        ?
        ?
        SKIP
ENDDO
RETURN
```

Notice that we added a title. Programmers often put titles and comments in their programs as notes to themselves. The comments don't have any effect on the actual program; they're just reminders to the person who wrote it. To put comments in dBASE programs like this, we must start the line with an asterisk (*). A lot of asterisks make the line stand out, but only one is necessary. Also note that there is a blank line between the GO TOP command and the start of the DO WHILE LOOP. This was only to make the loop stand out when looking at the program. Also, all of the commands inside of the DO WHILE loop are indented. This makes the commands inside the loop stand out even further. If you want to make your command file look like this one, just MODIFY COMMAND B:LABELS. Then, do a ^N to make room for the title and type it in. Don't forget to put at least one asterisk in front of it. Then position the cursor under the GO TOP command, and type a ^N. Then position the cursor next to the ? TRIM(FNAME) line, type a ^V (INSERT ON), and hit the space bar a few times to indent the line. Do the same for the other lines within the loop, then save it with a ^W. (Incidentally, if you need to delete a line from a command file, you can use ^Y.)

In the next chapter, we'll look at another capability that we can use with our command files: decision making.

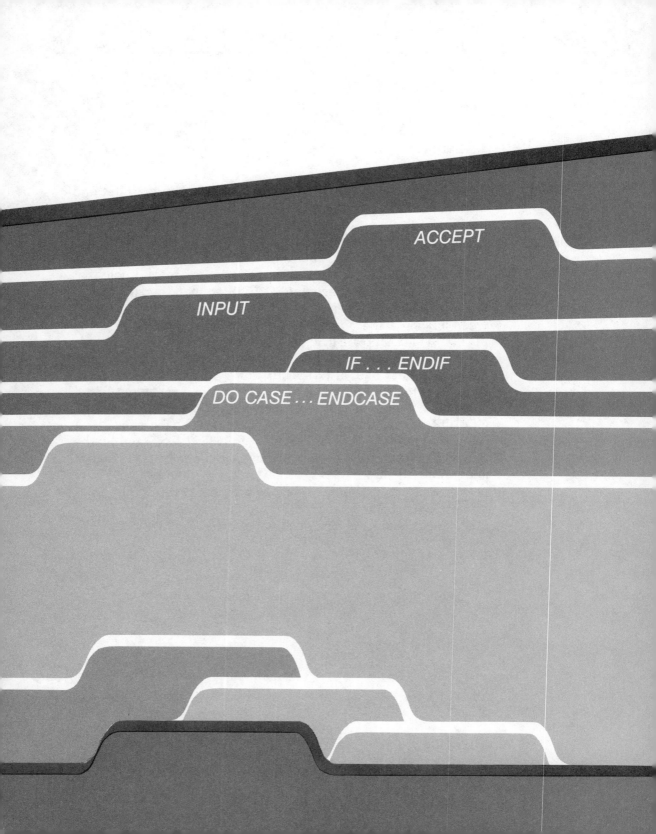

MAKING DECISIONS

12

The LABELS program we created in the last chapter has one limitation. It always prints out labels for everyone on the database, even though we might want labels for just San Diego residents or the 92122 zip code area. A better label program would allow us to specify only the labels we want printed. In this chapter, we'll learn to build this capability into our LABELS program.

Asking Questions with ACCEPT and INPUT

If the command file is going to print only certain labels for us, it needs to know what labels we have in mind. That is, it needs to *ask* us what labels we desire. We can make our command files ask us questions with the ACCEPT and INPUT commands. When we use either of these commands, we also type the question to be asked in apostrophes. We also need to provide a memory variable in which to store the answer to the question. To make the memory variable accessible outside of the command file, we need to define it as PUBLIC. We'll discuss PUBLIC variables in more detail later. For now, let's try out the ACCEPT command with a command file called B:TEST:

    MODIFY COMMAND B:TEST   <RET>

When the blank screen appears, type in these lines:

    PUBLIC NAME
    ACCEPT 'What is your name? ' TO NAME

and save it with ^W. Then DO B:TEST. We would see on the screen

    What is your name? _

dBASE will leave the question on the screen until we type in an answer. If we type in

    FRED ASTAIRE   <RET>

the dot prompt would appear because the program is over. This isn't too exciting, but if we now ask dBASE to

    ? NAME   <RET>

we see

    FRED ASTAIRE

If we were to DISPLAY MEMORY now, we'd see we have a memory variable called NAME, of the character type, with the contents FRED ASTAIRE. So we've been able to have the command file ask a question, wait for an answer, and remember the answer by storing it to a memory variable.

The INPUT command is very similar to the ACCEPT command, except that it is used when the answer to the question is a number. For example, try making a command file called B:TEST2 that looks like this:

```
PUBLIC ANSWER
INPUT ' Enter a number ' TO ANSWER
```

Save it, then DO B:TEST2, and the request appears

```
Enter a number _
```

Type in any old number, say 999 <RET>. The dot prompt reappears. Next type

```
    ? ANSWER <RET>
```

We see

```
999
```

When we DISPLAY MEMORY, we see that we have a memory variable called ANSWER, and it is numeric (N).

We'll see a practical application of the ACCEPT command in a moment.

Making Decisions with IF and ENDIF

We can embed some decision making into our command files by using the IF and ENDIF commands. IF, in dBASE, means the same thing as it does in English, i.e. "if (a condition is met), then (do something)." Each IF must be accompanied by an ENDIF. Let's look at a practical example.

Let's start by modifying the LABELS program. Let's change it so that before it prints labels, it asks us which zip code area we want labels for, then prints labels for only individuals who live in that zip code area. Here is what we should do:

```
MODIFY COMMAND B:LABELS   <RET>
```

This brings our labels program to the screen for us to edit. It should look something like the one in Program 12.1.

Now, just under the title, we need to add these three lines. The first, SET TALK OFF, will be used to keep the record numbers of the labels. The second, CLEAR, will clear the screen. Then we'll put in an ACCEPT statement so the command file will ask us a question.

```
SET TALK OFF
CLEAR
ACCEPT ' What zip code area ' TO AREA
```

So move the cursor down one line, and do a couple of ^Ns to make room, then type in the new lines so the command file looks like Program 12.2.

The ACCEPT command will present its question on the screen, then wait for an answer. It will store the answer to a memory variable named AREA. Now we need to type in two other lines, which will qualify the labels to be printed: IF ZIP=AREA and to end it, ENDIF. The first one goes right under the DO WHILE command line, and the ENDIF goes just above the SKIP command. You may want to add blank lines and indent the ? lines a little further as I have, but it is not necessary to do so. These are just for looks. In Program 12.3, you can see how the command file should look after you make these changes.

```
******** Mailing Labels Program.
GO TOP

DO WHILE .NOT. EOF()
    ? TRIM(FNAME),LNAME
    ? ADDRESS
    ? TRIM(CITY)+', '+STATE+ZIP
    ?
    ?
    ?
    SKIP
ENDDO
RETURN
```

Program 12.1

```
******** Mailing Labels Program.
SET TALK OFF
CLEAR
ACCEPT ' What zip code area ' TO AREA
GO TOP

DO WHILE .NOT. EOF()
    ? TRIM(FNAME),LNAME
    ? ADDRESS
    ? TRIM(CITY)+', '+STATE+ZIP
    ?
    ?
    ?
    SKIP
ENDDO
RETURN
```

—*Program 12.2*—

Double check to make sure you've typed in everything correctly, then save the command file with a ^W. Now, let's try it out. First, let's USE B:MAIL if you haven't already done so. Then let's

DO B:LABELS   <RET>

The first thing that should happen is that the screen clears and the following question appears:

What zip code area? _

Our command file is asking us a question, and is waiting for an answer. Let's type in 92123 <RET>. Then two labels appear on the screen.

Andy Appleby
345 Oak St.
Los Angeles, CA 92123

John Q. Smith
123 A. St.
San Diego, CA 92123

How about that? The command file asked which zip code area we wanted, then printed labels for people who live in that area. I'm

```
******** Mailing Labels Program.
SET TALK OFF
CLEAR
ACCEPT ' What zip code area ' TO AREA
GO TOP

DO WHILE .NOT. EOF()

    IF ZIP = AREA
        ? TRIM(FNAME),LNAME
        ? ADDRESS
        ? TRIM(CITY)+', '+STATE+ZIP
        ?
        ?
        ?
    ENDIF

    SKIP
ENDDO
RETURN
```

—Program 12.3—

impressed. Now, let's review why it did this. Let's take another look at the command file in Program 12.3.

When we asked dBASE to DO B:LABELS, it followed the instructions in our program. It ignored the title because of the leading asterisks, then it cleared the screen (CLEAR), then it presented the question "What zip code area?" and waited for an answer. This is because the ACCEPT command told dBASE to present the question in the apostrophes, then wait for an answer. dBASE waited until we typed in our reply, 92123, then it stored 92123 to a memory variable called AREA. Then the program began the loop through the database. Prior to printing each label, it checked to see IF ZIP = AREA. That is, it checked to see if the zip code on the record matched AREA, the zip code we typed in response to the "What zip code area?" question. If they matched, it printed the label. If they didn't match, all the lines between the IF and ENDIF were ignored. Either way, the SKIP command told dBASE to go to the next record. Then ENDDO sent dBASE through another loop, checking to see if the zip code on the next record matched the area we requested. It continued doing so until it got to the end of the database.

We can DO B:LABELS again, and this time when it asks

What zip code area? _

type in 91234 <RET> and, sure enough, we get

Ruth Doe
1142 J. St.
Los Angeles, CA 91234

This is the only person on our database in the 91234 zip code area.

We can print labels for a broader zip code area by typing in a partial zip code. If we DO B:LABELS and type in 92 as the zip code area to print labels for, we get

Andy Appleby
345 Oak St.
Los Angeles, CA 92123

John Q. Smith
123 A. St.
San Diego, CA 92123

Lucy Smithsonian
461 Adams St.
San Diego, CA 92122-1234

all the people in the 92XXX zip code areas. This feature is useful now, but it wasn't so handy in Chapter 3 when we asked for a list of Smiths and got Smithsonians in there too. dBASE listed all the 92XXX zip codes here because 9 and 2 were the first two digits of their zip codes.

Let's add the option to send mailing labels to the printer. Ask dBASE to MODIFY COMMAND B:LABELS <RET>, so we can edit it. Now, as shown in Program 12.4, add the lines I've added (the new lines are in darker print).

Once you've made the changes, save the command file with a ^W and the DO B:LABELS <RET>. This time we see

What zip code area? _

We'll type in 91234 <RET>, then we see

Shall I send labels to the printer? (Y/N)

We put in Y/N as a clue that the program is expecting a yes or no answer. If you have a printer hooked up to your computer, type in a Y<RET>. Otherwise, type N<RET>. Then the labels for the 92123 zip code area appear, either on the screen or printer, depending on how you've answered the question about the printer. Why is this?

In the command file we've added the command ACCEPT ' Shall I send labels to the printer? (Y/N) ' TO YN which causes dBASE to present the question on the screen and wait for an answer. The answer is stored in a memory variable called YN. We've also added these lines to the command file.

```
IF UPPER(YN) = "Y"
        SET PRINT ON
ENDIF
```

These lines say, "If the answer is Y, set the printer on." Notice the command actually checks to see if the uppercase equivalent is a Y.

```
********* Mailing Labels Program.
SET TALK OFF
CLEAR
ACCEPT ' What zip code area ' TO AREA


ACCEPT ' Shall I send labels to the printer? (Y/N) ' TO YN
IF UPPER(YN)="Y"
    SET PRINT ON
ENDIF

GO TOP

DO WHILE .NOT. EOF()
    IF ZIP = AREA
        ? TRIM(FNAME),LNAME
        ? ADDRESS
        ? TRIM(CITY)+', '+STATE+ZIP
        ?
        ?
        ?
    ENDIF
    SKIP
ENDDO
SET PRINT OFF
RETURN
```

Program 12.4

This is so that if we answered the question with a lowercase y, the printer would still be set on. Near the bottom of the command file, we've added the line

SET PRINT OFF

so that when the program was done printing labels, the printer was set back off automatically before returning to the dot prompt.

dBASE allows another method of decision making in command files: DO CASE.

Making Decisions with DO CASE

The IF . . . ENDIF clause is useful for allowing a program to make a simple either/or decision. Some programs may have to decide from several possibilities what to do next. The DO CASE . . . ENDCASE clause ensures that the program can do this. For example, notice in the program below that the first few lines present four menu options, and then an INPUT statement asks the user for his choice from the menu, and stores that answer in a memory variable called CHOICE:

```
CLEAR
? " 1. Add new names"
? " 2. Print Labels"
? " 3. Edit a record"
? " 4. Exit"

INPUT "Enter choice " TO CHOICE

DO CASE
    CASE CHOICE = 1
        APPEND
    CASE CHOICE = 2
        LABEL FORM TWOCOL
    CASE CHOICE = 3
        BROWSE
    OTHERWISE
        QUIT
ENDCASE
```

Beneath the menu is a DO CASE clause, starting with the command DO CASE, and ending with the command ENDCASE. Inside the DO CASE clause, the program decides what to do based upon the value of CHOICE. If choice = 1, the program appends If CHOICE = 2, the program prints labels from a label file called TWOCOL. If CHOICE = 3, the program goes into the BROWSE mode. If none of those situations occurs (OTHERWISE), the program quits.

We'll get a chance to use the DO CASE clause with a menu program in the next chapter. For now, let's talk about another form of decision making in programs: macro substitution.

Macro Substitution

Macro substitution is a powerful programming technique used in command files. A macro is simply a memory variable name with an ampersand (&) in front of it. When dBASE encounters a macro in a command file, it replaces that macro with the contents of the memory variable. For example, if you have a memory variable called FLD, and you have the word ZIP stored to that name, every time the &FLD is encountered in the program, dBASE will automatically substitute the word ZIP.

Let's discuss a practical example. We've set up our labels program so that it asks for a zip code area to print labels for. However, we may actually want to print labels for a certain city or a certain state. We need to modify the command file so that it asks which field we wish to search on, and also what value to look for. That is, when we run the new version of the command file, we want it to ask

Search on which field?

and we can type in any field name (such as CITY, STATE, or ZIP). Then it will ask

Look for what _ ?

and we can type in a characteristic to search for. For example, if we answer the first question with the word CITY, the second question will appear as

Look for what CITY?

and we can type in a city. If we were to answer this question with Los Angeles, then only labels for Los Angeles residents would be printed. If we answered the first question with ZIP, the second question would ask "Search for what ZIP?" and we could type in a zip code to search for. This gives the command file more flexibility.

To allow this flexibility, we must modify the LABELS command file in Program 12.5 to include macros (the three new lines are shown in darker print).

Once we've changed the program, we can save the command file and then DO B:LABELS. When we do so, the screen clears and we see

Search on which field?

Let's answer by typing in City <RET>. Then the next question to appear is

Look for what City?

and we can answer by typing in San Diego <RET>. Then it asks

Shall I send labels to the printer? (Y/N):

We'll answer N <RET> for now, and then we see the mailing labels for the San Diego residents.

John Q. Smith
123 A. St.
San Diego, CA 92123

Lucy Smithsonian
461 Adams St.
San Diego, CA 92122-1234

Let's try again. DO B:LABELS. The labels program asks

Search on which field?

```
******** Mailing Labels Program.
SET TALK OFF
CLEAR

ACCEPT ' Search on which field? ' TO FLD
ACCEPT ' Look for what &FLD ' TO COND

ACCEPT ' Shall I send labels to the printer? (Y/N) ' TO YN
IF UPPER(YN)="Y"
    SET PRINT ON
ENDIF

GO TOP

DO WHILE .NOT. EOF()
   IF &FLD = '&COND'
      ? TRIM(FNAME),LNAME
      ? ADDRESS
      ? TRIM(CITY)+', '+STATE+ZIP
      ?
      ?
      ?
   ENDIF
   SKIP
ENDDO

SET PRINT OFF
RETURN
```

— *Program 12.5* —

and we type State <RET>. Then the command file asks

Look for what State?

and we type CA <RET >. It asks about the printer, to which we can reply Y or N, then prints mailing labels for all California residents. Let's discuss why. Near the top of the LABELS program, we see these two lines:

ACCEPT ' Search on which field? ' TO FLD
ACCEPT ' Look for what &FLD ' TO COND

When we run the program, the first line causes dBASE to display the question, "Search on which field?" and it waits for an answer. If we type in CITY <RET> in response to this question, dBASE stores the word CITY to a memory variable called FLD. Then the next line is executed, but it has a macro in it, &FLD. This causes the contents of the FLD variable to be substituted into this line, so what we see on the screen next is the question, "Look for what CITY?" Whatever we answer to this question gets stored to a memory variable called COND. Hence, if we answer this question with San Diego, we have two memory variables in RAM. One is called FLD, and it contains the word CITY. The other memory variable is called COND, and it contains the words San Diego. I could have named the memory variables anything I like, but I chose FLD and COND because they remind me of FIELD (to search on) and CONDition (to search for).

Then the command file asks about the printer, and begins the DO WHILE loop. Within the DO WHILE loop is the command IF &FLD = '&COND'. Before this line makes a decision to print a label or not, it is going to have to substitute in the macros. Hence, the line becomes IF CITY = 'San Diego', and only labels for San Diego residents are printed.

Had we answered the question, "Search on which field?" with ZIP, and the question, "Look for what ZIP?" with 92111, memory variable FLD would contain the word ZIP, and COND would contain 92111. In this case, when the program needed to make a decision as to whether or not to print a label, the IF statement would become IF ZIP = '92111'.

Macro substitution is a bit abstract, and takes a little getting used to. The only strict rule on macros is that they must be character-type memory variables.

Usually, when creating command files, we come up with an idea for a program we want, then we need to figure out just how to write the program. This is not too easy if you are a beginner. In the next chapter, we'll talk about methods that can help make the transition from an idea to a working program.

PROGRAM DESIGN AND DEVELOPMENT

13

When we create a command file (program), we are actually *writing software*. There are four parts to writing software. First, we design the program by determining what it is to do for us. Second, we must write the program. In dBASE we do this by typing MODIFY COMMAND and then typing the program on the screen. Third, we run the program in order to test it. Fourth, since we often make mistakes when we first write the program, we need to make corrections to debug the program. Let's examine each of these steps in detail.

Step 1. The General Idea

It's a good idea to write down the general idea of a program on paper first. For example, let's say we want to develop a fancy mailing list system that's quick and easy to use. The general idea might read like this:

This system will be designed to manage a mailing list, and will operate from a menu of choices. When first run, the system will display the Mail Menu as so:

1. Add new names and addresses.
2. Sort the mailing list.
3. Print names and addresses.
4. Edit data.
5. Exit the system.

The option to print names and addresses will allow us to specify types of individuals to print data for. The system will be completely "menu-driven." That is, once we DO the main command file, jobs like adding new names, sorting, printing mailing labels, and editing will be performed by simply selecting menu options or answering questions on the screen. The system will be completely automated, so that an individual with no knowledge of dBASE III could still manage the mailing list.

Now that we have the general idea defined, we need to design a database that will support it.

Step 2. Design the Database Structure

We'll structure the database as follows:

#	FIELD NAME	TYPE	WIDTH	DECIMAL PLACES
1	LNAME	C	20	0
2	FNAME	C	15	0
3	ADDRESS	C	25	0
4	CITY	C	20	0
5	STATE	C	5	0

| 6 | ZIP | C | 10 | 0 |
| 7 | PHONE | C | 35 | 0 |

We've already created a database with the structure, MAIL, so this step is done already.

Step 3. Develop Pseudocode

It's a little easier to write a program if we first write a reasonable facsimile of it in plain English. Doing so is called writing *pseudocode*. When we write pseudocode, we should try to specify the logic and series of events that will occur in the program, so that when we have to translate the program to actual dBASE language, much of the task is already defined. This isn't particularly easy, of course, because we're not accustomed to thinking like machines. But it's still easier to write a program from pseudocode jotted down on a piece of paper than from pure thought. Here's a pseudocoded example of the Mail Menu program for our mailing system:

COMMAND FILE NAME: MENU.PRG

PURPOSE: Present a menu of options for managing the mailing list.

PSEUDOCODE:

Set dBASE talk off
Use the mailing list database
Set menu choice to 0

Repeat the Mail Menu until option to exit is selected
Clear the screen
Display the Mail Menu on the screen as follows:

Mail Menu

1. ADD new data

2. SORT data

3. PRINT data

4. EDIT data

5. EXIT the mailing system

Ask which option is desired

If option 1 selected
   Append new data
If option 2 selected
   Sort by last and first name
If option 3 selected
   Print mailing labels
If option 4 selected
   Edit data

Redisplay the Mail Menu (as long as option 5 was not selected)

Exit the mailing system

Notice that we've defined the logic of the MENU program here. We've also given it a title and mentioned its purpose. This is so that if it takes a long time to write the actual program, we can refer back to the pseudocode for reference. Notice that the pseudocode describes the task in English, but it looks like a program too. This intermediate step makes the next step a little easier. From this point, we'd need to write the actual program using proper dBASE III commands and syntax.

Step 4. Write the Program

Once we have a pseudocoded outline of the program, we need to write the actual program. In dBASE, we use MODIFY COMMAND for this. Let's now write the actual program. We cannot be as liberal with our sentences as we were in the pseudocode, because dBASE cannot understand English.
   Let's

```
MODIFY COMMAND B:MENU    <RET>
```

which brings us a blank screen to work with. Now we can type in the actual MENU program so that it looks like Program 13.1.

Now let's discuss how the actual program resembles the pseudo-code above it. First, the command file sets the dBASE talk off, and uses B:MAIL as the database. Then, it stores a zero to a memory variable called CHOICE. This is so that the DO WHILE CHOICE < 5 condition will be true when dBASE first enters the loop. Then it clears the screen and displays the mail menu using ? commands. Then it displays the question, "Enter your choice (1–5) from above, " and waits for an answer. Once an answer has been entered, the program performs the desired option. If the choice was 1, dBASE goes into APPEND mode. If the choice was 2, dBASE will sort by last name; if the choice was 3, dBASE will DO our other command file, B:LABELS, and so forth.

After the selected option has been performed, dBASE will eventually reach the ENDDO command at the bottom of the command file. The loop will repeat, redisplaying the mail menu and question. If the choice is 5 (exit) the DO WHILE CHOICE < 5 condition for the loop will cause the ENDDO not to repeat the loop, and the program will end.

Step 5. Run and Test the Program

Step 5 is not simply using the program, because as you probably know by now, we usually make a few mistakes in our program that need correcting. To test our program, of course, we still need to run it, so type in the command

    DO B:MENU   <RET>

After the screen is cleared, the Mail Menu is displayed.

Mail Menu

1. Add new names
2. Sort data
3. Print Data
4. Edit data
5. Exit the mailing system

```
******************** Mailing List System Mail Menu

SET TALK OFF
USE B:MAIL
STORE 0 TO CHOICE

********************* Present mail Menu
DO WHILE CHOICE < 5
    CLEAR
    ? '      Mail Menu'
    ?
    ? ' 1. Add new names'
    ? ' 2. Sort data'
    ? ' 3. Print Labels'
    ? ' 4. Edit data'
    ? ' 5. Exit the mailing system'
    ?
    INPUT ' Enter your choice (1-5) from above ' TO CHOICE

    ************* Perform appropriate task based on CHOICE
  DO CASE
      CASE CHOICE = 1
          APPEND

      CASE CHOICE = 2
          INDEX ON LNAME + FNAME TO B:NAMES
          USE B:MAIL INDEX B:NAMES

      CASE CHOICE = 3
          DO B:LABELS

      CASE CHOICE = 4
          EDIT
    ENDCASE
ENDDO
```

—Program 13.1—

Enter your choice (1–5) from above :

If we now type in 1 <RET>, dBASE will put us in the APPEND
mode.

Record no. 6
LNAME   :_   :
FNAME   :   :

```
ADDRESS :                          :
CITY      :                 :
STATE     :       :
ZIP       :            :
PHONE     :                              :
```

So, anyone who typed in the command DO B:MENU could now add new data to the database, even if they've never heard of the APPEND command. This is because the program has a line which states CASE CHOICE = 1, and beneath that is the APPEND command. Since CHOICE did = 1, dBASE goes into APPEND mode. We can then add as many names to the mailing list as we wish. When we exit the APPEND mode (by pressing <RET> instead of typing in an LNAME), the Mail Menu reappears.

Mail Menu

1. Add new names

2. Sort data

3. Print Data

4. Edit data

5. Exit the mailing system

Enter your choice (1-5) from above :

Why? Because none of the CASE clauses below the APPEND command in the program will be true. dBASE won't do the commands in CASE CHOICE = 2 or CASE CHOICE = 3, etc., because CHOICE = 1. When dBASE reaches the ENDDO command, CHOICE is less than 5, so the program loops around up to the DO WHILE CHOICE < 5 command, and the menu is redisplayed, and the INPUT question reappears. We could type in another option now, and whatever option we select (1–5) will be stored in CHOICE. Then, the appropriate function will take place (APPEND, INDEX, etc.).

Notice in the command file that if we select option #3, Print Labels, dBASE is told to DO a different command file, our LABELS program. In this case, dBASE will DO B:LABELS. As you may recall, the last line in LABELS is the RETURN command. When one command file calls another (as in this case where MENU calls LABELS), the RETURN command tells dBASE to go back to where it left off in the first program. Therefore, MENU will DO B:LABELS, and LABELS will print the mailing labels and then RETURN to MENU.

I'm assuming here that your program ran right the first time. More likely, it didn't and you got one of dBASE's many error messages. We usually don't see the errors in a program until we try to run the program. The computer catches them right away. The most common errors that occur in command files are syntax errors, which result from misspelling a command, a field name, or a variable name. Syntax errors also occur if we forget to put spaces between commands, or if we attempt to use a field or memory variable that does not exist.

When dBASE encounters an error in a command file, it will display an error message, and usually give us a chance to correct it. Let's take a hypothetical example. Suppose when I had asked dBASE to DO B:MENU, I got the message

```
Variable not found
   ?
CASE CHOCE = 1
Terminate command file? (Y/N)
```

At first glance, we may not see the problem. But on close inspection, we see that the word CHOICE is misspelled. dBASE attempted to find a memory variable called CHOCE, and couldn't. If we answer Y to the question Terminate command file?, dBASE will return to the dot prompt. Then you can MODIFY COMMAND B:MENU to correct the error.

In the next chapter, we'll expand our mailing label system with more command files, and pick up some programming techniques in the process.

In this chapter we'll develop new programs to create a *menu-driven* mailing system. The term *menu-driven* means that the person using the programs we develop need only run one program. He simply selects options from a menu we develop in order to perform various tasks. Programmers create menu-driven systems so that individuals who don't know the commands of a language can still use the computer. The MENU command file we developed in the last chapter is such a program. In this chapter, we will expand the MENU command file to a complete mailing list management system.

The procedure again will be to describe, pseudocode, write, and test each new program. Then we'll link all the programs with our MENU program, so that we will have a complete menu-driven mailing list system. The programs have been fully tested and *debugged* (cleared of errors), so if you type one in and it doesn't work, you've probably typed something incorrectly. You will no doubt have to debug after you type these in, but your debugging will be limited to checking to see where you've failed to copy the contents of the command files exactly as they appear in the text.

Make sure you have the disk with MAIL.DBF in drive B, and you may want to SET TALK OFF before doing these. Also, if you type in the command SET SAFETY OFF from the dot prompt, dBASE won't ask for confirmation before overwriting files when indexing.

The SORTER Command File

First we will develop a simple program (see Program 14.1) to allow for easy sorting. When we run sorter, the screen will clear and we'll see the following instructions on the screen:

```
How do you wish names sorted?
(Enter field name; LNAME, CITY, STATE, OR ZIP) :
```

When the sorting is complete, the program will inform us

SORT COMPLETE

Here is the pseudocode for SORTER.

PROGRAM	: SORTER.PRG
PURPOSE	: Allow for sort options to be displayed on the screen, then sort accordingly.
PSEUDOCODE :	

Clear the screen
Display Instructions
Ask which field to sort on
Index accordingly
Return

To type in the command file, use the MODIFY command:

MODIFY COMMAND B:SORTER \<RET>

When the screen is ready, type in the command file exactly as it appears in Program 14.1. Save it with a ^W.
  Now let's

USE B:MAIL \<RET>
DO B:SORTER \<RET>

If you typed it in correctly, the screen will clear, then the instructions appear on the screen.

How do you wish names sorted?'
(Enter field name; LNAME, CITY, STATE, OR ZIP) :

Type in

LNAME \<RET>

then we see the message SORT COMPLETE, and the dot prompt. To test to see if it ran properly, just

LIST \<RET>

The records should now be sorted by last name.

```
*************** SORTER.PRG
CLEAR
? ' How do you wish names sorted?'
ACCEPT '(Enter field name; LNAME, CITY, STATE, OR ZIP) ' TO FLD

INDEX ON &FLD TO B:MINDEX

?
? 'Sort complete'
RETURN
```

Program 14.1

1 Appleby	Andy	345 Oak St.	Los Angeles	CA	92123
4 Doe	Ruth	1142 J. St.	Los Angeles	CA	91234
5 SMITH	Betsy	222 Lemon Dr.	New York	NY	01234
2 Smith	John Q.	123 A. St.	San Diego	CA	92122
3 Smithsonian	Lucy	461 Adams St.	San Diego	CA	92122-1234

If something went wrong, you'll have to use MODIFY COMMAND again to edit your program.

After we link sorter to the MENU program, it will sort, then return to the Mail Menu.

The EDDY Command File

At present, when we select the option to edit from the menu program, it asks us which record number to edit. It would be much easier to edit individuals by last name rather than record number. We'll design the EDDY command file to allow us to do this. This command file would be pseudocoded as follows:

PROGRAM: EDDY.PRG

PURPOSE: To allow editing by last name rather than record number.

PSEUDOCODE:

Clear the screen
Start a loop to keep asking for edits until no more edits are desired.

Within loop
   Clear screen
   Ask what name to edit

   Count how many people on the database have that last name, and store count to a memory variable.

If nobody has that name
   Say 'there is no such person on the database'
   Wait for response

If one person has that name
 Find that person
 Edit that record

If several people have that name
 List all people with that name
 Ask which one to edit

Ask if more names to edit
 If Yes, continue loop
Otherwise, return

The command file is shown in Program 14.2.

```
****************** Edit names and address (EDDY.PRG)
CLEAR
SET EXACT ON
STORE 'Y' TO ANSWER

****************** Ask for names to edit while appropriate.
DO WHILE UPPER(ANSWER)="Y"
    CLEAR
    ACCEPT 'Edit whom? (Last name) ' TO WHOM
    COUNT FOR UPPER(LNAME) = UPPER(WHOM) TO WHOMS

    ************* If no such person, warn.
    IF WHOMS=0
        ?
        ? 'There is no &WHOM on the data base.'
    ENDIF

    ************* If 1 person with that name, edit.
    IF WHOMS=1
        LOCATE FOR UPPER(LNAME)=UPPER(WHOM)
        EDIT RECNO()
    ENDIF

    ************* If more than 1 person with that last
    ************* name, display and get record number.
    IF WHOMS > 1
        ?
        LIST FOR UPPER(LNAME)=UPPER(WHOM) LNAME,FNAME,ADDRESS
        ?
        ACCEPT 'Which one (by record number) ' TO RECNO
        EDIT &RECNO
    ENDIF

    ************* Ask if more names to edit.
    ?
    ACCEPT ' Edit more names? (Y/N) ' TO ANSWER
    CLEAR

ENDDO (while answer = 'Y')
SET EXACT OFF
RETURN
```
Program 14.2

In this program we use many of the commands we've already learned. Notice that we SET EXACT ON near the top of the program, so the searches will be exact rather than approximate. If one wishes to edit for Smith, there is no need to consider Smithsonians too. We SET EXACT OFF near the bottom of the program to return to the normal mode that dBASE uses (EXACT OFF). Also, when we COUNT or LIST FOR LNAME, we compare uppercase equivalents of each (UPPER), so that we don't miss anyone whose name might have been inadvertently entered in all caps. This is a fairly large program, and may take some time to get typed in.

To enter and save the program, use the commands

MODIFY COMMAND B:EDDY   <RET>

After the program is all typed in, save it with a ^W as usual. To run the program, type

DO B:EDDY   <RET>

When it runs, we'll see

Edit whom? (Last name) :

Let's see what happens if we type in a name that we haven't listed on our mailing list.

Jackson   <RET>

The program informs us that

There is no Jackson on the database
Edit more names? (Y/N) :

Our program has told us that we've tried to edit someone who doesn't exist on the data file. It is also asking if we want to edit more names. Let's type in a Y <RET> and try one that we know is on the list. The screen is waiting with the question

Edit whom? (Last name) :

This time we'll respond with

Appleby   <RET>

and we see on the screen:

```
Record No. 1
LNAME    :Appleby          :
FNAME    :Andy      :
ADDRESS :345 Oak St.                :
CITY      :Los Angeles    :
STATE    :CA    :
ZIP        :92123      :
PHONE    :                            :
```

The program found Appleby for us, and put his data into the edit mode. We can move the cursor down to the ADDRESS field and change Andy's address to 123 A. St. Then move down and change his city to San Diego. Andy's record should look like this now:

```
Record No. 1
LNAME    :Appleby          :
FNAME    :Andy       :
ADDRESS :123 A. St.               :
CITY      :San Diego       :
STATE    :CA    :
ZIP        :92123      :
PHONE    :                        :
```

When it does, type a ^W to save it. Now at the bottom of the screen, you should see the message

Edit more names? (Y/N) :

Let's try one more. Type in Y <RET>, so that the program again asks

Edit whom? (Last name) :

This time, type in

   Smith   <RET>

and we see on the screen:

```
Record#  LNAME  FNAME   ADDRESS
     5   SMITH  Betsy   222 Lemon Dr.
     2   Smith  John Q. 123 A. St.
```

Which one (by record number) _

Since the program found two Smiths this time, it is asking which one we want to edit. Let's pick Betsy. Type in 5 <RET>, and we'll see

```
Record No. 5
LNAME    :SMITH               :
FNAME    :Betsy    :
ADDRESS :222 Lemon Dr.               :
CITY     :New York         :
STATE    :NY   :
ZIP      :01234    :
PHONE    :                             :
```

Let's delete her by typing a ^U. This displays *DEL* at the top of the screen:

```
Record No. 5 *DEL*
LNAME    :SMITH        :
FNAME    :Betsy     :
ADDRESS :222 Lemon Dr.               :
CITY     :New York          :
STATE    :NY   :
ZIP      :01234     :
PHONE    :                             :
```

Betsy is now marked for deletion. We could bring her back with another ^U, but for now let's leave her marked for deletion. Save her new data with a ^W now, and once again the program asks

Edit more names? (Y/N) :

Let's answer N <RET>, at which point the program ends and the dot prompt reappears.

The DELNAMES Command File

This program will automatically display records that have been marked for deletion, and give us a chance to recall any of them prior to packing the file. Here is the pseudocode:

PROGRAM: DELNAMES.PRG

PURPOSE: Display names marked for deletion, and allow for recalls, prior to packing the database.

PSEUDOCODE:

Clear the screen
Set up a loop for recalling names
While recalling names
    Count how many records are marked for deletion

If no names are marked for deletion
    Display message 'no names to delete'
    Terminate loop

If names are marked for deletion
    Display names to be eliminated from the database
    Ask if O.K. to eliminate all names
    If not O.K.
        Ask which to recall, and redisplay names to be eliminated
    If O.K.
        Pack the database
Return

To enter the program, shown in Program 14.3, type

    MODIFY COMMAND B:DELNAMES   <RET>

Once the program is typed in, save it. Then

    DO B:DELNAMES   <RET>

which should bring up on the screen:

```
    5  *  SMITH  Betsy     222 Lemon Dr.
Delete these individuals? (Y/N)
```

You can answer either Y or N. If you answer Y, the program will pack the database, and Betsy will be eliminated. If you answer N, the program will ask

```
Keep which one? (by number) :
```

and we could unmark Betsy for deletion by simply typing in her record number, 5 <RET>. When we have decided whom we wish to delete, and whom we wish to recall, the program packs the database and returns to the dot prompt.

The DUPES Command File

Every good computerized mailing system needs a built-in check-for-duplicates program. Mailing systems tend to grow, so they need to be trimmed down to avoid duplicate mailings. The DUPES.PRG command file checks the database for identical street addresses in identical cities. When it finds duplicates, it tells us where they are so that we can view them through the EDIT command and decide whether or not to delete. It does not do any deleting itself, because in some cases we may want duplicates. For example, we may want to mail five items to the same address, because that address might be a large company with five individuals we wish to mail to.

Here is the pseudocode for the DUPES command file:

PROGRAM: DUPES.PRG

PURPOSE: Check for duplicate street addresses

PSEUDOCODE:

Clear the screen
Ask if duplicates should be sent to printer
If so, set printer on

```
**************** Before packing file, check.(DELNAMES.PRG)
CLEAR
STORE 'N' TO PERMIT

DO WHILE UPPER(PERMIT) = 'N'
   CLEAR
   COUNT FOR DELETED() TO DELS

   ******************** If nothing to delete, don't bother.
   IF DELS = 0
      ?
      ? 'No names to delete'
      STORE 'Y' TO PERMIT
   ENDIF

   ******************** If many names to delete,
   ******************** display and get permission first.
   IF DELS > 0
      LIST FOR DELETED() LNAME, FNAME, ADDRESS
      ?
      ACCEPT 'Delete all these individuals? (Y/N) ' TO PERMIT
      IF UPPER(PERMIT) = 'N'
         ACCEPT ' Keep which one (by number) ' TO RECNO
         RECALL RECORD &RECNO
      ENDIF (permit=n)
   ENDIF (dels > 0)
ENDDO (while permit = n)

PACK
RETURN
```

—*Program 14.3*—

Clear the screen
Index by address and city
Go to the top of the database
Print report title (Duplicate street addresses)
Store 0 to counter of duplicate addresses

Set up loop to end of the database
    Compare pairs of addresses by...
        Store top of pair to memory variable 1

    Store bottom of pair to memory variable 2
   If addresses match
    Display duplicate addresses
    Add 1 to counter of duplicate addresses
   Check next pair of addresses
  When done
   If no duplicates found
    Display message 'No duplicates'
 Return to dot prompt

  In Program 14.4, you can see the entire program. Again, it is fairly lengthy and might take some time to type in. Use the command MODIFY COMMAND B:DUPES <RET> to create the program.
  Once this command file is typed in and saved, we can run it with

   DO B:DUPES <RET>

The first thing it will ask is

Send duplicate addresses to printer? (Y/N) :

If you have a printer, you can answer Y <RET> if you like. Then the program will display all of the record numbers, addresses, and cities for which there are duplicate records. At this point, if you've followed along every step of the way, there are actually two duplicates on the database, and this program will display them as

   Duplicate Street Addresses

Record # 1 address is: 123 A. St. San Diego
Record # 2 address is: 123 A. St. San Diego
  Press RETURN to return to Mail Menu :

At this point if we press RETURN, the dot prompt will appear. After we get all of these command files linked to the MENU program, the Mail Menu will appear.

Linking the Command Files to the Mail Menu

Now we can link all of our command files together, so that all we have to do to use the mailing system is type in the command DO MENU, and select options from the Mail Menu displayed below.

Mail Menu
1. Add new names
2. Sort data
3. Print Labels
4. Edit data
5. Pack the database
6. Check for duplicates
7. Exit the mailing system

Enter your choice (1–7) from above :

We can choose whatever option we wish and the mailing system will perform accordingly. When we are done with the particular option we selected, the menu will reappear on the screen. We can keep selecting options as long as we wish. When we're done selecting, option #7 will return us to the dot prompt.

To link all of the command files into one integrated menu-driven mailing list system now requires that we modify MENU.PRG so that it calls up the various command files. Here is how MENU.PRG must look in order to provide links to these command files. The new or modified lines are in darker print in Program 14.5.

Once you type in and use the mailing list system for a while, you'll probably find room for new features or improvements. By all means, try writing your own command files. Mailing list programs are a good place to start learning some programming techniques. Run the programs in this book, then study them to see how they perform their tasks. In many ways, learning to program is learning to use other peoples' programming techniques.

When you start creating your own command files, the debugging process becomes more involved. Many beginning programmers are hampered by not knowing what to do when their program doesn't work quite as they expected. In the next chapter, we'll discuss debugging techniques.

```
*************** Check for duplicate addresses   (DUPES.PRG)

CLEAR
******************************** This routine checks for duplicate
******************************** street addresses by indexing on
******************************** addresss, then checking to see if
******************************** pairs of addresses match.

ACCEPT ' Send duplicate addresses to printer? (Y/N) ' TO YN

IF UPPER(YN)="Y"
   SET PRINT ON
ENDIF

CLEAR

************************** Create an index of street addresses

INDEX ON ADDRESS + CITY TO B:STREETS
GO TOP
************************** Now, starting at the top of the file,
************************** check to see if the address we're
************************** "looking at" is identical to the address
************************** directly underneath.
?
? '     Duplicate Street Addresses'
?
?
STORE 0 TO COUNTER
DO WHILE .NOT. EOF()
   STORE ADDRESS+CITY TO AD1
   SKIP 1
   IF .NOT. EOF()
      STORE ADDRESS+CITY TO AD2
   ENDIF

   ****** Compare the two addresses (upper case for accuracy)
   ****** If they match, print on report

   IF UPPER(AD1)=UPPER(AD2)
      SKIP -1
      ? ' Record # ' + STR(RECNO(),4) + ' address is: ',TRIM(ADDRESS),CITY
      SKIP 1
      ? ' Record # ' + STR(RECNO(),4) + ' address is: ',TRIM(ADDRESS),CITY
      ?
      STORE COUNTER + 1 TO COUNTER
   ENDIF
   STORE ' ' TO AD2
ENDDO   (While end of file has not been reached)
SET PRINT OFF

************* If none found, display message.
IF COUNTER = 0

   ? ' No Duplicates Found'
ENDIF

************* Pause, then return to Mail Menu.
?
?
WAIT ' Press RETURN to return to Mail Menu '

USE B:MAIL
RETURN
```

—Program 14.4—

```
********************** Mailing List System Mail Menu

    SET TALK OFF
    USE B:MAIL
    STORE 0 TO CHOICE

    ********************* Present mail Menu
    DO WHILE CHOICE < 7
        ? '      Mail Menu'
        ?
        ? ' 1. Add new names'
        ? ' 2. Sort data'
        ? ' 3. Print Labels'
        ? ' 4. Edit data'
        ? ' 5. Pack the data base'
        ? ' 6. Check for duplicates'
        ? ' 7. Exit the mailing system'
        ?
        INPUT ' Enter your choice (1-7) from above ' TO CHOICE

        ************* Perform appropriate task based on CHOICE
        DO CASE

            CASE CHOICE = 1
                APPEND

            CASE CHOICE = 2
                DO B:SORTER

            CASE CHOICE = 3
                DO B:LABELS

            CASE CHOICE = 4
                DO B:EDDY

            CASE CHOICE = 5
                DO B:DELNAMES

            CASE CHOICE = 6
                DO B:DUPES
        ENDCASE
ENDDO (while choice < 7)
```

Program 14.5

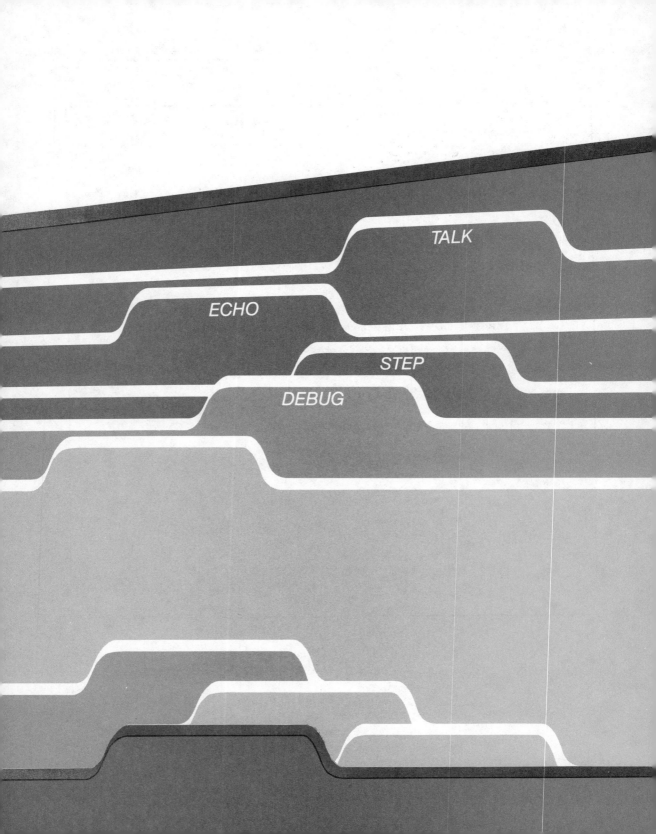

DEBUGGING TECHNIQUES

15

When our programs fail to perform as expected, we often stare at the screen helplessly and think, "Now what do I do?" Some errors are fairly obvious and easy to fix, such as when we misspelled CHOICE in the last chapter. Sometimes, however, dBASE will display a line as having an error in it, and we don't see the error. At that point, we may need to go deeper into our search for the error. Here are some good techniques that can help.

Public Memory Variables and DISPLAY

One of the best debugging techniques is to check the contents of all memory variables as soon as an error occurs in a command file. Check the current value of a memory variable for a clue to the problem. Unfortunately, dBASE III automatically erases all memory variables as soon as a command file terminates.

You can prevent dBASE from automatically erasing all memory variables by declaring them as PUBLIC in the beginning of the program. For example, if a program contains

PUBLIC CHOICE, YN, X, Y, Z

near the top of the program, the memory variables CHOICE, YN, X, Y, and Z will not be erased. If the program bombs, and you want to check the variables, use the DISPLAY MEMORY command from the dot prompt to check the status of these variables.

The DISPLAY STRUCTURE command will display the structure of the database, including field names. Use this command to check for the existence and correct spelling of field names used in the program. The DISPLAY STATUS command will display the names of all databases in use, as well as the names and contents of all active index files, as below

Select area - 1, Database in use: B:master.dbf Alias – MASTER
    Index file: B:master.ndx key – CODE

Currently selected database:
Select area - 2, Database in use: B:sales.dbf Alias – SALES
    Index file: B:sales.ndx key – CODE

This display shows that the currently selected database in Select area 2, is B:SALES.DBF. It has no alias, other than the name SALES in uppercase. The active index file associated with it is B:SALES.NDX, and is an index of the key field CODE. The DISPLAY STATUS command will also show the status of all dBASE SET parameters (e.g., SET TALK, SET SAFETY), and function key assignments.

When an error occurs, use these DISPLAY commands to check on the current status of dBASE. Perhaps you've simply misspelled a field or variable name or attempted to use a nonexistent field or variable. Perhaps the wrong database or wrong index file is in use. The DISPLAY commands will help you find out.

SET TALK ON

In the mailing list system command file, we SET TALK OFF at the top of the Mail Menu program. If we eliminate this line from the command file, and SET TALK ON before we DO the command file, dBASE's extraneous messages will be displayed on the screen. These extraneous messages can be useful to us for watching events as they occur in the command file. They may lead to clues to errors in our program.

SET ECHO ON

An exaggerated version of SET TALK ON is the SET ECHO ON command. This displays every command line in the dBASE program as it is being processed. Thus, we can see everything that the command file is doing as it is running. It goes by pretty fast, but we can slow it down considerably with SET STEP ON.

SET STEP ON

If you want to follow the logic of your command file as it is running, step by step, leave ECHO on, and SET STEP ON. Your command file will be processed one line at a time. As each line is processed, you can pause, continue, or stop processing. This is great for those hard-to-find little bugs that hide in tiny dark logical crevices.

SET DEBUG ON

The option to SET DEBUG ON can also be very helpful for getting at the hard-to-find errors. When the DEBUG parameter is on, all the outputs from SET ECHO ON and/or SET STEP ON are sent directly to the printer and are not displayed on the screen. Hence we can watch our command perform on the screen without distraction from the ECHO command. On the printer, the actual lines within the command file will appear as dBASE is doing them, as well as the results of each line. We can then study the hardcopy of the events that occured in the program. If other attempts failed, this will usually lead us to the source of the problem.

Make a Hardcopy of the Program

A printed copy of your program is very useful. To make a printed copy, be sure the printer is ready. Then use the TYPE command with the name of the command file, including the .PRG extension, to print the command file. For example, to print the MENU command file, type in the command

    TYPE MENU.PRG TO PRINT   <RET>

When you get a hardcopy, draw arrows from your DO WHILEs and their respective ENDDOs. Likewise for IF...ENDIF clauses. You may find dangling DO WHILEs that don't have ENDDOs associated with them, or IFs and ENDIFs which are crossed over and are throwing everything out of whack. In Program 15.1 is a printed command file with the DO...ENDDOs attached. Notice that they all match up, and that none of the arrows cross over one another.

It is easiest to do this working from the smaller, innermost DO loops and IF clauses to the larger, outermost loops and IF clauses. After you mark your routines in this way, study the program again in this light. You may find errors in your logic based on the arrows themselves.

Let's try out some debugging aids with a sample program which includes some errors. Using the command

    MODIFY COMMAND B:TEST   <RET>

we can create and save the command file in Program 15.2. Now when we

    DO B:TEST   <RET>

```
******************* Count to 5, 10 times.
STORE 1 TO OUTLOOP
STORE 1 TO INLOOP

******* Do outer-most loop 10 times
DO WHILE OUTLOOP < 11
? 'OUTER LOOP NUMBER : ' + STR(OUTLOOP,2)

    ************* For each outer loop, do 5 inner loops
    DO WHILE INLOOP < 6
       ? INLOOP
       STORE INLOOP + 1 TO INLOOP
    ENDDO (while inloop < 6)

STORE 1 TO INLOOP
STORE OUTLOOP + 1 TO OUTLOOP
ENDDO (while ouloop < 11)
```

Program 15.1

The program runs, but simply displays a dot prompt rather than the expected mailing labels for 92122 residents. Let's use the ECHO option to watch the program run.

Type in the command:

SET ECHO ON   <RET>

Then once again, run the program:

DO B:TEST   <RET>

This time, we can watch dBASE perform each step in the command file, as shown below:

```
SET TALK OFF
USE MAIL
GO BOTTOM
DO WHILE .NOT. EOF()
    IF ZIP = "92122"
SKIP
ENDDO
```

If the echoed lines go by too fast to read, you can slow them down further with the STEP option. Type in the command:

SET STEP ON   <RET>

Then run the program again:

DO B:TEST   <RET>

```
************************************************
* TEST.PRG                                      *
************************************************
SET TALK OFF
USE B:MAIL
GO BOTTOM

DO WHILE .NOT. EOF()
   IF ZIP = "92122"
      ? TRIM(FNAME), LNAME
      ? ADDRESS
      ? TRIM(CITY)+", "+STATE+ ZIP
      ?
      ?
      ?
   ENDIF
 SKIP
 ENDDO
```

—Program 15.2—

This time, dBASE will process only one line and wait for you to press a key before processing the next line. Press any key to see each line until the dot prompt shows again. You'll see a scenario like the one below:

```
SET TALK OFF
Type any key to step - ESC to cancel
USE MAIL
Type any key to step - ESC to cancel
GO BOTTOM
Type any key to step - ESC to cancel

Type any key to step - ESC to cancel
DO WHILE .NOT. EOF()

Type any key to step - ESC to cancel
    IF ZIP = "92122"
Type any key to step - ESC to cancel
SKIP
Type any key to step - ESC to cancel
ENDDO
Type any key to step - ESC to cancel
```

Here we can see that the command file only went through the loop once, rather than enough times to check all the records in the database. Check to see if dBASE is at the end of the file already. Type in the command:

```
? EOF()   <RET>
```

dBASE responds with:

```
.T.
```

Hmmmm. Looking back at the command file, we see that one of the earlier lines reads GO BOTTOM. That's causing dBASE to start at the bottom of the file, rather than the top. To fix the error, type in the command:

```
MODIFY COMMAND B:TEST   <RET>
```

and change the GO BOTTOM command to GO TOP, as in Program 15.3.

Save the command file, then test it again. First, disable the ECHO and STEP to see the program run in its natural state:

```
SET STEP OFF   <RET>
SET ECHO OFF   <RET>
```

Then

```
DO B:TEST   <RET>
```

```
********************************************
* TEST.PRG                                  *
********************************************
SET TALK OFF
USE B:MAIL
GO TOP

DO WHILE .NOT. EOF()
   IF ZIP = "92122"
      ? TRIM(FNAME),LNAME
      ? ADDRESS
      ? TRIM(CITY)+", "+STATE+ZIP
      ?
      ?
      ?
   ENDIF
SKIP
ENDDO
```

Program 15.3

The program prints one mailing label:

```
Lucy Smithsonian
461 Adams St.
San Diego, CA 92122-1234
```

Now you might want to make sure that the program was only supposed to print one label. You can check to make sure the loop is repeating by setting ECHO on again and running the command file. You'll see the commands inside the DO WHILE loop repeat several times.

Another way to make sure the program printed labels for all 92122 residents is to use the LIST command from the dot prompt to see how many 92122s are on the database. From the dot prompt, type in the command:

```
LIST FOR ZIP = "92122"
```

dBASE responds with:

Record#	LNAME	FNAME	ADDRESS	CITY	STATE	ZIP
5	Smithsonian	Lucy	461 Adams St.	San Diego	CA	92122

There is only one 92122 zip code resident on the database. Therefore, the program performed correctly.

Unfortunately, debugging isn't always this easy. Learning to become a good troubleshooter takes as much experience as learning to be a good programmer.

To summarize, the most common programming errors to watch out for are:

- Confusing character strings and numbers.

- Dangling DO WHILEs and ENDIFs. Also, crossed loops and IF clauses, which cause an ENDIF to respond to the wrong IF, or an ENDDO to respond to the wrong DO WHILE.

- Putting a command line in an IF...ENDIF clause that actually belongs outside the clause. This is a very common error which can wreak havoc on the program's results. Likewise, putting a command line inside a loop which belongs outside the loop. This can cause infinite loops to occur. Along this same line, forgetting to SKIP inside a 'DO WHILE .NOT.

EOF()' loop will cause an infinite loop to occur, because the loop will just keep rereading the first record over and over again.

- Misspelling a command, memory variable name, or field name. If we create a field called ADDRESS, and later attempt to ? ADRESS or INDEX ON ADRESS, an error is sure to occur. We called the field ADDRESS, and we're telling dBASE to look for ADRESS, which does not exist.

- Not bothering with design or pseudocode. When we come up with a good idea for a new program, we're tempted to just start typing it into the computer, and make it up as we go along. This can lead to a tangled mess of commands in a program that is very difficult to untangle later. A little pre-planning can save a lot of confusion.

Now let me give you a little pep talk on debugging. All programs have bugs. They are big ones at first, which eventually get refined down to very small ones. Even software systems that have been in use for a while (like dBASE II) have bugs in them. The professional does not take his bugs to heart. He does not sulk or pout over them, nor does he shake his fist at the CRT's blank stare (at least, not while anyone is looking). He knows that the computer can't do what he *means*, and so he is going to have to spell it out more clearly. The beginner, on the other hand, often feels intimidated, frustrated, or angered by his software bugs. This is not good. One should not get one's ego involved with one's software (at least, not until it's debugged and running).

The most important skill to develop in writing software is to break down big complex problems into smaller, workable pieces. The second most important skill is to say exactly what you mean, using the computer's extremely limited vocabulary. Experience helps us develop these skills. It's actually the debugging experience which best helps us learn to express ourselves in computer language.

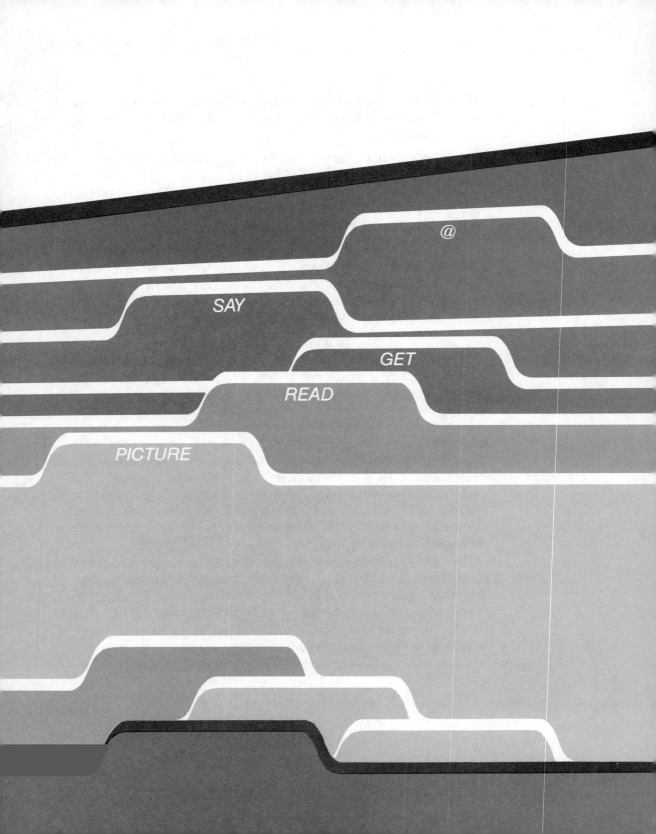

SETTING UP
SCREEN DISPLAYS
16

dBASE automatically provides us with many forms to fill out for adding or editing data. For example, when we USE B:MAIL and APPEND, we get the append form on the screen.

The append form is shown in the screen below.

```
Record No. 6
LNAME    :_                      :
FNAME    :              :
ADDRESS  :                            :
CITY     :              :
STATE    :      :
ZIP      :      :
PHONE    :                  :
```

In addition to these ready-made forms, dBASE allows us to create our own forms. For example, we might want to enter mail data using a form like this:

```
Record no. 6
Enter  ^W as last name to quit.

Last Name :               : First Name :          :
Address :                      :
City :          : State :      : Zip :          :
Phone :          :
```

This form is better than the first one because it provides instructions such as "Enter ^W as last name to quit," and it has the field names spelled out (Last Name instead of LNAME). To create such forms of our own, we need to use the @, SAY, GET, and READ commands.

Creating Forms with @, SAY, GET, and READ

The @ command tells dBASE where on the screen to position the cursor prior to printing something. It works by row and column number (@ ROW,COLUMN) where rows and columns are numbers. The upper left corner of the screen is row 0, column 0. The lower left corner is row 23 (on most screens), column 0. The upper right corner is row 0, column 80, and the lower right corner is row 23, column 80. The SAY command tells dBASE what to print at the cursor postion (SAY 'some message'). Hence, next to the dBASE dot prompt, if we were to type in the command

    @ 12,40 SAY 'Hi'   <RET>

we'd see the word "Hi" printed near the middle of the screen.

The GET command tells dBASE what information dBASE is to get from the screen (GET field name) when a READ command is encountered in the command file.

The best way to get a feel for these commands is to try them. The easiest method for using a custom screen is to create a format file. In dBASE, a format file is one that contains only @, SAY, and GET commands (and perhaps PICTURE and RANGE commands which we'll discuss later). Furthermore, a format file always has the file name extension .FMT. Let's create one for the MAIL database now.

You can use the MODIFY COMMAND editor to create a format file, but you must remember to use the file name extension .FMT. If you don't, dBASE will assign the extension .PRG, and the program won't work properly. So type in the command:

    MODIFY COMMAND B:ADDNAMES.FMT   <RET>

When the dBASE word processor message appears, type in the ADDNAMES.FMT format file exactly as shown in Program 16.1.
The RECNO() in the format file is the dBASE function which displays the number of a record. Notice that each line has a row and column

```
*************************** ADDNAMES.FMT
a 1,1 SAY "Record number: "
a 1,15 SAY RECNO()
a 2,1 SAY "Enter ^W as last name to quit."
a 4,1 SAY "Last Name " GET LNAME
a 4,35 SAY "First Name " GET FNAME
a 6,1 SAY "Address " GET ADDRESS
a 8,1 SAY "City " GET CITY
a 8,27 SAY "State " GET STATE
a 8,40 SAY "Zip " GET ZIP
a 10,1 SAY "Phone number " GET PHONE
```

Program 16.1

position (@ row,col), and a prompt (SAY "Last Name). Most lines also have the GET command to read in data for a particular field in the database (GET LNAME). In a moment, we'll see the format file set up a screen and read in data according to these instructions. Once you've typed in the entire format file, save it with a ^W as usual.

If you want to test the new format file, be sure that the MAIL database is in use:

    USE B:MAIL   <RET>

Then, use the SET FORMAT TO command to tell dBASE the name of the custom screen to use. In this case, we've named the format file ADDNAMES, so type in the command:

    SET FORMAT TO ADDNAMES   <RET>

When you append or edit records, dBASE will use the custom screen specified in the format file rather than its usual screens. Try it. Enter the command:

    APPEND   <RET>

You should see on the screen:

```
Record number: 6
Enter ^W as last name to quit.
Last Name :_                       : First Name :              :
Address :                   :
City :                  : State:       : Zip :         :
Phone number :                  :
```

Now you can type in as many new records as you like using all of the usual arrow key and control key commands to manage the cursor. When you're done, press RETURN or ^W, instead of entering a new last name. The dot prompt will be displayed on the screen once again.

To verify that the new records you typed in made it to the database, just enter the LIST command.

The same format file can be used with the EDIT command. Since we've already SET FORMAT TO B:ADDNAMES, we can just enter the EDIT command:

    EDIT 2   **<RET>**

and see the data for record number 2 in the custom screen ready to be edited:

```
Record number: 2
Enter ^W as last name to quit.
Last Name :Smith                    : First Name :John Q.            :
Address :213 A St.               :
City :San Diego             : State:CA        : Zip :92123        :
Phone number :(555)453-1212          :
```

Once again, you can use the arrow keys and control-key commands to make changes to the record.

When you are done using a custom screen, you should remember to put dBASE back into its normal screen mode. To do so, type in the SET FORMAT TO command without reference to a custom screen:

    SET FORMAT TO   **<RET>**

Now, let's take a look at ways to make custom screens a little fancier with templates.

Making Templates with PICTURE

The PICTURE command can be used with @, SAY, and GET to provide templates on the screen. For example, suppose we want our form to look like this:

```
Record Number 6
Enter ^W as last name to quit.

Last Name :_               : First Name :            :
Address :                  :
City :           : State :      : Zip :         :
Phone :(   )   -   :
```

Notice that the PHONE field has a template embedded in it that resembles a typical phone number format :( ) - :. The PICTURE command allows us to set up such a template, and also to limit the types of data that are acceptable for a given field. Here are some of the PICTURE data types:

Format Character	Acceptable Data
# or 9	Accepts only numeric digits (1,2,3...8,9,0) and +, −, and blanks.
A	Accepts only alphabetical characters (A–Z).
X	Accepts any data.
!	Translate data to uppercase

Let's try out an example. Let's MODIFY COMMAND B:ADD-NAMES.FMT to look like Program 16.2. Notice the only change is in the line which reads @ 10,1 SAY PHONE. We've added PICTURE '(999) 999-9999'. Now when we save the command file and SET FORMAT TO ADDNAMES, then APPEND we see

Record number: 6
Enter ^W as last name to quit.

Last Name :_   : First Name :   :
Address :   :
City :   : State :   : Zip :   :
Phone :( )   -   :

```
*********************** ADDNAMES.FMT
a 1,1 SAY "Record number: "
a 1,15 SAY RECNO()
a 2,1 SAY "Enter ^W as last name to quit."
a 4,1 SAY "Last Name " GET LNAME
a 4,35 SAY "First Name " GET FNAME
a 6,1 SAY "Address " GET ADDRESS
a 8,1 SAY "City " GET CITY
a 8,27 SAY "State " GET STATE
a 8,40 SAY "Zip " GET ZIP
a 10,1 SAY "Phone number " GET PHONE PICTURE "(999)999-9999"
```
Program 16.2

Fill out the form as below. When you type in the phone number, try typing in some alphabetical characters first. dBASE will beep and refuse to accept them, because the PICTURE format specifies numbers only.

Record number: 6

Enter ^W as last name to quit.

Last Name :Frisbee   : First Name :Hobart   :

Address :321 Third Ave.   :

City :Cucamonga   : State :CA   : Zip :91234   :

Phone :(213) 555-0101:

After all the data are typed in, the dot prompt reappears. If we now

> **LIST   <RET>**

we see

1	Appleby	Andy	123 A. St.	San Diego	CA	92123
2	Smith	John Q.	123 A. St.	San Diego	CA	92122
3	Smithsonian	Lucy	461 Adams St.	San Diego	CA	92122-1234
4	Doe	Ruth	1142 J. St.	Los Angeles	CA	91234
5	SMITH	Betsy	222 Lemon Dr.	New York	NY	01234
6	Rhodes	Dusty	P.O. Box 12345	Los Angeles	CA	91234
	(213) 555-1212					
7	Frisbee	Hobart	321 Third Ave.	Cucamonga	CA	91234
	(213) 555-0101					

   Notice that Hobart's phone number contains parentheses and a hyphen, even though we did not type these on the screen when we entered the phone number. This is because the PICTURE template specified that these characters are part of the field. When we have a great deal of data to enter, these templates can save us some repetitive typing.

Using the Custom Screen from a Menu

We can use the custom screen with the menu-driven mailing system we've developed in previous chapters. To use the custom screen for adding new records, type in the command:

MODIFY COMMAND B:MENU   <RET>

so that the menu program appears on the screen. Within the DO CASE clause of the MENU program is a CASE statement for adding new records, as shown below:

```
CASE CHOICE = 1
   APPEND
```

All we have to do is modify this statement. The CASE statement should first turn on the custom screen, the APPEND, then return to the normal screen. Change the CASE statement to read as follows:

```
CASE CHOICE = 1
   SET FORMAT TO B:ADDNAMES
   APPEND
   SET FORMAT TO
```

(Use ^N to make room for the new lines.) Then save the command file with ^W. To test it, DO B:MENU and select option number 1 from the main menu. When you have finished adding new names, the main menu will reappear on the screen as usual.

You may also want to use the custom ADDNAMES screen for editing records. If so, you'll need to make a couple of modifications to the EDDY.PRG command file. From the dot prompt, type in the command:

MODIFY COMMAND B:EDDY   <RET>

Then locate the routine which reads:

```
IF WHOMS = 1
   LOCATE FOR UPPER(LNAME) = UPPER(WHOM)
   EDIT RECNO()
ENDIF
```

All you need to do is specify the ADDNAMES format for the edit, then switch back to the normal screen. So just add two new lines, using ^N to make room:

```
IF WHOMS = 1
   LOCATE FOR UPPER(LNAME) = UPPER(WHOM)
   SET FORMAT TO B:ADDNAMES
   EDIT RECNO()
   SET FORMAT TO
ENDIF
```

There is also a routine in the EDDY.PRG command file that looks like this:

```
IF WHOMS > 1
   LIST FOR UPPER(LNAME) = UPPER(WHOM);
     LNAME,FNAME,ADDRESS
   ?
   ACCEPT 'Which one (by record number) ' TO RECNO
   EDIT &RECNO
ENDIF
```

Place the SET FORMAT TO commands around the EDIT command as shown below:

```
IF WHOMS > 1
   LIST FOR UPPER(LNAME) = UPPER(WHOM);
     LNAME,FNAME,ADDRESS
   ?
   ACCEPT 'Which one (by record number) ' TO RECNO
   SET FORMAT TO B:ADDNAMES
   EDIT &RECNO
   SET FORMAT TO
ENDIF
```

Then save the command file after making the changes. To test the modifications, enter the command:

```
DO B:MENU   <RET>
```

and select the menu option to edit data (option 4). Enter the name of the individual to edit, and you'll see his data on the custom screen ready for editing. When you're done editing, you'll be returned to the mailing system main menu.

Ranges

You can use the RANGE command with the @, SAY, and GET commands to limit the range of acceptable user input. For example, the menu below presents five possible choices. The @, SAY, GET, and READ commands wait for the user's response, then store that response to a variable called CHOICE. The RANGE command ensures that only a response within the range of 1 to 5 is accepted:

```
STORE 0 TO CHOICE
CLEAR
? "              MAIN MENU"
?
? "      1. Add new records"
? "      2. Sort the database"
? "      3. Edit a record"
? "      4. Print reports"
?
? "      5. Exit"
@ 10,6 SAY "Enter choice ";
   GET CHOICE RANGE 1,5
READ
```

Entering a number outside the range of 1 to 5 will cause dBASE to beep and display the message:

RANGE is 1 to 5 (hit space)

Pressing the space bar will remove the message and allow another try.

Notice in the command file above that the variable CHOICE is initially set to zero. If you are using a memory variable with a GET command, the memory variable *must* exist before it is used with GET. In this example, we've simply stored zero as an initial value for the CHOICE memory variable.

In this chapter, because we created a fairly small custom screen, we used the MODIFY COMMAND editor to create the format file.

dBASE III also comes with a special program called dFORMAT which you can use for creating custom screens by simply drawing the format you want on the screen. In the next chapter, we'll discuss the dFORMAT program, along with some other useful tips.

SOME USEFUL TIPS
17

Before ending this book, I'd like to give you some additional useful tips. I suspect you'll find them handy at some point in your work with dBASE III.

Using Abbreviations

To speed up our typing, dBASE allows us to abbreviate commands to four letters. Therefore, we can type in MODI COMM rather than MODIFY COMMAND to get the same result. Any command can be abbreviated. Here are some common commands and their abbreviations.

COMMAND	ABBREVIATION
REPORT FORM B:BYNAMES	REPO FORM B:BYNAMES
DELETE RECORD 6	DELE RECO 6
REPLACE ALL LNAME WITH 'Smith'	REPL ALL LNAME WITH 'Smith'
APPEND	APPE
SET DEFAULT TO B	SET DEFA TO B
MODIFY COMMAND B:LABELS	MODI COMM B:LABELS
MODIFY STRUCTURE	MODI STRU
DISPLAY STRUCTURE	DISP STRU
DISPLAY MEMORY	DISP MEMO

Custom Screens with dFORMAT

As we discussed in Chapter 16, you can use *format files* (.FMT) to create custom screens for editing and appending records. One way to do this is to use MODIFY COMMAND to create the format, which contains only @,SAY,GET, PICTURE, and RANGE commands. Optionally, you can use the dBASE III dFORMAT program. dFORMAT allows you to draw the custom screen as you wish it to appear, then it creates the format file with all the @, SAY, GET, and PICTURE commands in it. Let's look at an example.

Suppose you had a database named CLUB.DBF with the following structure:

```
Structure for database : C:club.dbf
Number of data records :  14
Date of last update : 10/27/84
        Field    Field name   Type        Width   Dec
            1    LNAME        Character      20
            2    FNAME        Character      20
            3    COMPANY      Character      20
            4    ADDRESS      Character      25
            5    CITY         Character      20
            6    STATE        Character       5
            7    ZIP          Character      10
            8    PHONE        Character      13
            9    EXP_DATE     Date            8
```

Furthermore, suppose you want to use a custom screen for appending and editing records, as shown in Figure 17.1.

To use dFORMAT to create the custom screen, you must first quit dBASE so that the DOS A> or C> prompt appears on the screen. Then run the dFORMAT program. dFORMAT is stored on the Sample Programs and Utilities disk that comes with dBASE III. If you are

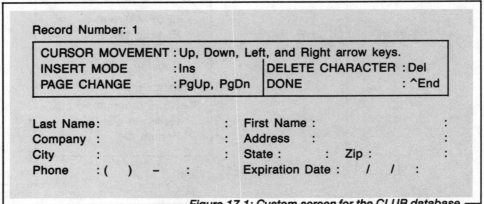

Figure 17.1: Custom screen for the CLUB database.

using a hard disk system and have already copied the dFORMAT.EXE and DFM.MSG files to the hard disk system, you can type in dFOR-MAT next to the C> prompt and press RETURN to use dFORMAT. If you are using a floppy-disk system, place the Sample Programs and Utilities disk in Drive A and type in the command dFORMAT next to the A> prompt, then press RETURN. A copyright notice appears briefly on the screen, then the dFORMAT main menu, which looks like Figure 17.2.

The entire dFORMAT User's Manual is stored on disk. To access the User's Manual, type in a question mark (?). The table of contents appears on the screen as in Figure 17.3.

If you press the space bar, you will move one page ahead through the manual; if you type B you will move one page back. You can also type in a page number you wish to turn to. For example, page 10 contains instructions for first time users, so you can enter the number 10 <RET> to view that page. Pressing RETURN brings you back to the main menu.

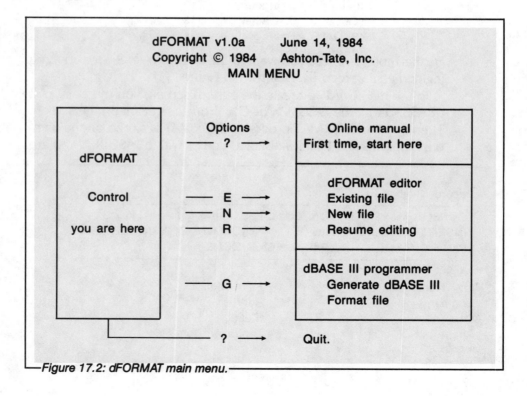

Figure 17.2: dFORMAT main menu.

dFORMAT On-line Manual — Contents

Topic	Explanation	Summary
Using this manual	10 *	20
dFM concepts	11	21
dFORMAT to dBASE III		
Format file generation	30	40
Input and text fields	31	41
Output fields	32	42
PICTURE formats	33	43
Programming dBASE commands	34	44
dFORMAT editor		
List of editor commands	60	66
Cursor and display movement	51	61
Inserting and deleting	52	62
Saving and quiting	53	63
Boxes and lines	55	65

APPENDICES

dFM conventions	80
dFM limitations	85

INDEX

! — }	91
A — C	92
D — F	93
G — M	94
N — R	95
S — Z	96

* First time? Enter 10 — then press the return key

p = PRINT, C->contents, RETURN->dFORMAT, SPACE = forward, B = back, or page number:

Figure 17.3: dFORMAT table of contents.

To create a custom screen, first think of a file name. In this example we'll use the name ADDNAMES.TXT. Select the New File option from the main menu by typing N. Then, type in a file name for the new screen. If you're using a floppy disk system, include the drive specification; e.g., B:ADDNAMES.TXT. Note: don't use .FMT as the extension; dFORMAT will create a format file later. A blank screen for composing your custom screen will appear.

To design the custom screen, use the arrow keys on the numeric keypad to move the cursor to where you want a prompt to appear. Then type the lines and prompts you want to appear on your custom screen. If you want the screen to display a value, such as the record number [RECNO()], use the > symbol to stand for SAY. In places where you want the screen to get data (read in information to put into a field), use the < symbol followed by the field name. If you want to use a PICTURE statement, use the exclamation point (!) to stand for the PICTURE command. Figure 17.4 shows a custom screen typed in for the CLUB.DBF file.

Notice that each field name is preceded by the < symbol. At each of these locations, dBASE will ask the user for data to put into the field (i.e., Last Name <LNAME becomes @ 1,1 SAY "Last Name" GET LNAME). Next to the EXP_DATE field is the symbol !"99/99/99". This will be translated to the PICTURE command "99/99/99" in the format file. At the top of the screen is the phrase "Record Number: >RECNO()", which will display the prompt "Record Number" and the record number.

Once you are done creating your custom screen, save it by pressing F2, and selecting the X option from the menu that appears.

Now you are ready to make the custom screen that you just drew into a dBASE format (.FMT) file. To do so, select the Generate option (G) from the main menu. dFORMAT will ask:

    Name of screen file:ADDNAMES.TXT

Press RETURN to use the ADDNAMES.TXT screen. dFORMAT will state:

    Will generate dBASE command file ADDNAMES.FMT (X to cancel)

Press RETURN to continue.

It only takes dFORMAT a couple of seconds to create the custom format file. Then, you'll be returned to the dFORMAT main menu. From there, select the quit option (Q) to exit dFORMAT.

```
Record Number: >RECNO()
┌──────────────────────────────────────────────────────────────┐
│ CURSOR MOVEMENT : Up, Down, Left, and Right arrow keys.        │
│ INSERT MODE        : Ins      │ DELETE CHARACTER : Del          │
│ PAGE CHANGE        : PgUp, PgDn │ DONE              : ^End       │
└──────────────────────────────────────────────────────────────┘

Last Name   <LNAME          First Name  <FNAME
Company     <COMPANY        Address  <ADDRESS
City        <CITY           State  <STATE      Zip  <ZIP
Phone       <PHONE!"(999)999-9999"  Expiration Date  <EXP_DATE!"99/99/99"
```

Figure 17.4: dFORMAT custom screen for the CLUB.DBF file.

Once you're back to the A> or C> prompt, you can use the TYPE command to view the custom format file. For example, if the format file is stored on the disk in drive B, enter the command:

TYPE B:ADDNAMES.FMT <RET>

You'll see the format file appear on the screen as in Figure 17.5.

```
* addnames.FMT
@2,0 SAY "Record Number:"
@2,16 SAY RECNO( )
@3,0 SAY "———————————————————————————————————————————"
@3,55 SAY "—————————"
@4,0 SAY "| CURSOR MOVEMENT : Up, Down, Left, and Right arrow key"
@4,55 SAY "s.  |"
@5,0 SAY "| INSERT MODE        : Ins    DELETE CHARACTER"
@5,56 SAY ": Del |"
@6,0 SAY "| PAGE CHANGE        : PgUp, PgDn  DONE"
@6,56 SAY ": ^End |"
@7,0 SAY "———————————————————————————————————————————"
@7,55 SAY "—————————"
@9,0 SAY "Last Name"
@9,11 GET LNAME
@9,34 SAY "First Name"
@9,46 GET FNAME
@11,0 SAY "Company"
@11,11 GET COMPANY
@11,34 SAY "Address"
@11,43 GET ADDRESS
@13,0 SAY "City"
@13,11 GET CITY
@13,34 SAY "State"
@13,41 GET STATE
@13,52 SAY "Zip"
@13,58 GET ZIP
@15,0 SAY "Phone"
@15,11 GET PHONE PICTURE "(999)999-9999"
@15,34 SAY "Expiration Date"
@15,51 GET EXP_DATE PICTURE "99/99/99"
```

Figure 17.5: A custom format file generated by dFORMAT.

To use the custom screen, load dBASE again. Then use the database (and any index files you've already created), set the format to the custom screen name as usual, and use the APPEND or EDIT command:

```
USE CLUB INDEX NAMES,ZIPS
SET FORMAT TO ADDNAMES
EDIT 2
```

The record to edit will appear on the custom screen, as shown in Figure 17.6. You can use all of the normal editing commands for controlling the cursor. When you are done editing, type ^W to return to the dot prompt.

When you are done with the custom screen, you should set dBASE back to its normal screen mode with the command:

```
SET FORMAT TO
```

If you change your mind about a custom screen and wish to redesign it, you can once again quit dBASE and call up the dFORMAT program. Select the Existing File option (E) from the main menu, and type in the name of the screen:

```
ADDNAMES.TXT
```

Then, you can make whatever changes you like. If you feel lost while in dFORMAT, press F1 to get help. When you're done making

```
Record Number: 2

┌────────────────────────────────────────────────────────────┐
│ CURSOR MOVEMENT : Up, Down, Left, and Right arrow keys.      │
│ INSERT MODE        : Ins    │ DELETE CHARACTER : Del         │
│ PAGE CHANGE        : PgUp, PgDn │ DONE              : ^End    │
└────────────────────────────────────────────────────────────┘

Last Name : Wallace          :   First Name : Doug            :
Company   : 3N Co.           :   Address    : 427 Zeppo St.   :
City      : San Francisco    :   State : CA   :   Zip : 91234 :
Phone     : (123)555–1212:       Expiration Date : 12/31/84 :
```

Figure 17.6: Custom append screen created by dFORMAT with data.

changes, save the new file with the F2 key, then select the Generate option once again to recreate the format (.FMT) file.

You can also edit the format (.FMT) file directly by using MODIFY COMMAND (e.g., MODIFY COMMAND B:ADDNAMES.FMT). You can also use a word processor, as long as it has a nondocument mode, to edit either the screen (ADDNAMES.TXT) or format (.FMT) file.

dFORMAT has many commands for drawing screens and boxes. All of the information you need is in the online manual. Consult the table of contents to find your way around the manual, and the P key to print any pages that appear on the screen.

Memo Fields

In some cases you might want to store long passages of text as data. For example, suppose you want to store references to journal articles on a database, including author, title, publication, date, pages, keywords (subjects) and an abstract. To make room for an abstract of any length, you could make the ABSTRACT field the Memo data type, as shown in the structure below:

```
Structure for database : C:library.dbf
Number of data records :  2
Date of last update : 10/19/84
Field    Field name   Type        Width   Dec
    1    AUTHOR       Character      20
    2    TITLE        Character      20
    3    PUB          Character      20
    4    DATE         Date            8
    5    PAGES        Character      10
    6    ABSTRACT     Memo           10
    7    KEYWORDS     Character      80
```

Even though dBASE automatically assigns a width of 10 characters to this field, the field can be up to 4,000 characters long.

When you use the APPEND command to add data to the reference database, or EDIT to modify data, the screen displays the usual entry form as below:

```
Record No.        1

AUTHOR        :                    :
TITLE         :                    :
PUB           :                    :
DATE          : / / :
PAGES         :              :
ABSTRACT      :memo:
KEYWORDS      :                          :
```

To put data into the ABSTRACT field, place the cursor in the field and press Ctrl-PgDn. The screen will clear and you'll automatically be in the dBASE word processor. From there you can type in your abstract, and use Ctrl and the dBASE MODIFY COMMAND arrow keys to compose and edit. When you are done typing or editing the abstract, type ^W or ^End to return to the APPEND or EDIT screen.

Data typed into memo fields are stored on an auxiliary database with the extension .DBT. For example, if you name the reference file LIBRARY, then the abstracts will be stored on a database named LIBRARY.DBT.

When you use the LIST command to view the records, the word "memo" will be displayed on the listing, as shown below:

```
# AUTHOR             TITLE            PUB
  DATE      PAGES    ABSTRACT KEYWORDS
1 Adams, A.A.        M68000 Programming    Microsystems.
  04/01/85  111–129  Memo 68000,    Programming
2 Stark, Robin D.    Software Design    Jour. of Software
                     Design
  03/01/85  9-27     Memo Programming,    Design,
                     Development
```

However, if you specify the field names:

LIST OFF AUTHOR,TITLE,PUB,DATE,PAGES,ABSTRACT

then the contents of the abstract field will be included in the listing:

```
Adams, A.A.          68000 Programming    Microsystems.
  04/01/85 111–129 An in-depth description of programming the
  32-bit M68000 processor at the assembly language level.
  Includes routines for custom I/O as well as general purpose
  applications.
```

Stark, Robin D.   Software Design   Jour. of Software
                                                  Design
03/01/85   19–27   Program design and development
                                  considerations when
working in a high-level database management language.
Discusses database and software design as well as modular
and structured programming.

The exact appearance of a memo field is sometimes difficult to display with a LIST or REPORT command. A command file can be used instead:

```
* * * * * * * * * * * * * * * * * * * * * * * *  Print library data.
USE LIBRARY
GO TOP
DO WHILE .NOT. EOF()
 ? "Author : ",AUTHOR
 ? "Title   : ",TITLE
 ? "Publication: ",PUB
 ? "Date    : ",DATE,"      Pages: ",PAGES
 ? "Keywords : ",KEYWORDS
 ?
 ? ABSTRACT
 ?
 ?
 SKIP
ENDDO (while not eof)
```

This command file displays the reference data as below:

```
Record no.                        1
Author           :   Adams, A.A.
Title            :   M68000 Programming
Publication:         Microsystems.
Date             :   04/01/85                    Pages: 111–129
Keywords         :   M68000,
                     Programming
An in-depth description of programming the 32-bit M68000
processor at the assembly language level. Includes routines
for custom I/O as well as general purpose applications.

Record no.                        2
Author           :   Stark, Robin D.
```

Title   :   Software Design
Publication: Jour. of Software
                    Design
Date   :   03/01/85   Pages: 19–27
Keywords   :   Programming, Design,
                    Development
Program design and development considerations when
working in a high-level database management language.
Discusses database and software design as well as modular
and structured programming.

The command file in program 17.1 performs the same task, but
incudes page breaks for the printer.

One slight disadvantage to memo fields is that you cannot perform
searching functions on them. For example, the command:

LIST FOR "Design" $ABSTRACT

will create an error, because you are attempting to list records with

```
*********************** Print library data.
USE LIBRARY
GO TOP
SET TALK OFF
SET PRINT ON
*********************** Start line feed counter (LF) at zero.
LF = 0
DO WHILE .NOT. EOF()
   ? "Author     : ",AUTHOR
   ? "Title      : ",TITLE
   ? "Publication: ",PUB
   ? "Date       : ",DATE,"              Pages: ",PAGES
   ? "Keywords   : ",KEYWORDS
   ?
   ? ABSTRACT
   ?
   ?
   LF = LF + 9
   ************* If 50 or more lines printed, start on
   ************* new page and reset the line counter.
   IF LF >= 50
      EJECT
      LF = 0
   ENDIF (lf >= 50)

   SKIP
ENDDO (while not eof())
SET PRINT OFF
```

Program 17.1

the word "Design" embedded in the abstract Memo field. However, this is usually not a problem. In the sample reference database we designed above, we've included a KEYWORD field which can be used to store keywords (subjects). Hence, to view all the references on the subject of design, just type in these commands:

```
LIST FOR "Design" $KEYWORDS
```

Another limitation to the memo field is that it cannot be used for sorting or indexing. For example, you cannot ask dBASE to

```
INDEX ON ABSTRACT TO ABS
```

However, it's pretty unlikely that you'd want to index on a memo field. In the LIBRARY example, you'd be more likely to index on the author field for alphabetical listings by author, and the DATE field for listings in chronological order.

Quick Lookups

If a database is indexed on a field, and you wish to look up something in that field, you can use the FIND or SEEK command rather than LOCATE or LIST FOR. FIND and SEEK are both very fast. For example, the MAIL database we created earlier could be indexed on last name or first and last name:

```
USE B:MAIL                                <RET>
INDEX ON LNAME + FNAME TO B:NAMES         <RET>
```

If you wanted to look up Miller with the FIND command, you'd first have to make sure the NAMES index is active, then perform the FIND:

```
USE B:MAIL INDEX B:NAMES   <RET>
FIND Miller                <RET>
```

If you wish to perform a FIND from within a command file, where the information you are looking up is stored in a memory variable, use the SEEK command instead, as in the command file below:

```
USE B:MAIL INDEX B:NAMES
ACCEPT "Look for whom? " TO LOOKFOR
```

SEEK LOOKFOR

If the FIND or SEEK command is successful, then the database is positioned to the first record that matches the value being looked for. If not succesful, then the message *No Find* appears on the screen, and the EOF() (end of file) function is true.

There are some important points to keep in mind about the FIND and SEEK commands. First, the FIND command *only* works on an indexed field. If a database is in use with multiple index files, the FIND command only works with the first listed index file. For example, if you open the MAIL database with the two index files as below:

USE B:TEST INDEX B:ZIPS, B:NAMES

the FIND or SEEK command can only be used to locate a zip code. To look up information in the NAMES index instead, just switch the order of the index files:

USE B:TEST INDEX B:NAMES, B:ZIPS

Both FIND and SEEK are limited to straightforward lookups; you *cannot* do anything fancy like

```
FIND Miller .OR. Smith
SEEK UPPER(SEARCH)
FIND LNAME > SEARCH
```

Also, you need to keep the data types straight. For example, if a database is indexed on a DATE field, and the field is of the Date type, then the information you're looking for must also be the Date type. Use the CTOD (Character to Date) function to help with this. For example, the command file below asks what date to look up, translates the date to the Date type, then uses the SEEK command to look up the date.

```
USE B:SALES INDEX B:DATES

ACCEPT "Look up what date? " TO LOOKFOR
STORE CTOD(LOOKFOR) TO LOOKFOR
SEEK LOOKFOR
IF EOF()
   ? "No such date!"
```

```
    ELSE
        LIST WHILE DATE = LOOK FOR
    ENDIF (eof)
```

After the SEEK command attempts to find the requested date, the IF EOF() command checks to see if the date was found or not. If EOF() is true (.T.), then the date was not found, and the command file displays the message *No such date!* If the end of the file was not encountered (ELSE), then the command file lists all records that have the requested date.

Complex Sorts

Combining dates, characters, and numbers in index files for sorts-within-sorts can be tricky. Generally, whenever you create an index file with multiple fields, all noncharacter fields should be converted to characters. The dBASE STR (string) function can help with this. Let's look at an example.

Earlier, we created a database called SALES with the following structure:

```
Structure for database : C:sales.dbf
Number of data records :    9
```

Field	Field name	Type	Width	Dec
1	CODE	Character	5	
2	TITLE	Character	15	
3	QTY	Numeric	5	
4	AMOUNT	Numeric	12	2
5	DATE	Date	8	

It has the following records in it:

Record#	CODE	TITLE	QTY	AMOUNT	DATE
1	AAA	Rakes	3	15.00	03/01/83
2	BBB	Hoes	2	12.50	03/01/83
3	CCC	Shovels	3	21.00	03/01/83
4	AAA	Rakes	2	10.00	03/01/83
5	CCC	Shovels	4	26.50	03/01/83
6	AAA	Rakes	2	11.00	03/02/83
7	CCC	Shovels	1	7.50	03/02/83

| 8 | BBB | Hoes | 2 | 12.50 | 03/02/83 |
| 9 | AAA | Rakes | 5 | 23.50 | 03/02/83 |

Suppose you want to sort this database in CODE order, by quantity within code. You could index on both CODE and QTY, as long as you convert the QTY field to a string, as shown below:

INDEX ON CODE + STR(QTY,3) TO TEST   <RET>

(The ,3 in the STR function means 3-wide.) When you list the records, you'll see them in code order, and within each code, in quantity order, as shown below:

Record#	CODE	TITLE	QTY	AMOUNT	DATE
4	AAA	Rakes	2	10.00	03/01/83
6	AAA	Rakes	2	11.00	03/02/83
1	AAA	Rakes	3	15.00	03/01/83
9	AAA	Rakes	5	23.50	03/02/83
2	BBB	Hoes	2	12.50	03/01/83
8	BBB	Hoes	2	12.50	03/02/83
7	CCC	Shovels	1	7.50	03/02/83
3	CCC	Shovels	3	21.00	03/01/83
5	CCC	Shovels	4	26.50	03/01/83

Now, suppose you want the records in ascending code order (A–Z), but the quantity in descending order (largest to smallest). You could accomplish this by indexing on the code plus the inverse of the quantity. That is, subtract the QTY field from some large constant (such as 999). However, the QTY field still must be converted to a string:

INDEX ON CODE + STR(1000–QTY,4) TO TEST

A LIST command will now display the records in ascending code order, and descending quantity order within codes:

Record#	CODE	TITLE	QTY	AMOUNT	DATE
9	AAA	Rakes	5	23.50	03/02/83
1	AAA	Rakes	3	15.00	03/01/83
4	AAA	Rakes	2	10.00	03/01/83
6	AAA	Rakes	2	11.00	03/02/83
2	BBB	Hoes	2	12.50	03/01/83
8	BBB	Hoes	2	12.50	03/02/83
5	CCC	Shovels	4	26.50	03/01/83

3	CCC	Shovels	3	21.00	03/01/83
7	CCC	Shovels	1	7.50	03/02/83

You might want to sort these records by date and quantity. For example, suppose you want the records to be displayed in date order, and descending quantity order. You would need to convert both the date and the inverse quantity to strings:

INDEX ON DTOC(DATE) + STR(1000 – QTY,4) TO TEST

If you list the database:

LIST DATE,QTY,CODE,TITLE,AMOUNT

you will see the records sorted by date and quantity:

Record#	date	qty	code	title	amount
5	03/01/83	4	CCC	Shovels	26.50
1	03/01/83	3	AAA	Rakes	15.00
3	03/01/83	3	CCC	Shovels	21.00
2	03/01/83	2	BBB	Hoes	12.50
4	03/01/83	2	AAA	Rakes	10.00
9	03/02/83	5	AAA	Rakes	23.50
6	03/02/83	2	AAA	Rakes	11.00
8	03/02/83	2	BBB	Hoes	12.50
7	03/02/83	1	CCC	Shovels	7.50

Now, you may want something a little different. Suppose you want the records in month order, disregarding the days, and the quantities in descending order. To do so, you'd want to index on the month (only) and the inverse quantity. Again, both must be converted to character strings:

INDEX ON STR(MONTH(DATE),2) + STR(1000 – QTY,4) TO TEST

Now you would see this list:

Record#	DATE	QTY	CODE	TITLE	AMOUNT
9	03/02/83	5	AAA	Rakes	23.50
5	03/01/83	4	CCC	Shovels	26.50
1	03/01/83	3	AAA	Rakes	15.00
3	03/01/83	3	CCC	Shovels	21.00
2	03/01/83	2	BBB	Hoes	12.50
4	03/01/83	2	AAA	Rakes	10.00
6	03/02/83	2	AAA	Rakes	11.00

8	03/02/83	2	BBB	Hoes	12.50
7	03/02/83	1	CCC	Shovels	7.50

If you add a few records for April with the APPEND command, then list, you will see:

Record#	date	qty	code	title	amount
9	03/02/83	5	AAA	Rakes	23.50
5	03/01/83	4	CCC	Shovels	26.50
1	03/01/83	3	AAA	Rakes	15.00
3	03/01/83	3	CCC	Shovels	21.00
2	03/01/83	2	BBB	Hoes	12.50
4	03/01/83	2	AAA	Rakes	10.00
6	03/02/83	2	AAA	Rakes	11.00
8	03/02/83	2	BBB	Hoes	12.50
7	03/02/83	1	CCC	Shovels	7.50
12	04/15/84	1000	AAA	Rakes	5000.00
10	04/01/84	99	AAA	Rakes	1234.56
11	04/15/83	57	CCC	Shovels	1777.44

Notice that the quantities go from highest to lowest within each month, but without regard to the particular day of the month. This sort order produces a nice report summarized by month. You could use MODIFY REPORT to create any report format you like, and specify MONTH(DATE) as the Group/Subtotal field. When you print the report, you'll see the data displayed as shown below:

```
Page No. 1
11/07/84
```

Sales by month and quantity

Date	Qty	Title	Amount
** Month number: 3			
03/02/83	5	Rakes	23.50
03/01/83	4	Shovels	26.50
03/01/83	3	Rakes	15.00
03/01/83	3	Shovels	21.00
03/01/83	2	Hoes	12.50
03/01/83	2	Rakes	10.00
03/02/83	2	Rakes	11.00
03/02/83	2	Hoes	12.50
03/02/83	1	Shovels	7.50

```
* *  Subtotal  * *
                    24                        139.50
* *  Month number: 4
04/15/84        1000  Rakes                  5000.00
04/01/84          99  Rakes                  1234.56
04/15/83          57  Shovels                1777.44
* *  Subtotal  * *
                  1156                        8012.00
* * *  Total  * * *
                  1180                        8151.50
```

The data are grouped and subtotalled by month and displayed in descending quantity order within each month.

You can do the same operations with the AMOUNT field, but be sure to specify two decimal places in the STR function for the amount. For example, for ascending amount order, use:

INDEX ON STR(AMOUNT,12,2) TO TEST

For descending order, use:

INDEX ON STR(999999.99 – AMOUNT,8,2) TO TEST

You should be aware that the index file contains the data in the converted format, so using the FIND or SEEK command will be tricky. You can get around this by using one index file of converted fields for displaying records in sorted order, and another index file with unconverted data for SEEK and FIND.

Record Numbers in Reports

If you'd like to include record numbers in a report, just make one of the columns contain the RECNO() function, as shown below:

```
Field                   RECNO()
    contents


                            # decimal places: 0 Total? (Y/N) N

Field
    header              1 Record No.
                        2
                        3
                        4
```

Width   10

That's all there is to it!

Custom Configurations

You can create a special file called CONFIG.DB, which will start up dBASE III with specified characteristics ready. To create a CON-FIG.DB file, use the nondocument mode from any word processor, or use MODIFY COMMAND from the dBASE dot prompt. Also, make sure that the file is on the same disk that you load dBASE III from (for example, drive A on a floppy disk system, or drive C on a hard disk). The file name must be spelled CONFIG.DB.

Inside the file, you can set up certain initial characteristics. For example, any of the dBASE SET commands (DEFAULT, EXACT, TALK, SAFETY, etc.) can be initialized. Also, any of the function keys (F1–F10) can be defined. If you like, a command file can also automatically run whenever you call up dBASE.

Take a look at the CONFIG.DB file below, which was typed in using command MODIFY COMMAND CONFIG.DB:

```
COLOR  =  BG
SAFETY  =  OFF
HELP  =  OFF
DEFAULT = B
COMMAND  =  DO MENU
WP = WS
```

The first line of the CONFIG file sets the color of the screen to aqua. The second line sets the SAFETY feature off. The third line sets the HELP feature off. The fourth line automatically sets the default drive to B, so that the USE and DO commands will automatically search the disk in drive B for files. Note: Appendix C, and the dBASE III manual for examples of other SET parameters.

The fifth line makes dBASE automatically run the program MENU rather than going straight to the dot prompt. The MENU program is assumed to be on drive B because of the DEFAULT setting in the line above. The last line, WP= WS, designates the WordStar program as the word processor used with Memo fields. That is, when a ^PgDn key is pressed to add or edit a Memo field, dBASE automatically uses the WordStar program, rather than the dBASE word processor, to enter/edit the Memo field. This also eliminates the 4,000 character limit on the length of a Memo field.

Exiting the WordStar program returns you to where you left off: at the Memo field of the append or edit screen.

Where Do I Go from Here?

Practice The only way to become fluent in a new language (such as dBASE III) is to use it. Create a database and work with it. If you're worried about experimenting on important data, just make a backup of the database first (COPY TO B:TEMP). Then, if you make a mess on the original data file, just ZAP the records from it and APPEND FROM TEMP. It's always a good idea to COPY TO B:TEMP when you work with a database. If anything at all goes wrong, including a power shortage, you have the security of a backup.

Read the manual. Few of us can stand to drudge through a technical user's manual, but it is important to do so to get a feel for all the capabilities and rules of this software. In this book, we've covered most of the dBASE III commands, and have tried to demonstrate their use through practical exercises. Read the manual to get additional information and more examples of commands.

Pace yourself. Don't try to work out problems that are over your head at the outset, or else you'll just end up frustrated. Learning to master the marvelous machine can be very enjoyable if you pace yourself. Work at a comfortable level and experiement to learn more. If you make it fun, you'll learn more in the long run.

INTERFACING dBASE III WITH OTHER SOFTWARE SYSTEMS

A

We can combine dBASE power with other software systems by transferring files to and from dBASE. In this appendix, we will discuss transferring data between dBASE and word processors, using the WordStar program as the example. We will also discuss transfer methods for spreadsheets, using the SuperCalc and Symphony packages as examples. We will then discuss transferring BASIC data files.

Interfacing with Word Processors

We can send dBASE reports to word processing systems for further editing or inclusion in other documents. To do so, we design our report using the MODIFY REPORT command in dBASE. Then print the report with the TO <filename> option. We can then load up our word processor, and read the report into the word processing system. Here is a typical scenario using the WordStar program as the word processor.

```
A> DBASE   <RET>
USE B:MAIL   <RET>
MODIFY REPORT B:BYNAME   <RET>
   (Define report format)
REPORT FORM B:BYNAME TO TRANSFER   <RET>
QUIT   <RET>
```

The TO B:TRANSFER option with the REPORT FORM commands sends a copy of the report to a disk file named TRANSFER.TXT. When we QUIT dBASE, the A> reappeared on the screen. Now we can load up WordStar. Let's say we want to pull the dBASE report into a document called MANUAL.TXT. We'd type in

```
WS B:MANUAL.TXT   <RET>
```

When the document appears on the screen, position the cursor to the place that you want the dBASE report to appear. Then enter a

```
^KR
```

The WordStar program asks NAME OF FILE TO READ? We reply with

```
TRANSFER.TXT   <RET>
```

That's all there is to it. The report which appeared on the screen when we asked dBASE to REPORT FORM B:BYNAME is now in our WordStar document, and is also in a disk file called TRANSFER.TXT.

Now, we may want to send our dBASE file to WordStar's MailMerge option for printing form letters. In this case, we need to create a database in MailMerge format. Let's say that we want to send our MAIL database to a MailMerge file from which to print form letters. After loading up dBASE, type in

```
USE B:MAIL   <RET>
```

Then we need to COPY it to another data file in MailMerge readable form. The command is

COPY TO B:MM DELIMITED WITH " <RET>

This creates a data file called MM.TXT which the MailMerge file can access to create form letters. Then we would have to create the form letter in WordStar. Recall that our MAIL database contains the fields LNAME, FNAME, ADDRESS, CITY, STATE, ZIP, PHONE. We would have to QUIT dBASE and load up the WordStar program. Then we could create a document called B:FORM.LET. Program A.1 contains a FORM.LET which can read the data file we've just created.

Notice that we've included PHONE in the .RV command, even though it is not used in the form letter anywhere. This is essential if the PHONE variable exists. The .RV command is expecting a certain number of fields, so it must have the same number of fields as the data file, regardless of whether or not we plan on using that field in our form letter. Even if we only wanted the first name for our form letter, we would still need to read in all of the fields. If you forget this important tidbit, your form letter might come out in a most unpleasant format.

After we create and save the form letter, we merely need to merge print it using the appropriate MailMerge command. That is, select WordStar option M from the WordStar Main Menu, and when it asks

```
.OP
.DF B:MM.TXT
.RV LNAME,FNAME,ADDRESS,CITY,STATE,ZIP,PHONE

&FNAME& &LNAME&
&ADDRESS&
&CITY&, &STATE&        &ZIP&

Dear &FNAME&,

        How do you like getting these form letters? You
probably wouldn't know the difference if it were not
for my dot matrix printer.

                        Ta ta for now,

                        Zeppo
```

Program A.1

NAME OF FILE TO MERGE PRINT?, tell it B:FORM.LET <RET>. A
letter for each individual in the MAIL database will then be printed.
Here is how the first one should come out:

Andy Appleby
123 A. St.
San Diego, CA 92123

Dear Andy,

How do you like getting these form letters? You
probably wouldn't know the difference if it were not
for my dot matrix printer.

Ta ta for now,

Zeppo

We could use our LABELS program to print mailing labels for all
these individuals, or we could create a WordStar MailMerge document to print names and addresses directly on envelopes, one envelope at a time. In Program A.2 is a MailMerge file to print envelopes
from our MM.TXT data file, which we'll call ENVEL.TXT.

After we create and save ENVEL.TXT, we can merge print it in the
usual WordStar fashion. However, when the merge print option asks
"PAUSE FOR PAPER CHANGE BETWEEN PAGES? (Y/N)," be sure to
answer Y. Then, you can insert each individual envelope, lining it up
so that the printer head is right where you want the printing to start.
The MailMerge option will print one envelope, eject it from the
printer, and wait for you to put in the next envelope.

If you want your form letter to go to certain individuals only, you
can specify this in your dBASE COPY command. Let's assume we
want our form letters to go to San Diego residents only. With the
dBASE dot prompt showing, and the MAIL database in use, type in
the command

    COPY TO B:MM FOR CITY = 'San Diego' DELIMITED WITH "
        <RET>

Only San Diego residents would appear on the MailMerge file, hence only individuals in San Diego would have form letters printed.

If you already have a MailMerge file and want to use some dBASE commands to manage it, you can send a copy of it to dBASE. To do so, you need to load up dBASE and CREATE an empty file with the CREATE command. Structure it so that it has the same fields as your MailMerge file. When dBASE asks INPUT DATA NOW?, say N. Then USE the newly created database, and

    APPEND FROM B:MM.DAT DELIMITED   <RET>

You can now sort your MailMerge file or do whatever you please with it in dBASE II. (This example assumed that the name of your existing MailMerge file was MM.DAT.) To get the dBASE database back into MailMerge readable form, just USE the dBASE file and

    COPY TO B:MM.DAT DELIMITED WITH "   <RET>

Interfacing with Spreadsheet Software

For our spreadsheet example, we will use the SuperCalc and Symphony packages as models. First, we will deal with getting information out of SuperCalc into dBASE. To do so, we need to load up the SuperCalc program and read in the desired file with the usual /L command. Next we need to get rid of borders because dBASE can't

```
.MT 0
.OP
.DF B:MM.TXT
.RV LNAME,FNAME,ADDRESS,CITY,STATE,ZIP,PHONE

                &FNAME& &LNAME&
                &ADDRESS&
                &CITY&, &STATE&     &ZIP&

.PA
```

Program A.2

handle these. Use the SuperCalc /GLOBAL BORDER command to get rid of the borders. Then we need to create an ASCII file of the data in SuperCalc. To do so, use the /O command as usual. Use the D for (D)isplay, and inform SuperCalc of the range (e.g., A1:E25). Then a prompt will ask if you want the data output to screen, printer or disk. Choose D for disk. When SuperCalc asks for the file name, give it any name you wish. We'll use DBCALC for our example. The SuperCalc package will add the extension .PRN to our file name. If you want to store the DBCALC file on drive B, use B:DBCALC as the filename.

Now DBCALC.PRN exists as an ASCII file, and can be read directly into a WordStar document if desired. To get this file into dBASE requires a little more juggling.

First, we need to load up dBASE so that the dot prompt is showing. Then, we need to CREATE a database that will pull in our SuperCalc file. The database we create must have a field for each column in the SuperCalc file. In our example we have five columns. I know this because the range I asked to have SuperCalc output was from A1 to E25, and E is the fifth letter of the alphabet.

We need to be careful about data types and widths here. The dBASE field widths must be identical to the SuperCalc column widths. We can see the width of each column in a SuperCalc file by simply placing the SuperCalc cursor under each field. Let's say our SuperCalc file had the first field as account number, the second as account title, the third as MTD balance, the fourth as QTD balance, and the fifth field as YTD balance. We would need to structure our dBASE file as follows:

```
FIELD     NAME,TYPE,WIDTH,DECIMAL PLACES
001       ACCNO,N,6,2
002       TITLE,C,20,0
003       MTD,N,12,2
004       QTD,N,12,2
005       YTD,N,12,2
006
INPUT DATA NOW? N
```

Now we need to USE this newly created file and

APPEND FROM DBCALC.PRN SDF   <RET>

Now we can dBASE a copy of our SuperCalc file to our heart's content.

To pull a dBASE III database into a Symphony spreadsheet, load up dBASE in the usual fashion and Use the file you want to transfer. Type LIST to make sure that your choosen file has some data in it.

Now you can copy the file, delimited, to another file with a new name with this command:

COPY TO TRANSFER DELIM WITH "

When that's done, quit dBASE.

Load up Symphony in the usual manner, and go to a blank spreadsheet. Put the cell pointer to the location where you want the dBASE database to be located. Press SERVICES and select the options File—Import—Structured, then type in the name of the file (e.g., TRANSFER.TXT). The spreadsheet now contains the dBASE III database. Although you can't see the contents of all the fields, they're there. Use the Width—Set commands from the menu to widen the fields and display all their contents. Don't forget to save the spreadsheet after reading in the TRANSFER.TXT file.

Note: you can also use this TRANSFER.TXT file as a WordStar Mail Merge file, or as a BASICA sequential data file.

To transfer a SYMPHONY database to dBASE III, first load up Symphony and use the SERVICES file—Retrieve to load up the database that you want to send. Go to the SHEET window by pressing WINDOW (F6) until the spreadsheet appears. Go to the _DB range by pressing GOTO (F5) and typing in the database name followed by _DB (e.g., MAIL_DB). Press DOWN to get to the first record in the database.

Now, decide on a width for each field. You must be very careful at this step, or the translation won't work. Position the cell pointer to the first field, then press MENU and select Width—Set. Press the right or left arrow key to expand or shrink the field until you get your desired width. Then, jot down the field name and the *exact* width of the field *before* you press RETURN. Do this for every field in the database, remembering to jot down the name and width of each on a piece of paper. Don't skip any fields. When you're done, add up the field lengths. Using the current example, you should end up with the list of field names and widths as shown below:

Field Name	Width
Last name	12
First name	9
Company	12
Address	16
City	17
State	5
Zip Code	10
	81 → Total width.

Now, position the cell pointer to the first field in the first record of the database (the very first *Last Name* in this example). Press SERV-ICES (F9) and select the options Print—Settings. Select Page—Breaks—No. Select Source—Range and highlight all the records in the database using the period and End Right End Down keys. Be sure that only the records in the database are highlighted. Press RETURN.

Select the Destination—File options, and type in a name for transferring the file (e.g., SYMTODB) and press RETURN. Select Margins—Left, and type in a zero <RET>. Select RIGHT and type in the value that is the sum of the field widths (81 in this example). Select Quit—Quit, then Go, and then Quit.

Next, exit Symphony with the usual SERVICES—Exit—Yes—Exit options.

Go into dBASE and create a database with a new name (MAIL). You need not use the exact field names, (e.g., use LNAME instead of *Last Name*), but their order must be correct. Also, the lengths must be *exactly* the lengths you jotted down while in Symphony. Once you create the database, dBASE will ask:

Input data records now?

Answer no. Then use the new database (with USE MAIL) and append the records from the transfer file using the SDF option, as shown below:

APPEND FROM SYMTODB.PRN SDF

Don't forget the .PRN extension which Symphony always adds.

Type LIST. If there are blank records at the top of the database, you can get rid of them by typing in the commands:

```
GO TOP
DELETE NEXT 5
PACK
```

Type LIST, and all the records should be fine.

If there is an offset error, such as part of the FNAME field in the LNAME field, it's because the widths you defined while in Symphony did not exactly match the widths you defined while creating the dBASE database. If the wrong data are in the wrong field, it's either because you didn't specify all the fields while creating the dBASE database, or you didn't highlight the entire database while in Symphony. In these cases, you'll have to start over.

Transferring dBASE III data in and out of Framework is quite easy. Framework has the @dbasefilter function that is designed specifically for loading dBASE III and dBASE III data into Framework. You can just use the standard Get file by Name option under the DISK menu, and type in the name of the dBASE III database to read in, being sure to specify .DBF in the file name. The Framework Write DosTextFile command can create an ASCII text file that can be read into dBASE III using the APPEND FROM (filename) DELIMITED procedure.

Interfacing with BASIC Data Files

The BASIC (or BASICA) language allows you to create data files with either variable-length records (sequential files), or fixed-length records (random access data files). Sequential files are easy to deal with. To send dBASE files to BASIC sequential data files, we merely need to load up dBASE, USE the data file of interest, then

```
COPY TO BASIC.DAT DELIMITED WITH "   <RET>
```

This will work fine for BASICA or CBASIC sequential files. To read BASICA sequential data files into dBASE, we must load up dBASE, and CREATE a database with a structure that matches the BASICA file. Then, we just:

> **APPEND FROM BASIC.DAT DELIMITED <RET>**

dBASE will then treat the new version of the BASIC data file as one of its own.

Random access files may present more of a problem. BASICA stores its random access files in binary notation, undelimited with fixed field lengths and no carriage return line/feed at the end. This is indeed a problem. The easiest method for getting a BASICA random access file into a dBASE database might be to first create a sequential file from the random access file in BASIC, then just read the data into dBASE using the commands mentioned above. A BASICA program capable of performing such a feat is shown in Program A.3.

```
10 REM ********* Send random access data to a sequential file
20 OPEN "R", #1, "RFILE.DAT", 60
25 FIELD #1, 20 AS F1$, 10 AS F2$, 15 AS F3$, 9 AS F4$,
   5 AS F5$, 10 AS F6$, 30 AS F7$

30 OPEN "O", #2, "SFILE.DAT"

40 FOR REC% = 1 TO 90000
50     GOSUB 1000    :REM Read next R/A record
55     REM *************** Assumes a zero marks the last record
60     IF LNAME$="0" THEN 100
70     WRITE #2, LNAME$,FNAME$,ADDRESS$,CITY$,STATE$,ZIP$,PHONE$
80 NEXT REC%

90 REM ********* Done with transfer

100 CLOSE
110 SYSTEM

1000 REM ******* Read random access record
1010 GET #1,REC%
1020 LNAME$=F1$
1030 FNAME$=F2$
1040 ADDRESS$=F3$
1050 CITY$=F4$
1060 STATE$=F5$
1070 ZIP$=F6$
1080 PHONE$=F7$
1090 RETURN
```

Program A.3

To send dBASE data into a BASICA random access file, we could use the COPY command mentioned above, then treat it as a sequential file, and write a BASICA program to translate the BASICA sequential file to a BASICA random file. In Program A.4, you will see the MBASIC code for that.

CBASIC and CB-86 handle random access files a little differently. Random files are stored in ASCII, delimited with commas, with variable-length fields. CBASIC random files will read a dBASE program that has been copied to another file delimited OK, but then the CBASIC or CB-86 program needs to deal with the nuisance of the padded fields. An easier way around this is to have dBASE mimic the CBASIC or CB-86 compiler. We need to CREATE a dBASE database with one field, with the total length of the fields equalling the record length of the CBASIC random access file. In the code below, we will

```
10 REM ********* Send sequential data to a random file
20 OPEN "R", #1, "RFILE.DAT", 60
25 FIELD #1, 20 AS F1$, 10 AS F2$, 15 AS F3$, 9 AS F4$,
   5 AS F5$, 10 AS F6$, 30 AS F7$

30 OPEN "O", #2, "SFILE.DAT"

40 FOR REC% = 1 TO 90000
50     IF EOF(2) THEN 100
60     INPUT #2, LNAME$,FNAME$,ADDRESS$,CITY$,STATE$,ZIP$,PHONE$
70     GOSUB 1000    :REM Write next R/A record
80 NEXT REC%

90 REM ********* Done with transfer

100 CLOSE
110 SYSTEM

1000 REM ****** Read random access record
1010 LSET LNAME$=F1$
1020 LSET FNAME$=F2$
1030 LSET ADDRESS$=F3$
1040 LSET CITY$=F4$
1050 LSET STATE$=F5$
1060 LSET ZIP$=F6$
1070 LSET PHONE$=F7$
1080 PUT #1,REC%
1090 RETURN
```

Program A.4

assume that the dBASE file CBASIC.DAT has already been created accordingly. (We're assuming here that if you have enough computer sophistication to write a random access data file system in CBASIC or CB-86, you don't need step-by-step instructions to create the appropriate database.) Now, using our MAIL.DBF database as an example, we can write the routine in Program A.5 to create true CBASIC/CB-86 random access data files.

Now the entire CBASIC.DAT file can be copied to another file with the SDF option and put in ASCII to get rid of the dBASE header. You may have to experiment with this a bit, but if you're already working with CB-86 random access files, I suspect that the experimentation will not take too long.

Pascal, PL/1, and other language programmers can follow the steps provided for MBASIC and CBASIC data files to work out a method for interfacing dBASE databases with their compilers.

```
SELECT 1
USE B:MAIL

SELECT 2
USE B:CBASIC.DAT

SELECT 1

DO WHILE .NOT. EOF()
    SELECT 2
    APPEND BLANK
    STORE TRIM(LNAME) + ','+TRIM(FNAME)+','+TRIM(ADDRESS)+',';
        +TRIM(CITY)+','+TRIM(STATE)+','+TRIM(ZIP)+',';
        +TRIM(PHONE) TO CRECORD

    ******************** Pad entire record with blanks
    DO WHILE LEN(CRECORD) < 155
        STORE CRECORD + ' ' TO CRECORD
    ENDDO

    REPLACE CBFIELD WITH CRECORD

    SELECT 1
    SKIP
    ENDDO   (while not EOF)
    CLOSE DATABASES
    QUIT
```

Program A.5

GRAPHICS WITH dBASE III

B

You might ask, "Since when does one do graphics with a database management system?" We're not talking about doing anything too fancy here, just drawing some pictures or perhaps a bar graph on the screen. We can't use any high-resolution graphics here either, just the computer's standard character set.

The Character Set

The first thing we need to know about our machine is what characters we have to work with. Obviously we can use the ones on our keyboard, but most computers and printers have extra graphics characters hidden away in their memories. We can pull the little devils out of hiding with the CHR function. The CHR function tells us the character that goes along with a number. For instance, CHR(42) is an asterisk, CHR(32) is a blank space. Each letter and number on the keyboard is assigned an ASCII number, and the CHR function translates a number into its appropriate character. ASCII stands for American Standard Code for Information Interchange, a standard for assigning numbers to characters on computer keyboards. We can see the ASCII character set just by writing and doing the command file in Program B.1.

When we do this command file, we get the following results:

```
ASCII Character Set
32.
33. !
34. "
35. #
36. $
37. %
38. &
39. '
```

```
******* Generate ASCII Chart.
SET TALK OFF
? ' ASCII Character Set'
?

STORE 32 TO COUNTER
DO WHILE COUNTER < 128
   ? STR(COUNTER,3) + '. ' + CHR(COUNTER)
   STORE COUNTER + 1 TO COUNTER
ENDDO
```

Program B.1

40. (

41.)

42. *

43. +

44. ,

45. –

46. .

etc.

Where are all the fancy graphics characters? They are hidden away in numbers greater than 127, beyond the standard character set. I can't guarantee that your particular terminal has a graphics set, so don't be disappointed if you don't get good results. The characters whiz by on the screen pretty fast, so let's create the command file in Program B.2 with three columns so that more characters are displayed on the screen.

This will yield an unpredictable result, but mine came out looking like those in Figure B.1.

You will probably notice that if you SET PRINT ON before printing the ASCII chart, the graphics characters look different on the screen than on the printed copy. This is because the ASCII numbers above 127 are free turf for manufacturers, so different companies assign different characters to these ASCII numbers. Keep a copy of your graphics chart on paper. When you want to use a graphics character, you can just look up its number, and tell dBASE to ? CHR(___).

```
***********************Display graphics set.
CLEAR
SET TALK OFF
? 'Graphics characters'
?
STORE 127 TO N

DO WHILE N < 255
    ? STR(N,3)+CHR(N)+'    '+STR(N+1,3)+CHR(N+1)+'    '+STR(N+2,3)+CHR(N+2)
    STORE N+3 TO N
ENDDO
```

Program B.2

127 _	128	129 ▪
130 ▪	131 ▀	132 ▄
133 ▌	134 ▪▪	135 ▛
136 ▪	137 ▚	138 ▐
139 ▜	140 ▄▄	141 ▙
142 ▟	143 █	144
145 ▪	146 ▪	147 ▚
148 ▄	149 ▌	150 ▄
151 ▛	152 ▄	153 ▄
154 ▟	155 ▚	156 ▄
157 ▙	158 ▟	159 ▐
160 ▪	161 ▐	162 ▪
163 ▟	164 ▄	165 ▐
166 ▄	167 ▛	168 ▐
169 ▜	170	171 ▐
172 ▄	173 ▐	174 ▄
175 ▌	176	177 ▐
178 ▄	179 █	180 ▄
181 ▐	182 ▟	183 ▐
184 ▄	185 ▚	186 ▐
187 ▐	188 ▄	189 ▐
190 ▟	191 █	192
193 ▙	194 ▐	195 ▀
196 ▄	197 █	198 ▪▪
199 ▛	200 ▪	201 ▚
202 █	203 ▜	204 ▄▄
205 ▙	206 ▟	207 █
208 ▄	209 ▪	210 ▪
211 ▙	212 ▄	213 ▐
214 ▜	215 ▛	216 ▄
217 ▙	218 ▐	219 ▜
220 ▄	221 ▐	222 ▄
223 ▐	224	225 ▐
226 ▪	227 ▜	228 ▄
229 ▐	230 ▄	231 ▐
232 ▄	233 ▜	234 ▄
235 ▐	236 ▄	237 ▐
238 ▄	239 █	240
241 ▪	242 ▄	243 █
244 ▄	245 ▐	246 ▟
247 ▐	248 ▄	249 ▚
250 ▟	251 ▚	252 ▐
253 ▐	254 ▟	255 █

—Figure B.1: Graphics Characters—

Drawing Pictures on the Screen

Suppose I want to draw Figure B.2 on the screen. Frivolous, you say? Yes indeed.

Ideally, we would draw the picture on a piece of graph paper, and put each asterisk in a separate box on the paper. Now, we can easily see the row and column number of each character. Doing things the hard way, we could then write a command file that says

```
@ 1,1 SAY '*'
@ 1,2 SAY '*'
@ 1,3 SAY '*'
```

etc., but that is too many @ R,C SAY '*' to write. Instead, we will CREATE a database called FACE and structure it as such:

field name	type	width	dec
Row	Numeric	3	0
Col	Numeric	3	0

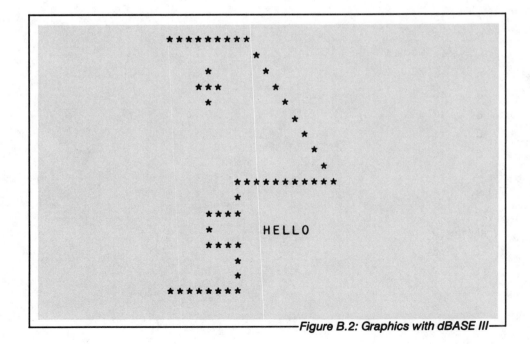

Figure B.2: Graphics with dBASE III

Then we can APPEND our coordinates into the database, each as a record.

ROW	COL
1	1
1	2
1	3
1	4
1	5
1	6
1	7
1	8
1	9
2	10
3	11
4	12
5	13
6	14
7	15
8	16
8	15
8	14
8	13
8	12
8	11
8	10
8	9
9	9
10	9
11	9
11	8
11	7
11	6
12	6
13	6

14	6
14	7
14	8
14	9
15	9
16	9
17	9
17	8
17	7
17	6
17	5
17	4
17	3
17	2
17	1
3	5
4	4
4	5
4	6
5	5

Now we can create a command file that draws from the data we put in the FACE database. This is shown in Program B.3.

```
********** Draw a database's contents.
CLEAR
SET TALK OFF
USE B:FACE
DO WHILE .NOT. EOF()
   @ ROW,COL SAY '*'
   SKIP 1
ENDDO
@ 12,11 SAY 'HELLO'
```

Program B.3

When we DO DRAW, we get the face displayed on the screen. We could also make a general-purpose command file, as shown in Program B.4, that could draw the contents of any database. This would allow us to make up even more amusing pictures.

To send pictures to the printer, just SET DEVICE TO PRINT above the 'DO WHILE' loop. After the picture is drawn, SET DEVICE TO SCREEN, as in the routine in Program B.5.

A General-Purpose Bar Graph Routine

Before you spend a bundle on a graphics package for your computer, you might want to try keying in GRAPH.PRG, the command

```
******** Draw requested picture.
CLEAR
SET TALK OFF
ACCEPT 'Use which data base' TO FILENAME
USE &FILENAME
CLEAR
DO WHILE .NOT. EOF()
    a ROW,COL SAY '*'
    SKIP 1
ENDDO
```

—Program B.4—

```
******** Draw requested picture.
CLEAR
SET DEVICE TO PRINT

DO WHILE .NOT. EOF()
    a ROW,COL SAY '*'
    SKIP 1
ENDDO
SET DEVICE TO SCREEN

RETURN
```

—Program B.5—

file I've listed on the last few pages of this appendix. Once you get it typed in and saved (under the file name GRAPH.PRG), you can DO it with dBASE, and it will ask the following of questions:

```
Enter graph title          :                    :
How many columns?           :          :
How wide each column?       :          :
Low end of Y axis           :          :
High end of Y axis          :          :
```

Just answer each question on the screen, and follow your answer with RETURN. Let's say you want to title your graph "Sample Graph" and plot six columns of data on it, each column ten spaces wide. On the Y (vertical) axis, you want the low end to be zero and the high end to be 100. Just answer each question as follows:

```
Enter graph title          :Sample
How many columns?          :6        :
How wide each column?      :10       :
Low end of Y axis          :0        :
High end of Y axis         :100      :
```

At that point the screen will clear and GRAPH will ask for the value to be plotted in each column, and the title of each column, as below:

```
Column 1 data? :    :    Title:    :
Column 2 data? :    :    Title:    :
Column 3 data? :    :    Title:    :
Column 4 data? :    :    Title:    :
Column 5 data? :    :    Title:    :
Column 6 data? :    :    Title:    :
```

Make sure you key in values within the Y-axis range you've specified (0–100 in this example). Then, GRAPH will plot the graph on your screen for you. When it is done, it will just stay there until you press the RETURN key. At that point, the screen will clear, and ask

Send Graph to printer? (Y/N) :

If you answer Y, the graph will then be sent to your printer. Below, I've provided a sample graph in Figure B.3, created on my Okidata Microline printer with GRAPH.PRG.

The GRAPH.PRG command file is also presented, with some notes on configuring it to other printers and terminals. Figure B.3 shows a sample graph. Enjoy!

Program B.6 shows the entire GRAPH command file. Inside the program, notice the graphics characters used for the screen are set up in the routine.

```
****** Store graphics characters for screen.
STORE STR(196,3) TO XCHAR
STORE STR(179,3) TO YCHAR
STORE STR(219,3) TO BCHAR
```

That is, I use an ASCII 45 for the X character (X-axis line), an ASCII 129 for the Y-character (Y-axis line), and an ASCII 150 for the bar itself. For the printer, I use these characters (stored in a routine near the middle of the command file).

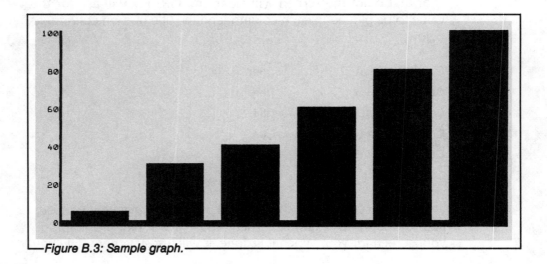

Figure B.3: Sample graph.

```
******************************* GRAPH.PRG
**************** General purpose bar graph routine.
CLEAR
SET TALK OFF

***************************** Get Graph data.
STORE "                         " TO TITLE
STORE 0 TO NO_COL,COL_WIDTH,LR,HR
a 2,1 SAY "Enter graph title      " GET TITLE
a 3,1 SAY "How many columns?      " GET NO_COL PICT "99"
a 4,1 SAY "How wide each column? " GET COL_WIDTH PICT "99"
a 5,1 SAY "Low end of Y axis?     " GET LR PICT "9999999"
a 6,1 SAY "High end of Y axis?    " GET HR PICT "9999999"
READ

CLEAR
STORE 1 TO LP
DO WHILE LP <= NO_COL
   IF LP < 10
      STORE STR(LP,1) TO LPS
   ELSE
      STORE STR(LP,2) TO LPS
   ENDIF (lp<=no_col)
   STORE "     " TO COL&LPS
   STORE SPACE(COL_WIDTH-2) TO TITLE&LPS
   a LP,1 SAY "Column " + LPS + " data? ";
     GET COL&LPS PICT "99999"
   a LP,24 SAY "Title " GET TITLE&LPS
   STORE LP+1 TO LP
ENDDO
READ
CLEAR
? "Working....."

X=1
STORE "        " TO BLINE
DO WHILE X <= NO_COL
   IF X < 10
      STORE STR(X,1) TO XS
   ELSE
      STORE STR(X,2) TO XS
   ENDIF
   STORE BLINE+TITLE&XS+"  " TO BLINE
   X=X+1
ENDDO

******************** Store graphics characters.
STORE STR(196,3) TO XCHAR
STORE STR(179,3) TO YCHAR
STORE STR(219,3) TO BCHAR

******************** Create vertical lines.
STORE 1 TO CNTR
STORE ' ' + CHR(&YCHAR) TO LINE

******************** Create horizontal line.
STORE ' '+CHR(&XCHAR) TO TLINE
```

Program B.6

```
STORE 1 TO CNTR
DO WHILE CNTR <= (NO_COL*COL_WIDTH)
    STORE TLINE+CHR(&XCHAR) TO TLINE
    STORE CNTR+1 TO CNTR
ENDDO (while cntr)

********************** Create bar character.
STORE ' ' TO BAR
STORE 1 TO CNTR
DO WHILE CNTR < COL_WIDTH-1
    STORE BAR + CHR(&BCHAR) TO BAR
    STORE CNTR+1 TO CNTR
ENDDO (while cntr)

********************** Draw graph background.
CLEAR
STORE 1 TO CNTR
STORE 0 TO BCOUNT
?
DO WHILE CNTR < 21
    STORE '     ' TO LEFT
    IF ((CNTR-1)/4 = INT((CNTR-1)/4)) .OR. CNTR = 1
       IF CNTR < 20
          STORE STR(HR-((BCOUNT/5)*HR),5) TO LEFT
          STORE BCOUNT+1 TO BCOUNT
       ENDIF (cntr < 20)
    ENDIF (cntr-1 evenly divisible by 4)
    ? LEFT + LINE
    STORE CNTR+1 TO CNTR
ENDDO (while cntr < 21 lines printed)
? STR(LR,5) + TLINE
? '  '+BLINE

****************** Set up looping variables for graph.
STORE 7 TO C
STORE 'COL' TO VBASE
STORE ' ' TO VNAME
STORE (HR-LR)/10 TO DIV
STORE 1 TO OUTLOOP

***************** Set up outer loop.
DO WHILE OUTLOOP <= NO_COL
    STORE 1 TO CW
    IF OUTLOOP > 9
       STORE 2 TO CW
    ENDIF (outloop > 9)
    STORE VBASE + STR(OUTLOOP,CW) TO VNAME
    @ 21,C SAY ' '
    STORE "&VNAME" TO NM
    STORE 2*(VAL(&NM)/DIV) TO COL
    STORE 21 TO ROW

  ****************** Draw bars on screen.
  DO WHILE COL > 0
     @ ROW,C SAY BAR
     STORE ROW - 1 TO ROW
     STORE COL - 1 TO COL
  ENDDO (While COL > 0)
```

Program B.6 (continued)

```
STORE C + COL_WIDTH TO C
STORE OUTLOOP + 1 TO OUTLOOP

ENDDO  (outloop)

******************** Center title over graph
@ 0,((NO_COL*(COL_WIDTH+2))/2)-(LEN(TRIM(TITLE))/2);
 SAY TITLE
@ 23,0 SAY ' '

**************** Prepare for printer copy.
WAIT "Press a key..."
CLEAR
WAIT 'Send graph to printer? (Y/N) ' TO YN
CLEAR
? "Working....."
IF UPPER(YN)='Y'
   STORE STR(143,3) TO XCHAR
   STORE STR(213,3) TO YCHAR
   STORE STR(255,3) TO BCHAR
   STORE CHR(&XCHAR) TO TLINE
   STORE 1 TO CNTR
   DO WHILE CNTR < (NO_COL*COL_WIDTH)
      STORE TLINE+CHR(&XCHAR) TO TLINE
      STORE CNTR+1 TO CNTR
   ENDDO (cntr)

   **************** Create printer bar.
   STORE 1 TO CNTR
   STORE ' ' TO BAR
   STORE ' ' TO SPACES
   DO WHILE CNTR < COL_WIDTH-1
       STORE BAR + CHR(&BCHAR) TO BAR
       STORE SPACES + ' ' TO SPACES
       STORE CNTR + 1 TO CNTR
   ENDDO (while cntr < 8)

   ********************* Generate printer report.
   CLEAR
   SET PRINT ON
   ************* Center title on printer graph
     STORE ' ' TO TCENTER
     MID = ((NO_COL*(COL_WIDTH+2))/2)-(.5*LEN(TRIM(TITLE)))
     DO WHILE LEN(TCENTER) < MID
        STORE TCENTER + ' ' TO TCENTER
     ENDDO  (len tcenter)
     ? TCENTER + TITLE
     ?
   ********************* Start graph loops.
   STORE 1 TO LCOUNT
   STORE 1 TO CCOUNT
   STORE 0 TO BCOUNT

   DO WHILE LCOUNT < 21
      STORE '     ' TO LEFT
      IF ((LCOUNT-1)/4 = INT((LCOUNT-1)/4)) .OR. LCOUNT =1
        IF LCOUNT < 20
```

Program B.6 (continued)

```
            STORE STR(HR-((BCOUNT/5)*HR),5) TO LEFT
            STORE BCOUNT+1 TO BCOUNT
       ENDIF (lcount < 20)
    ENDIF (lcount-1 evenly divisble by 4)
    STORE LEFT+ CHR(&YCHAR) TO GLINE
    DO WHILE CCOUNT <= NO_COL
       STORE 1 TO CW
       IF CCOUNT > 9
          STORE 2 TO CW
       ENDIF (ccount > 9)
       STORE 'COL' + STR(CCOUNT,CW) TO VNAME
       STORE "&VNAME" TO NM
       IF LCOUNT > 20-(2*(VAL(&NM)/DIV))
          STORE GLINE + BAR  TO GLINE
       ELSE
          STORE GLINE + SPACES TO GLINE
       ENDIF (lcount > 20)
       STORE GLINE+" " TO GLINE
       STORE CCOUNT+1 TO CCOUNT
    ENDDO (for ccount)

       ? GLINE
       STORE ' ' TO GLINE
       STORE 1 TO CCOUNT
       STORE LCOUNT + 1 TO LCOUNT
    ENDDO   (for lcount)

***************** Done with printer graph, print bottom lines.
? STR(LR,5)+ TLINE
? ' '+BLINE
?
?
SET PRINT OFF
ENDIF  (if printer was selected)
RETURN
```

Program B.6 (continued)

```
****** Set up graphics characters for printer.
STORE STR(143,3) TO XCHAR
STORE STR(213,3) TO YCHAR
STORE STR(255,3) TO BCHAR
```

If this program doesn't work, or if your graph comes out looking funny, you may want to try different ASCII characters. You should use the command file at the beginning of this appendix to display the screen and printer character sets for you.

dBASE III
VOCABULARY

C

Command	Definition
!	Displays a field's contents in uppercase [LIST !(LNAME)].
#	Not equal to.
$	Substring function, used for finding a character string embedded within larger character string (LIST FOR 'Lemon' $ADDRESS).
&	Used for macro substitution (IF &FLD = '&COND'). Macros must be stored in memory variables as character strings.
()	Used for logical and mathematical grouping [? (10+10)*5].
*	Multiplies two numbers (? 10*10).
**	Exponent symbol. ? 99 ** 2 displays 99 squared. X = 1234 ** (1/3) stores the cube root of 1234 to memory variable X.
;	Splits long command lines into two separate lines.
^	Exponent symbol. ? 34 ^5 displays 34 raised to the fifth power (45435424.00) In text, the ^ symbol usually means "hold down the Ctrl key."
+	Adds two numbers or links two character strings together (? 10+10).
−	Subtracts two numbers or links two character strings with trailing blanks removed.
.AND.	Two things true simultaneously (LIST FOR 'Oak' $ADDRESS .AND. CITY='San Diego').
.NOT.	A condition is not true (DO WHILE .NOT. EOF).
.OR.	One or another of two conditions is true (LIST FOR CITY='San Diego' .OR. CITY='Los Angeles').
/	Divides two numbers (? 10/5).

Command	Definition
<	Less than (LIST FOR LNAME < 'Smith').
<=	Less than or equal to (LIST FOR LNAME <= 'Smith').
=	Equal to (LIST FOR LNAME = 'Smith').
>	Greater than (LIST FOR LNAME > 'Appleby').
>=	Greater than or equal to (LIST FOR DATE >= CTOD ("03/01/83").
?	Displays the contents of a field, memory variable, or the results of a mathematical equation (? 1+1).
??	Displays the contents of a field, memory variable, or expression without starting on a new line [?? SQRT(X)].
@	Formats screen and printer displays (@ 5,1 SAY 'Hi').
ACCEPT	Displays a prompt on the screen and waits for a response. Stores answer to a memory variable as Character data (ACCEPT 'Do you want more?' TO YN).
ALIAS	Allows a database to be accessed through two different names (USE MAIL ALIAS NAMES).
ALL	Refers to all records in the database (DISPLAY ALL, DELETE ALL, REPLACE ALL).
APPEND	Allows us to add new data to our database.
APPEND BLANK	Adds a new record to the bottom of a database, with all fields blank [APPEND BLANK].
APPEND FROM	Reads the records from another database into the database in use. Adds new records to the bottom of database in use (APPEND FROM TEMP).
ASC	Displays the ASCII value of a character [? ASC("A") displays 65].

Command	Definition
ASSIST	Aids in the use of dBASE III by presenting menus and help screens [ASSIST].
AT	Shows the position at which one character string starts in another [?AT("B","AABBCC") displays 3 because B appears as the third character in "AAB-BCC"].
AVERAGE	Computes the average of a numeric field in a database [AVERAGE AMOUNT FOR MONTH (DATE) = 12].
B:	Signifies drive B for storing data files (CREATE B:MAIL).
B->	Refers to a field from a database opened in work area 2 (or B) with the SELECT command. C-> refers to a field opened in work area 3 or C, and so forth (LIST CODE,B->TITLE,QTY,AMOUNT).
BOF()	Beginning of file. Opposite of EOF() [? BOF()].
BROWSE	Displays a "screenful" of the database and allows us to scan and make changes to the database.
/C	Used with the SORT command to ignore upper-/lowercase in a sort (SORT ON LNAME/C,FNAME/C TO B:TEMP).
CANCEL	Aborts command file execution and returns to the dot prompt [CANCEL].
CDOW	Displays the day of the week as a character (Sunday, Monday, etc.) for a Date field or memory variable [? CDOW(DATE)].
CHANGE	Globally edits a specific field in a database [CHANGE FIELD PHONE FOR CITY = "San Diego"].
CHR	Displays the ASCII character for a number [? CHR(65) displays "A" ? CHR(7) rings the bell].

Command	Definition
CLEAR	Clears the screen.
CLEAR ALL	Closes all database, index, format, and relational databases. Undoes all SELECT commands [CLEAR ALL].
CLEAR GETS	Releases GET variables from READ access [CLEAR GETS].
CLEAR MEMORY	Erases all current memory variables.
CLOSE	Closes open files, of either alternate, database, format, index, or procedure types [CLOSE DATABASES].
CMONTH	Displays the month for a Date field or memory variable as a character (e.g. January) [? CMONTH(DATE)]
COL()	Displays the current column position of the cursor on the screen [? COL()].
COMMAND	Creates or edits a command file (MODIFY COMMAND B:MENU).
CONTINUE	Used with the LOCATE command, to find the next record with a particular characteristic.
COPY	Copies the contents of one database into another database (COPY TO TEMP).
COPY FILE	Copies a non-dbf file to another file [COPY FILE MYPROG.PRG TO MYPROG.BAK].
COPY STRUCTURE	Copies the structure of a database to another database without copying the contents [COPY STRUCTURE TO MAIL2].
COUNT	Counts how many records in a database meet some criterion [COUNT FOR MONTH(DATE) = 12 TO DECEMBER].

Command	Definition
CREATE	Allows us to create a database, and define its structure (CREATE MAIL).
CREATE LABEL	Creates a format file for mailing labels (same as MODIFY LABEL) (CREATE LABEL B:TWOCOL).
CREATE REPORT	Creates a custom report format (same as MODIFY REPORT) (CREATE REPORT B:BYNAME).
CTOD	Converts a date, stored as a character ("01/01/85") to a Date data type [LIST FOR DATE = CTOD("01/01/85")].
/D	Used with SORT to sort from largest to smallest, rather than smallest to largest (SORT ON ZIP/D TO B:TEMP).
DATE()	Displays dBASE 'internal' date [i.e. ? DATE()].
DAY	Displays the day of the month for a Date data type as a number [? DAY (DATE).
DEBUG	A debugging aid which displays echoed command lines to the printer (SET DEBUG ON).
DEFAULT	Changes the default drive for storing data files (SET DEFAULT TO B).
DELETE	Marks a record for deletion (DELETE RECORD 7).
DELETED()	Evaluates to "true" if record is marked for deletion [LIST FOR DELETED()].
DELIMITED	Copies dBASE databases to other data file formats (COPY TO MM.TXT DELIMITED WITH ,).
DIR	Shows files on diskette (DIR B:*.PRG displays command file names on drive B).
DISPLAY	Shows information about a database, or its contents (DISPLAY ALL, DISPLAY STRUCTURE).

Command	Definition
DISPLAY MEMORY	Displays all current memory variables (DISPLAY MEMORY).
DISPLAY STATUS	Displays the current status of databases and index files in use, SET parameters, and function key (F1–F10) assignments (DISPLAY STATUS).
DO	Runs a command file (DO B:MAIL).
DO CASE	Sets up a clause of mutually exclusive options in a command file. Terminated with the ENDCASE command.
DO WHILE	Used with ENDDO to set up a loop in a command file [DO WHILE .NOT. EOF()].
DTOC	Converts a date field or memory variable to a Character data type [LIST FOR DTOC(DATE)="01/01/85"].
ECHO	A debugging aid, displays all statements in a command file as processed (SET ECHO ON).
EDIT	Displays existing data in a record and allows us to change its contents (EDIT 17).
EJECT	Starts the paper in the printer on a new page (EJECT).
ELSE	Performs a set of commands if the criterion in an IF statement is false.
ENDDO	Used with the DO WHILE command to mark the bottom of a loop in a command file.
ENDIF	Marks the end of an IF clause in a command file.
EOF()	End of File. Used primarily in DO WHILE loops in command files [DO WHILE .NOT. EOF()].
ERASE	Deletes a specified file from the directory (ERASE TEMP.DBF).

Command	Definition
EXACT	Determines how searches will function (SET EXACT ON).
EXIT	Escapes from a DO WHILE loop without terminating execution of the command file (EXIT).
EXP	Natural exponent of a number [? EXP(1)].
FIELD	Refers to individual fields in a record (CHANGE FIELD . . .).
FILE	Refers to a disk file. DISPLAY FILES shows disk files.
FIND	Used to look up information in an index file (FIND Miller).
GET	Used with the READ command to accept field and memory variable data from the screen (@ 5,1 SAY 'Last name' GET LNAME).
GO BOTTOM	Goes to the last record in a database.
GO TOP	Starts at the first record in a database.
HELP	Provides help on the screen for a command or function [HELP RECNO()].
IF	Determines whether or not to perform commands in a command file based upon some criteria (IF ZIP='92122').
INDEX	Creates an index file of sorted data, (INDEX ON LNAME TO NAMES), or uses an existing index to display data in sorted order (USE B:MAIL INDEX B:NAMES).
INPUT	Displays a prompt on the screen, and waits for a response. Used with numeric data (INPUT 'How many labels per page' TO PER:PAGE).
INSERT	Puts a new record into a specified position in the database (GOTO 4 <RET> INSERT BEFORE <RET>).

Command	Definition
INT	Integer portion of a number, with decimal places truncated (not rounded) [? INT(1.99999) displays 1.].
JOIN	Creates a third database based upon the contents of two existing databases (JOIN TO B:NEWDB FOR CODE = S.CODE).
LABEL	Prints mailing labels in the format specifed in a file created with the MODIFY LABEL command (LABEL FORM B:TWOCOL TO PRINT).
LEN	Displays the length of a string [? LEN(TRIM(LNAME))].
LIST	Shows the contents of a database.
LIST FOR	Lists data that have some characteristic in common (LIST FOR LNAME = 'Smith').
LOCATE	Finds a record with a particular characteristic (LOCATE FOR LNAME = 'Smith').
LOG	Calculates the natural logarithm of a number [? LOG(2.72)].
LOOP	Skips all commands between itself and the ENDDO command in a DO WHILE loop (LOOP).
LOWER	Converts upper- to lowercase [? LOWER(LNAME)].
M->	Specifies a memory variable. Useful when a field and memory variable share the same name (? M->LNAME).
MEMORY	Displays memory variables in RAM (DISPLAY MEMORY).
MODIFY	Changes a database's structure, or creates/edits a command file (MODIFY STRUCTURE, MODIFY COMMAND B:MENU).
MONTH	Returns the month of a Date field or variable as a number (1–12) [LIST FOR MONTH(EXPDATE) = 12].

Command	Definition
OFF	Leaves record numbers out of displays (LIST OFF). Also, turns off parameters (SET PRINT OFF).
ON	Sets dBASE parameters into 'on' mode (SET PRINT ON).
PACK	Permanently deletes records marked for deletion from the database.
PCOL	Displays the current column position of the printer head [? PCOL()].
PICTURE	Used with the GET command to make templates and define acceptable character types [@ 12,1 SAY 'Phone number' GET PHONE PICTURE '(999)999-9999'].
PRINT	Sends displays to the printer (SET PRINT ON, REPORT FORM BYNAME TO PRINT).
PRIVATE	Specifies memory variables that are automatically erased when a command file terminates [PRIVATE ALL LIKE M*].
PROW	Displays the current row position of the printer head [? PROW()].
PUBLIC	Specifies memory variables that are not to be erased when a command file terminates (PUBLIC CHOICE, LP, X, Y, Z).
QUIT	Exits dBASE III back to the operating system's A> prompt.
RANGE	Specifies a range of acceptable values with @, SAY, GET, READ commands (@ 12,5 SAY "Enter choice" GET CHOICE RANGE 1,5).
READ	Used with @, SAY, and GET to read in field and memory variable data from the screen.

Command	Definition
RECALL	Brings back a record marked for deletion (RECALL RECORD 14).
RECNO()	Record number [LIST FOR RECNO() >= 10 .AND. RECNO() <= 20 list all records in the range of record number 10 to 20].
RECORD	Refers to a single record (DELETE RECORD 4).
REINDEX	Recreates all active index files (REINDEX).
RELEASE	Erases current memory variables (RELEASE ALL).
RENAME	Changes the name of a disk file (RENAME B:OLD.DBF TO B: NEW.DBF).
REPLACE	Changes the current contents of a field with new data. Used in global deletes (REPLACE ALL LNAME WITH 'Smith' FOR LNAME = 'SMITH').
REPORT	Allows us to either create a report format (MODIFY REPORT), or display data in report format (REPORT FORM B:BYNAME).
RESTORE	Recalls memory variables that were saved to disk with the SAVE command back into RAM (RESTORE FROM B:THOUGHT).
RETURN	Returns control from a command file to the dot prompt or another command file.
RETURN TO MASTER	Returns control from a subprogram back to the first-run program, (usually the Main Menu program) (RETURN TO MASTER).
ROUND	Rounds a number to a specified number of decimal places [? ROUND(RATE*HOURS),2)].
ROW()	Displays the current row position of the cursors on the screen [? ROW()].

Command	Definition
RUN	Executes a program outside of dBASE III. For example, RUN WS runs the WordStar program (RUN DATE).
SAVE	Stores a copy of memory variables to a disk file (SAVE TO B:THOUGHT).
SAY	Used with @ to position output on the screen or printer (@ 5,2 SAY 'Hi').
SDF	Standard Data Format. Copies dBASE files to other database formats (COPY TO BASIC.DAT SDF FOR RECNO() < 100).
SEEK	Looks up the contents of a memory variable in an index file [STORE CTOD("01/01/85") TO LOOKUP <RET>, SEEK LOOKUP].
SELECT	Assigns databases in use to any one of ten work areas numbered 1 through 10, or lettered A through J (SELECT 1, SELECT A).
SET	Displays a menu of SET parameters and allows changes to be made via a menu of options (SET).
SET ALTERNATE	Transfers all screen activity (except @, SAYs) to a data file, after the file name is specified and the alternate is on (SET ALTE TO B:file, SET ALTE ON).
SET BELL	Determines whether or not the bell sounds when a field is filled on an APPEND, EDIT, or custom screen (SET BELL OFF).
SET CARRY	When the CARRY option is on, a newly appended record automatically receives the contents of the previous record, which may then be edited (SET CARRY ON).
SET COLOR	Changes color of screen to blue (B), green (G), red (R), or white (W), or combinations. Set up blinking (*) and intensity (+) (SET COLOR TO B+).

Command	Definition
SET CONFIRM	Determines whether pressing the RETURN key is necessary after filling a screen prompt (SET CONFIRM ON).
SET CONSOLE	When console is off, nothing is displayed on the screen (SET CONSOLE OFF).
SET DEBUG	Sends output of an ECHO to the printer when on (SET DEBUG ON).
SET DECIMALS	Sets the minimum number of decimals displayed in the results of mathematical calculations (SET DECIMALS TO 2).
SET DEFAULT	Determines which disk drive dBASE uses when looking for disk files with the USE, DO, INDEX, SELECT, and other commands that access files (SET DEFAULT TO B).
SET DELETED	Determines whether or not records marked for deletion are displayed with LIST, DISPLAY, ?, REPORT, and LABEL commands (SET DELETED ON hides deleted records).
SET DELIMITER	Determines how field entries are displayed on the screen with APPEND, EDIT, and custom screens (SET DELIMITER TO "[]" encloses fields in brackets).
SET DEVICE	Determines whether @, SAY commands display data on the screen or on the printer (SET DEVICE TO PRINTER, SET DEVICE TO SCREEN).
SET ECHO	A debugging aid that displays each line of a command file as it is being processed (SET ECHO ON).
SET ESCAPE	Determines whether or not a command file terminates when Esc is pressed (SET ESCAPE OFF aborts the power of the Esc key).

Command	Definition
SET EXACT	Determines how dBASE compares two values either with an exact match or with first letters only. With EXACT off, Smith will match Smithsonian (SET EXACT ON).
SET FILTER	Limits display of data to those records which match a criterion (SET FILTER TO LNAME = "Smith" will limit output of LIST, REPORT, LABEL, etc. to Smiths).
SET FIXED	Sets the number of decimal places that will appear with all numeric displays. Usually used in conjunction with the SET DECIMALS command (SET FIXED ON).
SET FORMAT	Specifies a custom screen display stored in a format (.FMT) file to be used with EDIT and APPEND commands (SET FORMAT TO B:ADDNAMES, SET FORMAT TO).
SET FUNCTION	Reprograms the function keys (F1–F10) to perform custom tasks. DISPLAY STATUS shows current settings (SET FUNCTION 10 TO 'BROWSE').
SET HEADING	Determines whether field names will be displayed above data in DISPLAY, LIST, SUM, and AVERAGE commands (SET HEADING OFF removes field names from displays).
SET HELP	Determines whether or not the message *Do you want some help?* appears during an error (SET HELP OFF removes the prompt).
SET INDEX	Specifies index file(s) to make active with a database (SET INDEX TO B:NAMES, B:ZIPS).
SET INTENSITY	Determines whether or not field entries are displayed on the screen in reverse video (SET INTENSITY OFF removes reverse video).
SET MARGIN	Adjusts the left-hand margin for printer displays (SET MARGIN TO 5).

Command	Definition
SET MENUS	Determines whether or not cursor control commands appear in a menu above APPEND, EDIT, BROWSE, and other displays (SET MENUS ON displays the menus).
SET PATH	Specifies directory paths to search for disk files (SET PATH TO \C:DBIII will cause dBASE to search path DBIII on drive C if file not found on current drive).
SET PRINT	Determines whether displays will be echoed to the printer (SET PRINT ON causes all screen displays to be printed; SET PRINT OFF returns to normal mode).
SET PROCEDURE	Advanced programming technique whereby subprograms are combined into a single file and assigned procedure names (SET PROCEDURE TO B:ROUTINES).
SET RELATION	Sets up a relationship between two data files in use, based upon a field that they have in common (SET RELATION TO CODE INTO B:MASTER).
SET SAFETY	Determines whether on not the message *(file name)* already exists. *overwrite it?* appears when a file is about to be overwritten (SET SAFETY OFF disables).
SET STEP	Debugging aid used to limit command file execution to a single line at a time (SET STEP ON).
SET TALK	Determines whether or not dBASE displays a response to various commands. Usually, SET TALK OFF is used in command files to eliminate dBASE messages.
SET UNIQUE	Used with the INDEX command to display an ordered listing of unique field values. Can be used as an aid in checking for duplicates (SET UNIQUE ON).
SKIP	Skips to next record in the database. Can also skip more or less than 1 record (SKIP 10, SKIP − 3).

<u>Command</u>	<u>Definition</u>
SORT	Rearranges records on a database into sorted order. Requires that records be sorted to another database (SORT ON LNAME TO B:TEMP).
SPACE	Generates blanks [LNAME = SPACE(20) creates a memory variable called LNAME that consists of 20 blank spaces].
SQRT	Displays the square root of a number [? SQRT(64), STORE SQRT(64) TO X].
STEP	A debugging aid, pauses after each line in a command file is processed (SET STEP ON).
STORE	Stores a value to a memory variable (STORE 1 TO COUNTER).
STR	Converts a number to a string. Useful for complex sorting with index files [INDEX ON CODE + STR-(AMOUNT,12,2) TO TEST].
STRUCTURE	Refers to the structure, rather than the contents of a database (DISPLAY STRUCTURE).
SUBSTR	Isolates a portion of a string [? SUBSTR("ABC-DEFG",3,2) displays CD, a substring starting at the third character, 2 characters long].
SUM	Adds a column of fields, and displays the total (SUM AMOUNT).
TALK	Sets dBASE's miscellanous messages on or off (SET TALK OFF).
TEXT	Starts a block of text in a command file, terminated with the command ENDTEXT.
TIME	Displays the current system time [? TIME()].
TOTAL	Summarizes and totals a database to another database. File must be either presorted or preindexed. (TOTAL ON CODE TO B:SALESUMM).

Command	Definition
TRIM	Removes trailing blanks from a field's contents [LIST TRIM(FNAME),LNAME].
TYPE	Displays the contents of a DOS ASCII file [TYPE MYREOPRT.TXT].
UPDATE	Revises the file in use by adding or replacing data from another database (UPDATE ON CODE FROM B:SALES REPLACE PRICE with B->PRICE).
UPPER	Converts lowercase letters to uppercase [INDEX ON UPPER(LNAME) TO NAMES].
USE	Tells dBASE which database to work with (USE B:MAIL).
VAL	Changes character strings to numerics [? VAL(AD-DRESS)].
WAIT	Stops execution of a command file, and waits for user to press a key. Key press is stored to a memory variable (WAIT TO DATA).
YEAR	Displays the year of a Date field or variable in 19XX format [LIST FOR YEAR(DATE) = 1984].
ZAP	Permanently removes all records from a database and active index files.

CONVERTING dBASE II FILES TO dBASE III FILES

D

If you have some dBASE II databases and command files that you want to convert to dBASE III, you can do so very easily with the dCONVERT program.

The dCONVERT Program

The dBASE III Sample Programs and Utilities disk contains the program dCONVERT. This program can be used to convert dBASE II databases and command files to dBASE III. To use it, put the Sample Programs and Utilities disk in drive A, or copy the dCONVERT.EXE program to your hard disk. To run dCONVERT, enter the command DCONVERT from the A> or C> prompt. A menu of options appears on the screen, as shown in Figure D.1.

You can use the arrow keys on the numeric keypad to highlight an option, then press RETURN to select the option. Option 9 displays instructions for using dCONVERT.

If you have a computer with two floppy disk drives, you may want to put the converted files on a separate disk. To do so, first create a blank format diskette using the usual DOS FORMAT command.

```
dBASE CONVERT - - dBASE III File Conversion Aid v1.06 6/14/84
        ©  1984 By Ashton-Tate    All Rights Reserved


                    dBASE II --> dBASE III

        1 - - Database File              (.DBF)
        2 - - Memory Variable File       (.MEM)
        3 - - Report Format File         (.FRM)
        4 - - Command File               (.PRG)
        5 - - Screen Format File         (.FMT)
        6 - - Index File Help            (.NDX)
        7 - - Un-dCONVERT III->II        (.DBF)

        9 - -      Instructions
        0 - -      Exit

(Use cursor arrow keys to move between choices; hit RETURN to
select choice.)
```

Figure D.1

Then, load the Sample Programs and Utilities disk into drive A, and enter the command:

DCONVERT A: B:

When the dCONVERT menu appears on the screen, you can remove the Sample Programs disk from drive A, and put in the disk with the files that you wish to convert. dCONVERT will stay in memory and allow you to convert as many files as you wish. The original files in drive A will remain unchanged and the modified files will be stored on the disk in drive B.

Converting Databases

Option number 1 from the dCONVERT menu will change any dBASE II database to dBASE III format. When you select this option, dCONVERT will display the names of all .DBF files, and ask you to type in the name of the file to convert. After you type in the file name, dCONVERT will display the message *Working . . .,* and then it will inform you when it's done.

Since colons are not allowed in dBASE III field names, they will be replaced with underscore characters. Other than that, the structure and contents of the dBASE III file will be identical to that of the dBASE II file. The converted file will have the same name as the original file. The original file will have the same first name, but the extension will be changed to .DBB.

Option 7 from the dCONVERT menu allows you to convert files from dBASE III to dBASE II. However, the dBASE III database must fit the rules of dBASE II: 32 fields or fewer, maximum record length of 1,000, and no more that 6,535 records.

Converting Index Files

The easiest way to convert an index file is to convert the .DBF file, then create the index files again with the INDEX ON command. Optionally, you can use dCONVERT to help make the conversion.

Select option 6 from the dCONVERT menu, and then enter the name of the index file to convert (NAMES). When the conversion is done, load up dBASE and use the appropriate dBASE III database (MAIL). Then run the program created by dCONVERT, which has the same name as the index file, and the extension .RX. To convert the NAMES index file, type in the command DO NAMES.RX from the dot prompt. The NAMES.RX command file will reindex the file for you.

Converting Report Formats

Option number 3 from the dCONVERT menu allows you to convert dBASE II REPORT FORM (.FRM) files to dBASE III format. Simply select the option and specify the name of the format file to convert. From the dBASE III dot prompt, use the REPORT FORM command to display the report. Then, you can use the MODIFY REPORT to make changes to the report.

Converting Memory Files

If you use .MEM files (disk files with memory variables stored in them), use option 2 from the dCONVERT menu to convert them to dBASE III. The dBASE III .MEM file will be about 25 percent larger than the dBASE II .MEM file, primarily because dBASE III stores numbers with more digits of accuracy. Note: colons embedded in memory variable names will be converted to underlines.

Converting Custom Screen Files

Option 5 from the dCONVERT menu allows you to convert dBASE II custom screen files (.FMT) to dBASE III. Colons embedded in field names will be replaced by underscore characters to match field names in the dBASE III database.

Converting Command Files

dCONVERT can even convert dBASE II command files (.PRG or .CMD) to dBASE III, but with limited accuracy. The converted programs will have the commands SET HEADING OFF and SET SAFETY OFF near the top of the program. These options remove headings from LIST and DISPLAY commands, and disable the dBASE III prompts which ask for permission before overwriting files. This is done to make the dBASE III program perform as close as possible to the original dBASE II program. Of course, you can remove these new lines to take advantage of the headings and safety features.

In some situations, dCONVERT will be unable to make an appropriate change. In this case dCONVERT will display a warning message on the screen and continue converting the rest of the command file. The converted command file will have notes, beginning with the characters *!!, that will inform you of those sections of the program that may require further attention.

Some dBASE II commands, such as RESET, SET HEADING TO, SET DATE, SET RAW, TEST, have no dBASE III equivalent. dCONVERT will eliminate these and inform you of the change with a screen message. If your command file needs a capability that is not available in dBASE III, you'll have to figure out how to perform a similar task. For example, dBASE III does not support the SET LINKAGE command. However, the SET RELATION command performs a similar task, so you can set up the relationship between the two files in a different manner.

Generally speaking, dCONVERT does an excellent job of converting dBASE II programs to dBASE III. The problems that it cannot solve are few and far between.

Selections from The SYBEX Library

ADVANCED BUSINESS MODELS WITH 1-2-3
by Stanley R. Trost
250 pp., illustr., Ref. 0-159

Take full advantage of the power of still best-selling 1-2-3, quickly and easily! If you are a business professional who wants to use the 1-2-3 software package for forecasts, budgets, financial analysis, data base management, or graphing, this book will provide you with models that are ready for use in everyday business situations. In addition, this book will guide you to advanced knowledge of 1-2-3, allowing you to create your own models from the examples in the text.

ADVANCED TECHNIQUES IN dBASE II
by Alan Simpson
250 pp., illustr., Ref. 0-228

If you are an experienced dBASE II programmer and would like to begin customizing your own programs, this book is for you. It is a well-structured tutorial that offers programming techniques applicable to a wide variety of situations. Data base and program design are covered in detail, and the many examples and illustrations clarify the test.

REAL WORLD UNIX™
by John D. Halamka
209 pp., Ref. 0-093

This book is written for the beginning and intermediate UNIX user in a practical, straightforward manner, with specific instructions given for many business applications.

DOING BUSINESS WITH MULTIPLAN™
by Richard Allen King and Stanley R. Trost
250 pp., illustr., Ref. 0-148

This book will show you how using Multiplan can be nearly as easy as learning to use a pocket calculator. It presents a collection of templates for business applications.

UNDERSTANDING dBASE II™
by Alan Simpson
260 pp., illustr., Ref. 0-147

Learn programming techniques for mailing label systems, bookkeeping, and data management, as well as ways to interface dBASE II with other software systems.

THE THINKTANK™ BOOK
by Jonathan Kamin
200 pp., illustr., Ref. 0-224

Learn how the ThinkTank program can help you organize your thoughts, plans, and activities.

THE COMPLETE GUIDE TO MULTIMATE™
by Carol Holcomb Dreger
250 pp., illustr., Ref. 0-229

A concise introduction to the many practical applications of this powerful word processing program.

INTRODUCTION TO WORDSTAR®
by Arthur Naiman
202 pp., 30 illustr., Ref. 0-134

Makes it easy to learn WordStar, a powerful word processing program for personal computers.

ESPIONAGE IN THE SILICON VALLEY
by John D. Halamka
200 pp., illustr., Ref. 0-225

Discover the behind-the-scenes stories of famous high-tech spy cases you've seen in the headlines.

ASTROLOGY ON YOUR PERSONAL COMPUTER
by Hank Friedman
225 pp., illustr., Ref. 0-226

An invaluable aid for astrologers who want to streamline their calculation and data management chores with the right combination of hardware and software.